$40.00

# Plug-in CSS
## 100 POWER SOLUTIONS

Robin Nixon

New York  Chicago  San Francisco
Lisbon  London  Madrid  Mexico City
Milan  New Delhi  San Juan
Seoul  Singapore  Sydney  Toronto

**The McGraw·Hill** Companies

Cataloging-in-Publication Data is on file with the Library of Congress

McGraw-Hill books are available at special quantity discounts to use as premiums and sales promotions, or for use in corporate training programs. To contact a representative, please e-mail us at bulksales@mcgraw-hill.com.

### Plug-in CSS: 100 Power Solutions

1234567890   DOC DOC   10987654321

ISBN    978-0-07-174876-6
MHID       0-07-174876-8

**Sponsoring Editor**
Roger Stewart

**Editorial Supervisor**
Jody McKenzie

**Project Manager**
Vastavikta Sharma,
Glyph International

**Acquisitions Coordinator**
Joya Anthony

**Technical Editor**
Alan Solis

**Copy Editor**
Mike McGee

**Proofreader**
Carol Shields

**Indexer**
Jack Lewis

**Production Supervisor**
George Anderson

**Composition**
Glyph International

**Illustration**
Glyph International

**Art Director, Cover**
Jeff Weeks

**Cover Designer**
Pehrsson Design

*For Julie*

## About the Author

**Robin Nixon** has worked with and written about computers since the early 1980s (his first computer was a Tandy TRS 80 Model 1 with a massive 4KB of RAM!). During this time, he has written in excess of 500 articles for many of the UK's top computer magazines. *Plug-in CSS* is his seventh book.

Robin lives on the southeast coast of England with his wife, Julie, a trained nurse, and their five children, and also finds time to foster three disabled children, as well as work full time from home as a technical author.

### Also by Robin Nixon

*Learning PHP, MySQL and JavaScript*, O'Reilly 2009, ISBN 978-0596157135

*Ubuntu: Up and Running*, O'Reilly 2010, ISBN 978-0596804848

*Plug-in PHP*, McGraw-Hill 2010, ISBN 978-0071666596

*Plug-in JavaScript*, McGraw-Hill 2010, ISBN 978-0071738613

### About the Technical Editor

**Alan Solis** has more than 30 years experience designing, writing, and maintaining software for companies ranging from small start-ups to large corporations. He currently is designing and maintaining web sites and web applications using PHP, JavaScript, Java, and various relational databases.

In his spare time, Alan enjoys creative writing and is a published short story and poetry author. Alan lives in the San Jose, California, area with his wife, Cheryl.

# Contents at a Glance

# Contents

## Part I   About CSS and These Plug-ins

# Acknowledgments

I would like to thank Wendy Rinaldi for giving me the opportunity to put together another book of handy plug-ins, and Roger Stewart for acting as my personal editor on the book. I also want to thank Joya, Alan, Melinda, Jody, Mike, Vastavikta, and everyone else who helped create this book, without whom it would not have been the same. McGraw-Hill is an exceptionally professional and friendly company to work with, and it has once again been a pleasure.

# Introduction

When the World Wide Web was first invented by Tim Berners-Lee, simply having a means to create hypertext links to other documents (including ones on remote computers), and to combine text and images using basic formatting, were revolutionary concepts that we take for granted today.

But slowly web developers started getting used to the initial 20 elements provided by HTML (Hypertext Markup Language) 1, and began adding more and more features in each new specification of the language. Luckily, though, the people driving this development realized early on that if these extensions to the language were not handled sensibly, they could end up as an unwieldy, tangled web of tags. Thus, it was decided to include cascading style sheets (CSS) within the specification so the content of web pages could be completely separate from the design and layout.

Because of this, over time, HTML arguments such as `color='blue'` within `<font>` tags became deprecated in favor of using the syntax `style='color:blue;'`. In fact, even that type of usage is frowned upon by purist web developers, since the design and content remain combined. Instead, to fully separate the two, it became possible to embed all the styles within a pair of `<style>` ... `</style>` tags, inside a document's `<head>` section, which is great for placing all of a document's styles in a single place, and yet still keep them as part of the document.

And what about those times when two separate styles were needed—such as one for displaying a page in a browser, and another one to lay it all out in a print-friendly manner? The solution to this was to totally remove all style settings to external style sheets that a document can pull in on demand, as required.

Nowadays, although all the older and deprecated features still work (but for how long is unknown), most good web sites separate out the content and styles into separate documents. By simply loading in a different style sheet, a document (or even an entire web site) can be given a totally new look and feel. In fact, this system is so flexible that you can even create style sheets to output web pages through a voice synthesizer, Braille printer, or a reader for blind people.

In these days of widely varying browser capabilities and screen dimensions, CSS is becoming more important than ever, because you can now create different style sheets for iPhones, iPads, Android devices, PCs and Macs, and so on, and by simply loading in the relevant one at the start, your web pages will look as good as they possibly can on all platforms.

## Much More than Just Styles

CSS is more than simply a method to restyle a document. It includes dynamic functionality, too. For example, using the `hover` pseudo class you can change the appearance of an element when the mouse passes over it.

Also, all browsers have their own style properties that extend CSS by adding effects such as fading elements in and out, or moving them about. The only problem with them is that they are unique to each browser (or rendering engine).

Still, by correctly specifying the CSS for each browser it is possible to offer eye-catching effects for those browsers that support them—effects that gracefully degrade to standard functionality on browsers that don't.

## What this Book Provides

This book provides 100 ready-to-go CSS classes and groups of classes that you can simply drop into your web pages. And if you are new to CSS, don't worry that you'll be using plug-ins you don't understand, because they are fully documented and their functionally clearly explained, often with tips on how you can further tailor them to your requirements.

Each property, class, pseudo class, and every other aspect of CSS is detailed as it is encountered, and for beginners there's also an in-a-nutshell guide to CSS before the plug-ins, explaining the box model and much more to get you up to speed.

## Includes CSS 3, HTML, and HTML 5

With the adoption of CSS 3 features in all modern browsers, this book also provides plug-ins to take advantage of this latest version, including native text and box shadowing, rounded borders, and even web fonts, so you can break away from the same old fonts the Web has put up with for so many years.

Also all the plug-ins come with HTML examples and screen shots showing you exactly how to use them in real-world situations. What's more, some of the plug-ins show ways to use CSS in conjunction with the emerging HTML 5 standard to make your web pages even more interactive and dynamic, helping you create more cutting-edge web sites.

## About the Plug-ins

All this book's plug-ins are ready to use and can be either typed in (if you don't have Internet access), copied and pasted, or downloaded from *plugincss.com*, where they are stored as in a compressed *.zip* file.

When you visit the web site, you can navigate through the plug-ins chapter by chapter, view the CSS highlighted in color for clarity, and can also click through and try out the plug-ins directly on the web site before downloading them for your own use.

### What Is and Isn't Included

Although the first aim of this book is to provide newcomers to CSS with a comprehensive resource of plug-ins to draw on, it has a secondary goal: to help you move up to the next level and create your own CSS toolkit. Therefore, all the plug-ins are thoroughly documented and explained in detail, and advice is given on ways to improve and extend them, as well as on how to adapt them to your own requirements.

And while this book isn't a design manual or a teaching guide, I do hope that by reading through the explanations, rather than just including the plug-ins in your projects, you'll pick up a number of tips and tricks that many developers take years to discover, and by osmosis will learn more about CSS.

### Plug-in License

You are free to use any of the plug-ins in this book in your own projects, and may modify them as necessary, without attributing this book—although if you do attribute them, it will always be appreciated.

However, you may not sell, give away, or otherwise distribute the plug-ins themselves in any manner, whether printed or in electronic format, without the written permission of the publisher.

## The Companion Web Site

A companion web site (plugincss.com) accompanies this book, where all 100 plug-ins are available for download, along with example HTML files for you to experiment with.

The web site is best used in conjunction with this book. As you read a chapter, call it up on the web site, too, and list each plug-in on the screen with color-highlighted syntax. This makes it very easy to see the structure of each program.

When you wish to, you can click a link to copy and paste a particular plug-in right into your own style sheets. Or, if you prefer, you can download all the plug-ins to your computer, from where you can pick the one(s) to upload to your own web site.

# PART I
# About CSS and
# These Plug-ins

# CHAPTER 1

## How to Use the Plug-ins

Because CSS is supported by all major browsers, you might think that using it is as easy as having a text editor and a web browser. Well, you *could* get by with just those, but there's actually a lot more to it if you want to produce pages that display to their best on all major browsers.

First of all, although CSS is available on almost all web browsers, it varies slightly between them in the way certain features are implemented, including differing amounts of spacing around elements, and even sizes of elements. This means you need to be able to test your web pages on all the main browsers to ensure they display well in all cases.

Therefore, if you use Mac OS X or another operating system such as Linux, you really need to also have access to a Windows computer because recent versions of Internet Explorer are available only for that operating system.

## Downloading and Installing Web Browsers

Table 1-1 lists the five major web browsers and their Internet download locations. While all of them can be installed on a Windows PC, some of them are not available for OS X or Linux. The web pages at these URLs are smart and offer up the correct version to download according to your operating system, if available. Before proceeding with this book, I recommend that you ensure you have installed as many of these browsers on your computer as you can.

If you're running any version of Windows from XP onwards, you will be able to install all the browsers, but on other operating systems it's not quite so easy. For example, on Mac OS X (because development of IE for the Mac was halted many years ago when it reached version 5), you can install all the browsers except for Microsoft Internet Explorer. And although it's possible to install the Wine windows application interface on a Mac and run Internet Explorer using it, I have found it to be a laborious process with inconsistent results. Therefore, I wouldn't recommend that method. Neither would I suggest you rely on those web sites that take screen shots of a web page in different browsers, because they can't tell you whether the mouse, keyboard, and other features are working well, or at all.

Instead, your best option is to either perform a dual install of Windows alongside Mac OS X, or ensure you have access to a Windows PC. After all, unless you intend to develop only for Mac computers, people using a Windows operating system will represent the majority of your users by far.

As for Linux, not only does it not have access to Internet Explorer, there is no version of Safari either, although all the other browsers do come in Linux flavors. And, as with OS X,

| Web Browser | Download URL | Windows | Mac | Linux |
|---|---|:---:|:---:|:---:|
| Apple Safari | *apple.com/safari* | ✓ | ✓ | |
| Google Chrome | *google.com/chrome* | ✓ | ✓ | ✓ |
| Microsoft Internet Explorer | *microsoft.com/ie* | ✓ | | |
| Mozilla Firefox | *mozilla.com/firefox* | ✓ | ✓ | ✓ |
| Opera | *opera.com/download* | ✓ | ✓ | ✓ |

**TABLE 1-1**  Web Browser Download URLs and Supported Operating Systems

while various solutions exist that incorporate Wine for running Internet Explorer, they only seem to work with some distributions and not others, so it can be a bit of a minefield trying to find a bulletproof way for you to run Windows browsers on Linux.

So what it all comes down to is that, if you will be developing on a non-Windows computer, I recommend you arrange to have access to a Windows PC, or have Windows installed as a dual boot (or a virtual machine) alongside your main operating system so you can fully test your web sites before publishing them to the web at large.

## Older Versions of Microsoft Internet Explorer

The latest version of Internet Explorer (IE8 at the time of writing, although IE9 is definitely in the works) has made tremendous strides towards compatibility with the other major browsers, but there are still large numbers of users running IE7 and even IE6. According to *statcounter.com*, as of mid 2010 the breakdown of browsers by use was that shown in the screen grab in Figure 1-1.

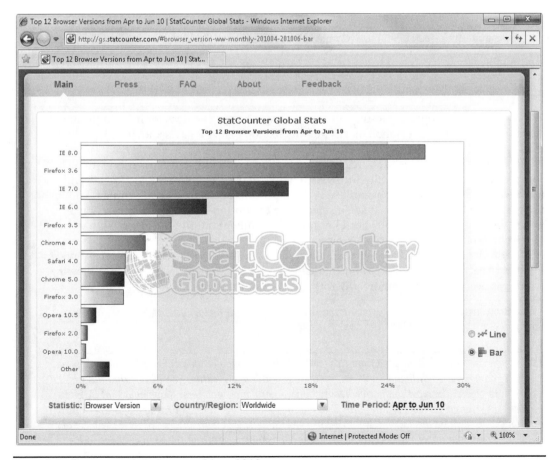

**FIGURE 1-1**  Browser market share as of June 2010

Because each version of Internet Explorer works differently (with IE6 and IE7 having over 25 percent of all users between them), besides testing your web pages in the latest versions of the main browsers you also need to test them in these older versions, too. I know, it's a pain, but it has to be done. Luckily, though, there's a trick to make this easier than it might otherwise be.

## Emulating Internet Explorer 6 and 7

To aid developers who have designed web sites to work specifically with older versions, the developers of Internet Explorer created a meta tab that you can add to the head of a web page to make IE think it is an earlier version of itself. Here are the two main meta tags you would use.

```
<meta http-equiv="X-UA-Compatible" content="IE=7" />
<meta http-equiv="X-UA-Compatible" content="IE=5" />
```

And this is an example of how you would incorporate the IE7 tag:

```
<html>
   <head>
      <meta http-equiv="X-UA-Compatible" content="IE=7" />
      <title>My Website</title>
   </head>
   <body>
   ... Website Contents ...
```

There is no IE=6 option (presumably because the rendering engines for IE5 and IE6 are so similar), so using the IE=5 option makes Internet Explorer enter what is known as "quirks" mode, in which it behaves like both IE5 and IE6.

Incidentally, if you wish to force Internet Explorer into full standards mode (to be as compatible as possible with other browsers), you can use the option IE=8. Or, without the meta tag, Internet Explorer will use its own proprietary and optimal settings, known as "edge" mode—which you can also select with the option IE=edge. Of course, once you have finished testing, you should remove or comment out these meta tags unless you wish to use one for a particular reason.

In addition, you should always ensure you have a suitable HTML doctype declaration at the start of each document. For example, the most commonly found doctype is the following, which has been fully tested and works with all the plug-ins in this book.

```
<!DOCTYPE HTML PUBLIC "-//W3C//DTD HTML 4.01 Transitional//EN"
"http://www.w3.org/TR/html4/loose.dtd">
```

---

**TIP** *If you use a different doctype from this, certain plug-ins may behave differently, and you may find you have to slightly modify them. I often use both the preceding "loose" doctype and the IE7 meta tag to get the most compatible results with other major browsers. Remember that if IE behaves strangely when all other browsers appear to work well with your web pages, the solution could be to change the doctype and/or IE5/IE7 meta tags. If you are interested in the subject of browser compatibility and its various nuances, I recommend visiting the Quirks Mode web site at* quirksmode.org.

## The Companion Web Site

To save you the effort of typing them all in, you can download the plug-ins from this book's companion web site at *plugincss.com* (see Figure 1-2).

Click the Download link to download the file *plug-ins.zip*, which is an archive file (easily extractable on all operating systems) containing all the plug-ins. Once extracted, you'll find all the plug-ins in numerical order, saved in the file *PC.css*. There is also a file called *ReadMe.txt* which contains the latest details about the plug-ins, including any improvements or updates that have been made since this book was published.

Additionally, there are various example files showing the use of each plug-in, which you can load into a browser to try out for yourself.

Accompanying these are a couple of JavaScript files called *PJ.js* and *PC.js*, which are explained toward the end of this chapter in the section on JavaScript, and which are used by the plug-ins in Chapter 12.

**FIGURE 1-2**   The companion web site at plugincss.com

---

**CAUTION**  *By default, Windows computers may not show the file extensions unless you have enabled this facility, in which case the files will simply show as* index *(instead of* index.html*) or* PC *(instead of* PC.css*) and so on.*

---

## About the Document Object Model

When HTML was invented, one of the fundamental design decisions was to base it around a Document Object Model (DOM). This is a means of separating out all the different elements within a web page into discrete objects, each with their own properties and values. It was a very smart decision because it led to the introduction of style sheets, enabling a web page's content to be completely separated from its styling, and also makes HTML documents easily modifiable by languages such as JavaScript to provide dynamic user interaction.

When a web page is placed into a DOM, it is a simple matter for you to style every aspect of it with CSS. For example, each heading will be within pairs of tags such as <h1> ... </h1> and a single CSS instruction can set the styling of all such occurrences within a document, changing the font used, its size, any font decoration, and so on. This lets you completely change the design of a page without altering the HTML and, as you'll see in some of the later plug-ins, some style settings can even apply dynamic effects to page elements (such as changing their color and other properties) when the mouse passes over them, or even create transition effects by using proprietary browser extensions.

### How the DOM Works

The Document Object Model separates the different parts of an HTML document into a hierarchy of objects, each one having its own properties. The term property is used for referring to an attribute of an object such as the HTML it contains, its width and height, and so on.

The outermost object possible is the *window* object, which is the current browser window, tab, iframe, or popped-up window. Underneath this is the *document* object, of which there can be more than one (such as several documents loaded into different iframes within a page). And inside a document there are other objects such as the head and body of a page.

Within the head there can be other objects, such as the title and meta objects, while the body object can contain numerous other objects, including HTML tags with headings, anchors, forms, and so forth.

Figure 1-3 shows a representation of the DOM of an example document, with the title "Hello" and a meta tag in the head section, and three HTML elements (a link, a form, and an image) in the body section. Of course, even the simplest of web pages has more structure than is shown here, but it serves to illustrate how the DOM works. Starting from the very outside is the window, inside which there's a single document, and within the document are the various elements or objects, which connect to each other.

In the figure, properties are shown with a darker background and in italics. For example, the value "robots" is a property of name, which is a property of meta, and so on. Although it isn't shown in the figure, the meta tag should have another matching property called content, which would contain a string specifying which robots may access the web page.

Other properties are "http://google.com", which is a property of the href tag (itself a property of a, and so on), and "Hello", which is a property of title. All the other items are objects or object argument names. If the figure extended further down and sideways, other objects and properties attached to the ones shown would come into view. A couple of the places where these would appear are shown by unconnected dotted lines.

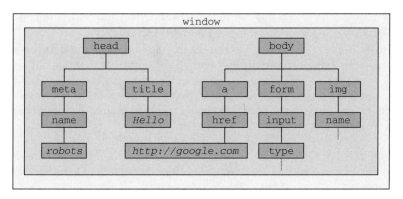

**Figure 1-3**   Example of a DOM showing head and body sections

Representing this as HTML code, the structure of the head section looks like this:

```html
<head>
   <meta name="robots" content="index, follow" />
   <title>Hello</title>
</head>
```

And the body section of HTML might look like this:

```html
<body>
   <img src="/images/welcome.jpg" />
   <a href="http://google.com">Visit Google</a>
   or enter your username and password to continue...
   <form id="login" method="post" action="login.php">
      <input type="text" name="name" />
      <input type="password" name="password" />
      <input type="submit" />
   </form>
</body>
```

Remembering that these two sections of HTML are part of the same document, we would bring them both together inside an <html> tag, like this:

```html
<html>
   <head>
      <meta name="robots" content="index, follow" />
      <title>Hello</title>
   </head>
   <body>
      <img src="/images/welcome.jpg" />
      <a href="http://google.com">Visit Google</a>,
      or enter your username and password to continue...
      <form id="login" method="post" action="login.php">
         <input type="text" name="name" />
         <input type="password" name="password" />
         <input type="submit" />
      </form>
   </body>
</html>
```

Of course, a web page can look quite different from this, but it will usually follow the same form, although that's not always the case because most browsers are very forgiving and allow you to omit many things, such as the closing tags at the end, and the opening ones, too, if you choose. I don't recommend you do this though, because one day you might want to convert your page to XHTML, which is a lot stricter. So it's always a good idea to close every tag, and make sure you do so in the right order. For example, you shouldn't close a document by issuing </html> followed by </body> because the proper nesting of tags would be broken by this reversal.

For the same reason, you should also get into the habit of self-closing any tags that do not have a closing version, such as <img src="..." />, which does not have a matching </img> tag, and therefore requires a / character right before the final > in order to properly close it. In the same way, <br> becomes <br />, and so on.

You should also remember that arguments within tags must have either single or double quotation marks to be XHTML compatible, even though nearly all browsers allow you to omit them.

---

**NOTE** *In the early days of the Web, when most users had very slow dial-up modems, it was common to see all manner of things such as quotation marks and various tags omitted from web pages. But nowadays, most of your users will have fairly decent bandwidth speeds, and there's no longer any reason to do this.*

---

# About Cascading Style Sheets

Using CSS, you can apply styles to your web pages to make them look exactly how you want. This works because CSS is connected to the DOM so you can quickly and easily restyle any element. For example, if you don't like the default look of the <h1>, <h2>, and other heading tags, you can assign new styles to override the default settings for the font family and size used, or decide whether bold or italics should be set, and many more properties, too.

One way you can add styling to a web page is by inserting the required statements into the head of a web page between the <head> and </head> tags. So, to change the style of the <h1> tag, you might use the following code:

```
<style>
   h1 { color:red; font-size:3em; font-family:Arial; }
</style>
```

Within an HTML page, this might look like the following (see Figure 1-4):

```
<html>
   <head>
      <style>
         h1 { color:red; font-size:3em; font-family:Arial; }
      </style>
   </head>
   <title>Hello World</title>
   <body>
      <h1>Hello there</h1>
   </body>
</html>
```

**Figure 1-4**   Styling the <h1> tag, with the original style shown in the small window

## Importing a Style Sheet

When you wish to style a whole site, rather than a single page, a better way to manage style sheets is to completely remove them from your web pages to separate files, and then import the ones you need. This lets you have different style sheets for different layouts (such as web and print), without changing the HTML.

This can be achieved a couple of different ways, the first of which is by using the CSS @import directive like this:

```
<style>
   @import url("/css/styles.css");
</style>
```

This statement tells the browser to fetch a style sheet with the name *styles.css* from the */css* folder. The @import command is quite flexible in that you can create style sheets that themselves pull in other style sheets, and so on. Just make sure that there are no <style> or </style> tags in any of your external style sheets, otherwise they will not work.

### Importing CSS from within HTML

You can also include a style sheet with the HTML <link> tag like this:

```
<link rel="stylesheet" type="text/css" href="/css/styles.css" />
```

This has the exact same effect as the @import directive, except that <link> is an HTML-only tag and is not a valid style directive, so it cannot be used from within one style sheet to pull in another, and also cannot be placed within a pair of <style> ... </style> tags.

Just as you can use multiple @import directives within your CSS to include multiple external style sheets, you can also use as many <link> statements as you like in your HTML.

## Local Style Settings

There is also nothing stopping you from individually setting or overriding certain styles for the current page on a case-by-case basis by inserting style statements directly within HTML, like this (which results in italic blue text within the tags):

```
<div style="font-style:italic; color:blue;">Hello</div>
```

But this should be reserved only for the most exceptional circumstances since it breaks the separation of content and layout.

## IDs and Classes

A better solution for setting the style of an element is to assign an *ID* to it in the HTML, like this:

```
<div id='iblue'>Hello</div>
```

What this does is state that the contents of the div with the ID `iblue` should have the style defined in the `#iblue` style setting applied to it. The matching CSS statement for this might look like the following

```
#iblue { font-style:italic; color:blue; }
```

Note the use of the # symbol, which specifies that only the ID with the name `iblue` should be styled with this statement.

If you would like to apply the same style to many elements, you do not have to give each one a different ID because you can specify a *class* to manage them all, like this:

```
<div class="iblue">Hello</div>
```

What this does is state that the contents of this element (and any others that use the class), should have the style defined in the `iblue` class applied to it. Once a class is applied, you can use the following style setting, either in the page header or within an external style sheet for setting the styles for the class:

```
.iblue { font-style:italic; color:blue; }
```

Instead of using a # symbol, which is reserved for IDs, class statements are prefaced with a . (period) symbol.

---

**NOTE** *You can apply styles to elements in many more ways than using single IDs or classes. These are explained in detail in Chapter 2.*

---

# CSS and Semicolons

In order to separate CSS statements when they appear on the same line, you must place semicolons after each. But if there is only one statement on a line (or in an inline style setting within an HTML tag), you can omit the semicolon.

To avoid hard-to-find CSS errors, you may prefer to always use a semicolon after every CSS setting while developing your style sheets, only removing the unnecessary ones later if you need to optimize your style sheets for maximum download speed and minimum size.

# Using the Plug-ins in Your Own Web Sites

Once you have downloaded the *plug-ins.zip* file from the *plugincss.com* web site (and extracted the files from it), the recommended way for you to access them is to load the entire set stored in the file *PC.css* as an external style sheet, with a command such as:

```
<link rel="stylesheet" type="text/css" href="css/PC.css" />
```

Here, */css* is the folder where you have saved the file (relative to the current folder) and *PC.css* is the filename of the style sheet (the initials P and C are short for Plug-in and CSS).

This method of inclusion ensures that you can add new elements to your web pages that require additional plug-ins, without having to copy and paste the additional ones in separately. The file is not very different in size from an average image, thus the speed of loading and bandwidth consumed are about the same, so normally it won't be an issue to include the entire file. But should you need to only include some of the plug-ins, they are clearly commented and you can easily copy and paste them into another style sheet, or into the `<style>` section of your web page.

**NOTE** *Some of the JavaScript-aided plug-ins require a couple more lines of HTML to include. If you wish to use them, please refer to the section entitled* JavaScript-Aided Plug-ins *a little further on.*

## Class Name Conflicts

In order to keep the plug-ins easy to access, I have tried to always use short, self-explanatory class names, even including a number of single-letter classes such as `i` (which applies italics to text).

However, if your own style or that of a third party use any of the same class names, then one or other class will take precedence (according to rules explained in the next chapter), and the other styles may only be partially implemented, if at all. In such cases, you are unlikely to be able to successfully use both at the same time.

# JavaScript-aided Plug-ins

Some of the plug-ins in this book perform actions that are simply not possible to achieve with CSS alone. They do this by using two JavaScript libraries of plug-ins. These are *PJ.js*, from the companion book to this, *Plug-in JavaScript*, and *PC.js*, which was specially written for this book. The *PJ.js* functions provide a wide range of positioning, sizing, and transition effects, which are then called upon by the *PC.js* functions to achieve various enhanced CSS effects.

Using these libraries is very easy and clearly explained in the sections that access them, and simply consists of including the following line of HTML in the head of a web page:

```
<script src="PJ.js"></script><script src="PC.js"></script>
```

This line loads in the libraries from the current folder (but you can also import them from elsewhere) and performs the basic initialization required by them. Both of these files are also included in the *plug-ins.zip* file downloadable from the *plugincss.com* web site.

### Including JavaScript-aided CSS Alongside Pure CSS

In order to use all of the plug-ins in this book (both pure CSS and JavaScript-aided), and to set up and forget their inclusion, I recommend you add the following two lines to the head section of *all* your web pages that use them:

```
<link rel="stylesheet" type="text/css" href="PC.css" />
<script src="PJ.js"></script><script src="PC.js"></script>
```

Remember to preface the filenames with the correct path(s) if you are importing these files from somewhere other than the current folder.

---

**NOTE** *There is a smaller version of the* PJ.js *file called* PJsmall.js, *which is also available in the* plug-ins.zip *download. It contains all the same functions and works in exactly the same manner, but it has been compressed to around half the size of* PJ.js. *Therefore, where file size and/or available bandwidth are an issue, you may wish to use this smaller file instead of* PJ.js.

### Users Without JavaScript

There is a slight downside to using the JavaScript-aided plug-ins, in that a very small number of users have JavaScript disabled on their browser. Therefore, you may choose to not use the JavaScript-aided plug-ins, which would be a shame since they provide some great enhancements.

Or you could include an HTML segment such as the following to ask your readers to enable JavaScript on your web site (in which case you should remember that those enhanced features that cannot degrade gracefully will simply not be available to users without JavaScript):

```
<noscript>
<h1>JavaScript Enhanced</h1>
This website is enhanced with JavaScript and you will be able to
view it at its best only if you enable JavaScript in your browser.
</noscript>
```

Alternatively, a much friendlier method (albeit a little more time-consuming), is to offer an alternative <noscript> ... </noscript> section of HTML for each time you use JavaScript-aided CSS. That way your non-JavaScript users will never know the difference.

---

## Summary

You should now have a basic picture of how style sheets work, how CSS and the DOM relate to each other, and how to import the plug-ins. In the next chapter, we'll take a crash course on CSS, at the end of which you will be able to understand and use all the plug-ins in this book. You will also be able to create your own variations by tweaking or extending them.

# CHAPTER 2

## CSS Crash Course

The subject of Cascading Style Sheets (CSS) is a large one, covering a wide range of different techniques, and there are many books that have been written solely about how to use it and how it works. But in this chapter, I have distilled as much of this information as possible into an easily digestible primer that provides all the information you need to use the plug-ins in this book.

If you are already used to CSS, I recommend you at least skim through this chapter to get a quick refresher on the subject since the rest of the book draws on this information.

## CSS Rules

Before looking at the inner workings of style sheets, let's examine the structure of CSS and break down the rules for constructing CSS statements.

Each statement starts with a selector, which is what the rule affects. For example, in the following assignment, `h1` is the selector being given a font size 240 percent larger than the default:

```
h1 { font-size:240%; }
```

By providing a new value to the `font-size` property of the selector, this ensures that the contents of all `<h1>` ... `</h1>` pairs of tags will be displayed at a font size 240 percent larger than the default size. This is achieved by placing one or more assignments within the `{` and `}` symbols that follow the selector (in this case: `font-size:240%;`).

The part before the `:` (colon) symbol is the *property*, while the remainder is the *value* applied to it. Lastly, there is a `;` (semicolon) to end the statement, which in this instance is not required (but would be if another assignment were to follow on the same line). For the sake of avoiding tricky to track down errors, in this book I always include the semicolons even when they are not necessary.

### Multiple Assignments

You can create multiple property assignments in a couple of different ways. First, you can concatenate them on the same line, like this:

```
h1 { font-size:240%; color:blue; }
```

This adds a second assignment that changes the color of all `<h1>` headers to blue. You can also place the assignments one per line, like the following:

```
h1 { font-size:240%;
color:blue; }
```

Or you can space the assignments out a little more so they line up below each other in a column at the colons, like this:

```
h1 {
    font-size:240%;
        color:blue;
}
```

This way you can easily see where each new set of rules begins, because of the selector in the first column, and because the assignments that follow are neatly lined up with all property values starting at the same horizontal offset.

There is no right or wrong way to lay out your CSS, but I recommend you at least try to keep each block of CSS consistent with itself, so it can be easily taken in at a glance. This is the approach I have taken in this book, in that I always try to make groups of assignments as tidy and symmetrical as I can so the individual CSS rules are easy to follow.

## Comments

It is a good idea to comment your CSS rules, even if you only describe the main groups of statements rather than all or most of them. You can do this in two different ways. First, you can place a comment within a pair of /* ... */ tags, like this:

```
/* This is a CSS comment */
```

Or you can extend a comment over many lines, like this:

```
/* A Multi
   line
   comment */
```

---

**CAUTION**  *If you use multiline comments, you should be aware that you cannot nest more comments within them, otherwise you will get unpredictable errors.*

## Style Types

A number of different style types exist, ranging from the default styles set up by your browser (and any user styles you may have applied), through inline or embedded styles to external style sheets. The styles defined in each type have a hierarchy of precedence, from low to high.

## Default Styles

The lowest level of style precedence is the default styling applied by a web browser. These styles are created as a fallback for when a web page doesn't have any styles and are intended to be a generic set of styles that will display reasonably well in most instances.

Pre-CSS, these were the only styles applied to a document, and only a handful of them could be changed by a web page (such as font face, color and size, and a few element-sizing arguments).

## User Styles

User styles are the next highest precedence of styles, and are supported by most modern browsers, but are implemented differently by each. If you would like to learn how to create your own default styles for browsing, use a search engine to enter your browser name followed by **user styles** (for example, enter **firefox user styles** for the Mozilla Firefox browser). Figure 2-1 shows a user style sheet being applied to Microsoft Internet Explorer 8 by clicking Internet Options | General | Accessibility.

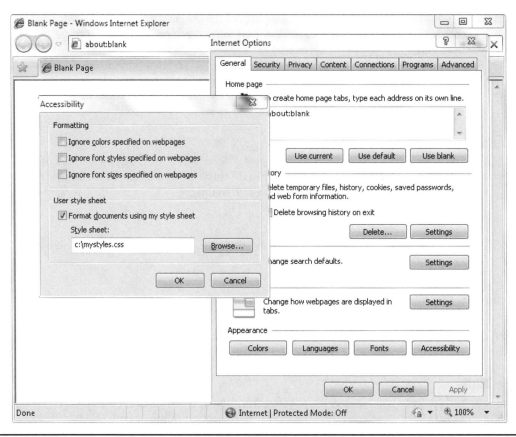

**FIGURE 2-1**    Applying a user style sheet to Internet Explorer 8

If a user style is assigned that has already been defined as a browser default, it will then override the browser's default setting. Any style not defined in a user style sheet will retain their default values as set up in the browser.

## External Style Sheets

The next types of styles are those assigned in an external style sheet. These settings will override any assigned either by the user or by the browser. External style sheets are the recommended way to create your styles because you can produce different style sheets for different purposes, such as styling for general web use, for viewing on a mobile browser with a smaller screen, for printing purposes, and so on, and then apply just the one needed for each type of media.

## Internal Styles

Internal styles are those you create within `<style>` ... `</style>` tags; they take precedence over all the preceding style types. At this point, though, you are beginning to break the separation between styling and content since any external style sheets loaded in at the same time will have a lower precedence.

## Inline Styles

An inline style is where you assign a property directly to an element. It also has the highest precedence of any style type. It is used like this:

```
<a href="http://google.com" style="color:green;">Visit Google</a>
```

In this example, the link specified will be displayed in green, regardless of any default or other color settings applied by any other type of style sheet, whether directly to this link or generically for all links.

When you use this type of styling, you are breaking the separation between layout and content; therefore, it is recommended you do so only when you have a very good reason.

# Selectors

The means by which you access one or more elements is called selection, and the part of a CSS rule that does this is known as a selector. As you might expect, there are many different varieties of selector.

## Type

The type selector works on types of HTML elements such as <p> or <i>. For example, the following rule will ensure that all the contents within <p> ... </p> tags are fully justified:

```
p { text-align:justify; }
```

## Descendant

Descendant selectors let you apply styles to elements that are contained within other elements. For example, the following rule sets all text within <b> ... </b> tags to red, but only if they occur within <p> ... </p> tags (like this: <p><b>Hello</b> there</p>):

```
p b { color:red; }
```

Descendant selectors can continue nesting indefinitely, so the following is a perfectly valid rule to make bold text within a list element of an unordered list display in blue:

```
ul li b { color:blue; }
```

## Child

The child selector is similar to the descendant selector, but is more constraining about when the style will be applied by selecting only those elements that are direct children of another element. For example, the following code uses a descendant selector that will change any bold text within a paragraph to red, even if the bold text is itself within italics (like this <p><i><b>Hello</b> there</i></p>):

```
p b { color:red; }
```

In this instance, the word "Hello" displays in red. However, when this more general type of behavior is not required, a child selector can be used to narrow the scope of the selector. For example, the following child selector will set bold text to red only if the element is a direct child of a paragraph, and is not itself contained within another element:

```
p > b { color:red; }
```

Now the word "Hello" will not change color because it is not a direct child of the paragraph.

## ID

If you give an element an ID name (like this: <div id='mydiv'>), then you can directly access it from CSS in the following way, which changes all the text in the div to italic:

```
#mydiv { font-style:italic; }
```

### Reusing IDs

IDs can be used only once within a document; therefore, only the first occurrence found will receive the new property value assigned by a CSS rule. But in CSS, you can directly reference any IDs that have the same name, as long as they occur within different element types, like this:

```
<div id='myid'>Hello</div>
<span id='myid'>Hello</span>
```

Because IDs normally apply only to unique elements, the following rule will apply an underline to only the first occurrence of myid:

```
#myid { text-decoration:underline; }
```

However, you can ensure that CSS applies the rule to both occurrences like this:

```
span#myid { text-decoration:underline; }
div#myid  { text-decoration:underline; }
```

Or more succinctly, like this (see the section on grouping a little further on):

```
span#myid, div#myid { text-decoration:underline; }
```

---

**CAUTION**  *If you use this form of selection, you should remember that any JavaScript that also must access these elements cannot easily do so because the commonly used* getElementByID() *function will return only the first occurrence. To reference any other instances, the programmer would have to search through the whole list of elements in the document, a cumbersome task to undertake.*

## Class

A much better way to reference multiple elements at a time is with a class. When you want to share the styling of a number of elements in a page, you can assign them all the same class name (like this: <span class='myclass'>) and then create a single rule to modify all those elements at once, as in the following rule, which creates a 10-pixel left-margin offset for all elements using the class:

```
.myclass { margin-left:10px; }
```

In modern browsers, HTML elements may also use more than one class by separating them with spaces, like this: `<span class='thisclass thatclass otherclass'>`, which is the technique used in this book to provide multiple styles to elements. Older browsers only allow a single class, so if you are targeting them, you should put the most important class first.

### Narrowing Class Scope

You can narrow the scope of action of a class by specifying the types of elements to which it should apply. For example, the following rule applies the setting only to paragraphs that use the class `main`:

```
p.main { text-indent:30px; }
```

In this example, only paragraphs using the class `main` (like this: `<p class="main">`) will receive the new property value. Any other element types that may try to access the class (such as `<div class="main">`) will be ignored.

## Attribute

Many HTML tags support attributes and using this type of selector can save you from having to use IDs and classes for referencing them. For example, you can directly reference attributes in the following manner, which sets all elements with the attribute `type="submit"` to a width of 100 pixels:

```
[type="submit"] { width:100px; }
```

If you wish to narrow the scope of the selector to, for example, only form input elements with that attribute type, you could use the following rule instead:

```
form input[type="submit"] { width:100px; }
```

---

**NOTE** *Attribute selectors also work on IDs and classes so that, for example, [class="classname"] performs in exactly the same way as the ID selector .classname (except that the latter has a higher precedence). Likewise, [id="idname"] is equivalent to using the class selector .idname. The # and . prefaced class and ID selectors can, therefore, be viewed as shorthand for attribute selectors, but with a higher precedence.*

## Universal

The wildcard or universal selector matches any element, so the following rule will make a complete mess of a document by giving a green border to all of its elements:

```
* { border:1px solid green; }
```

It's therefore unlikely that you will use the * on its own, but as part of a compound rule it can be very powerful. For example, the following rule will apply the same styling as earlier, but only to all paragraphs that are subelements of the element with the ID boxout, and only as long as they are not direct children:

```
#boxout * p {border:1px solid green; }
```

Here, the first selector following #boxout is a * symbol, and so it refers to any element within the boxout object. The following p selector then narrows down the selection focus by changing the selector to apply only to paragraphs (as defined by the p) that are subelements of elements returned by the * selector. Therefore, this CSS rule performs the following actions (in which I use the terms object and element interchangeably to refer to the same thing):

1. Finds the object with the ID of boxout.
2. Finds all subelements of the object returned in step 1.
3. Finds all p subelements of the objects returned in step 2 and, since this is the final selector in the group, also finds all p sub- and sub-subelements (and so on) of the objects returned in step 2.
4. Applies the styles within the { and } characters to the objects returned in step 3.

The net result of this is that the green border is applied only to paragraphs that are grandchildren (or great-grandchildren, and so on) of the main element.

## Grouping

Using CSS, it is possible to apply a rule to more than one element, class, or any other type of selector at the same time by separating the selectors with commas. So, for example, the following rule will place a dotted orange line underneath all paragraphs, the element with the ID of idname, and all elements using the class classname:

```
p, .idname, #classname { border-bottom:1px dotted orange; }
```

# The Cascade

One of the most fundamental things about CSS properties is that they *cascade*, which is why they are called Cascading Style Sheets. But what does this mean? Well, cascading is a method used to resolve potential conflicts between the various types of style sheet a browser supports, and apply them in order of precedence according to who created them, the method used to create the style, and the types of properties selected.

## Style Sheet Creators

Three main types of style sheet are supported by all modern browsers. In order of precedence from high to low, they are:

1. Those created by a document's author
2. Those created by the user
3. Those created by the browser

These three sets of style sheets are processed in reverse order. First, the defaults in the web browser are applied to the document. Without these defaults, web pages that don't use style sheets would look terrible. They include the font face, size and color, element spacing, table borders and spacing, and all the other reasonable styling a user would expect.

Next, if the user has created any user styles to employ in preference to the standard ones, these are applied, replacing any of the browser's default styles that may conflict.

Lastly, any styles created by the current document's author are then applied, replacing any that have been created either as browser defaults or by the user.

## Style Sheet Methods

Style sheets can be created in three different ways, or methods. In high to low order of precedence, they are:

1. As inline styles

2. In an embedded style sheet

3. As an external style sheet

Again, these methods of style sheet creation are applied in reverse order of precedence. Therefore, all external style sheets are processed first, and their styles are applied to the document.

Next, any embedded styles (within `<style>` ... `</style>` tags) are processed, and any that conflict with external rules are given precedence and override the others.

Lastly, any styles applied directly to an element as an inline style (such as `<div style="...">` ... `</div>`) are given the highest precedence, and override all previously assigned properties.

## Style Sheet Selectors

Selecting elements to be styled is done in three different ways. Going from highest to lowest order of precedence, they are:

1. Referencing by individual ID

2. Referencing in groups by class

3. Referencing by element tags (such as `<p>` or `<b>`)

Selectors are processed according to the number and types of elements affected by a rule, which is a little different than the previous two methods for resolving conflicts. This is because rules do not have to apply only to one type of selector at a time, and may reference many different selectors. Therefore, a method is needed to determine the precedence of rules that can contain any combination of selectors. This is done by calculating the specificity of each rule by ordering them from the widest to narrowest scope of action.

This specificity is calculated by creating three-part numbers based on the selector types in the earlier numbered list. These compound numbers start off looking like [0, 0, 0]. When processing a rule, each selector that references an ID increments the first number by 1, so that the compound number would become [1, 0, 0]. Let's say there are three ID references in a particular rule; thus, the compound number becomes [3, 0, 0].

Then, the number of selectors that reference a class is placed in the second part of the compound number. Let's say there were five of them, making the number [3, 5, 0].

Finally, all selectors that reference element tags are counted and this number is placed in the last part of the compound number. Let's say there were two, so the final compound number becomes [3, 5, 2], which is all that is needed to compare this rule's specificity with any another.

In cases with nine or fewer of each type in a compound number, you can convert it directly to a decimal number, which in this case is 352. Rules with a lower number than this will have lower precedence, and those with a higher number will have greater precedence. Where two rules share the same value, the most recently applied one wins.

### Using a Different Number Base

Where there is more than nine of a type in a number, you have to work in a higher number base. For example, the compound number [11, 7, 19] doesn't convert to decimal by simply concatenating the three parts. Instead, you can convert the number to a higher base, such as base 20 (or higher if there are more than 19 of any type).

To do this, multiply the three parts out and add the results like this, starting with the rightmost number and working left:

```
        20x19 =    380
      20×20×7 =   2800
   20×20×20×11 = 88000
Total in decimal = 91180
```

On the left, replace the values of 20 with the base you are using, then once all the compound numbers of a set of rules are converted from this base to decimal, it is easy to determine the specifity, and therefore the precedence of each. Thankfully, all this is handled for you by the CSS processor, but knowing how it works helps you to properly construct rules and understand what precedence they will have.

## The !important Tag

Where two or more style rules are equivalent, only the most recently processed rule will take precedence. However, you can force a rule to a higher precedence than other equivalent rules using the !important tag, like this:

```
p { color:#ff0000 !important; }
```

When you do this, all previous equivalent settings are overridden (even ones using !important) and any equivalent rules that are processed later will be ignored. So, for example, the second of the two following rules would normally take precedence, but because of the use of !important in the prior assignment, it is ignored:

```
p { color:#ff0000 !important; }
p { color:#ffff00 }
```

## The Difference between Divs and Spans

Both divs and spans are types of containers, but they have different qualities. By default, a div has infinite width (at least to the browser edge), which can be seen by applying a border to one, like this:

```
<div style="border:1px solid green;">Hello</div>
```

A span, however, is only as wide as the text it contains. Therefore, the following line of HTML shows the border only around the word "Hello," and it does not extend to the right-hand edge of the browser:

```
<span style="border:1px solid green;">Hello</span>
```

Also, spans follow text or other objects as they wrap around and can therefore have a complicated border. For example, in the following web page, CSS has been used to make the background of all divs yellow, all spans cyan, and to add a border to both before creating a few example spans and divs:

```
<html
    <head>
        <title>Div and span example</title>
            <style>
                div, span { border:1px solid black;   }
                div        { background-color:yellow;  }
                span       { background-color:cyan;    }
            </style>
    </head>
    <body>
        <div>This text is within a div tag</div> This isn't.
        <div>And this is again.</div><br />

        <span>This text is inside a span tag.</span> This isn't.
        <span>And this is again.</span><br /><br />

        <div>This is a larger amount of text in a div that
        wraps around to the next line of the browser</div><br />

        <span>This is a larger amount of text in a span that
        wraps around to the next line of the browser</span>
    </body>
</html>
```

Figure 2-2 shows what this page looks like in a web browser. Although it is printed only in shades of gray in the paperback version of this book, the figure clearly shows how divs extend to the right-hand edge of a browser and force following content to appear at the start of the first available position below them.

The figure also shows how spans keep to themselves and only take up the space required to hold their contents, without forcing following content to appear below them. For example, in the bottom two examples of the figure, you can also see that when divs wrap around the screen edge, they retain a rectangular shape, whereas spans simply follow the flow of the contents within them.

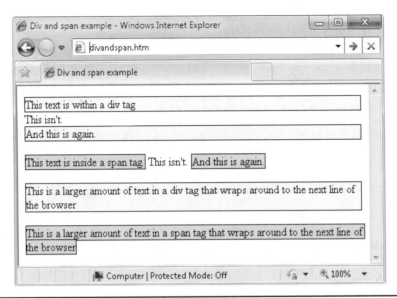

**FIGURE 2-2** A variety of divs and spans of differing widths

Therefore, since divs can only be rectangular, they are better suited for containing objects such as images, boxouts, quotes, and so on, while spans are best used for holding text or other attributes that follow one after another inline (such as sections of text).

## Measurements

CSS supports an impressive range of different units of measurement, enabling you to tailor your web pages precisely to specific values or relative dimensions. The ones I generally use (which you will likely find the most useful) are pixels, points, ems, and percent.

- **Pixels**   The size of a pixel varies according to the dimensions and pixel depth of the user's monitor. One pixel equals the width/height of a single dot on the screen, and so this measurement is best suited to monitors.
  Example: `#classname { margin:5px; }`

- **Points**   A point is equivalent in size to 1/72 of an inch. The measurement comes from a print design background and is best suited for that medium, but is also commonly used on monitors.
  Example: `#classname { font-size:14pt; }`

- **Inches**   An inch is the equivalent of 72 points and is also a measurement type best suited for print.
  Example: `#classname { width:3in; }`

- **Centimeters**   Centimeters are another unit of measurement best suited for print. One centimeter is a little over 28 points.
  Example: `#classname { height:2cm; }`

- **Millimeters**   A millimeter is one-tenth of a centimeter (or almost 3 points). Millimeters are another measure best suited to print.
  Example: `#classname { font-size:5mm; }`
- **Picas**   A pica is another print typographic measurement, which is equivalent to 12 points.
  Example: `#classname { font-size:1pc; }`
- **Ems**   An em is equal to the current font size and is, therefore, one of the more useful measurements for CSS since it is used to describe relative dimensions.
  Example: `#classname { font-size:2em; }`
- **Exs**   An ex is also related to the current font size; it is equivalent to the height of a lowercase letter "x". This is a less popular unit of measurement and is typically used as a good approximation for helping set the width of a box that will contain some text.
  Example: `#classname { width:20ex; }`
- **Percent**   This unit is related to the em in that it is exactly 100 times greater (when used on a font). Whereas 1 em equals the current font size, the same size is 100 in percent. When not relating to a font, this unit is relative to the size of the container of the property being accessed.
  Example: `#classname { height:120%; }`

# Fonts

Using CSS, you can style four main font properties: family, style, size, and weight. Between them, you can fine-tune the way text displays in your web pages and/or when printed, and so on.

## Font Family

The `font-family` property assigns the font to use. It also supports listing a variety of fonts in order of preference so that styling can fall back gracefully when the user doesn't have the preferred font installed. For example, to set the default font for paragraphs, you might use a CSS rule such as this:

```
p { font-family: Verdana, Arial, Helvetica, sans-serif; }
```

Where a font name is made up of two or more words, you must enclose the name in quotation marks, like this:

```
p { font-family: "Times New Roman", Georgia, serif; }
```

---

***TIP***   *Because they should be available on virtually all web browsers and operating systems, the safest font families to use on a web page are Arial, Helvetica, Times New Roman, Times, Courier New, and Courier. The Verdana, Georgia, Comic Sans MS, Trebuchet MS, Arial Black, and Impact fonts are safe for Mac and PC use, but may not be installed on other operating systems such as Linux. Other common but less safe fonts are Palatino, Garamond, Bookman, and Avant Garde. If you use one of the less safe fonts, make sure you offer fallbacks of one or more safer fonts in your CSS, so your web pages will degrade gracefully on browsers without your preferred fonts.*

## Font Style

With this property, you can choose to display a font normally, in italics or obliquely. The following rules create three classes (`normal`, `italic`, and `oblique`) that can be applied to elements to create these effects:

```
.normal  {font-style:normal;  }
.italic  {font-style:italic;  }
.oblique {font-style:oblique; }
```

## Font Size

As described in the earlier section on measurements, you can change a font's size in many ways. But these all boil down to two main types: fixed and relative. A fixed setting looks like the following rule, which sets the default paragraph font size to 14 point:

```
p { font-size:14pt; }
```

Alternatively, you may wish to work with the current default font size, using it to style various types of text such as headings. In the following rules, relative sizes of some headers are defined, with the <h4> tag starting off 20 percent bigger than the default, and with each larger size being another 40 percent larger than the previous one:

```
h1 { font-size:240%; }
h2 { font-size:200%; }
h3 { font-size:160%; }
h4 { font-size:120%; }
```

## Font Weight

Using this property, you can choose how boldly to display a font. The main values you will use are likely to be `normal` and `bold`, like this:

```
.bold { font-weight:bold; }
```

# Text

Regardless of the font in use, you can further modify the way text displays by altering its decoration, spacing, and alignment. A crossover exists between the text and font properties though, such that effects like italics or bold text are achieved via the `font-style` and `font-weight` properties, while others such as underlining require the `text-decoration` property.

## Decoration

With the `text-decoration` property, you can apply effects to text such as `underline`, `line-through`, `overline`, and `blink`. For example, the following rule creates a new class called `over` that applies overlines to text (the weight of over, under, and through lines will match that of the font):

```
.over { text-decoration:overline; }
```

## Spacing

A number of different properties allow you to modify line, word, and letter spacing. For example, the following rules change the line spacing for paragraphs by modifying the line-height property to be 25 percent greater, the word-spacing property is set to 30 pixels and letter-spacing is set to 3 pixels:

```
p {
   line-height   :125%;
   word-spacing  :30px;
   letter-spacing:3px;
}
```

## Alignment

Four types of text alignment are available in CSS: left, right, center, and justify. In the following rule, default paragraph text is set to full justification:

```
p { text-align:justify; }
```

## Transformation

Four properties are available for transforming text: none, capitalize, uppercase, and lowercase. For example, the following rule creates a class called upper that will ensure all text is displayed in uppercase when it is used:

```
.upper { text-transform:uppercase; }
```

## Indenting

Using the text-indent property, you can indent the first line of a block of text by a specified amount. For example, the following rule indents the first line of every paragraph by 20 pixels, although a different unit of measurement or a percent increase could also be applied:

```
p { text-indent:20px; }
```

# Colors

Colors can be applied to the foreground and background of text and objects using the color and background-color properties (or by supplying a single argument to the background property). The colors specified can be one of the named colors (such as red or blue), colors created from hexadecimal RGB triplets (such as #ff0000 or #0000ff), or colors created using the rgb() CSS function.

The standard 16 color names as defined by the W3C (*w3.org*) standards organization are aqua, black, blue, fuchsia, gray, green, lime, maroon, navy, olive, purple, red, silver, teal, white, and yellow. The following rule uses one of these names to set the background color for an object with the ID of object.

```
#object { background-color:silver; }
```

In the following rule, the foreground color of text in all divs is set to yellow (because on a computer display hexadecimal levels of `ff` red, plus `ff` green, plus `00` blue creates the color yellow):

```
div { color:#ffff00; }
```

Or, if you don't wish to work in hexadecimal, you can specify your color triplets using the `rgb()` function, as in the following rule, which changes the background color of the current document to aqua.

```
body { background-color:rgb(0, 255, 255); }
```

---

**TIP**    *If you prefer not to work in ranges of 256 levels per color, you can use percentages in the* `rgb()` *function instead, with values from 0 to 100, ranging from the lowest (zero) amount of a primary color, through to the highest (100), like this:* `rgb(58%, 95%, 74%)`. *You can also use floating point values for even finer color control, like this:* `rgb(23.4%, 67.6%, 15.5%)`.

---

## Positioning Elements

Elements within a web page fall where they are placed in the document, but can be moved about by changing an element's `position` property from the default of `static` to one of `absolute`, `relative`, or `fixed`.

An element with absolute positioning is removed from the document and any other elements that can will flow into its released space. You can then position the object anywhere you like within the document using the `top`, `right`, `bottom`, and `left` properties. It will then rest on top of (or behind) other elements.

So, for example, to move an object with the ID of `object` to the absolute location of 100 pixels down from the document start and 200 pixels in from the left, you would apply the following rules to it (you can also use any of the other units of measurement supported by CSS):

```
#object {
   position:absolute;
   top      :100px;
   left     :200px;
}
```

Likewise, you can move the object relative to the location it would occupy in the normal document flow. So, for example, to move `object` 10 pixels down and 10 pixels to the right of its normal location, use the following rules:

```
#object {
   position:relative;
   top      :10px;
   left     :10px;
}
```

The final positioning property setting lets you move an object to an absolute location, but only within the current browser viewport. Then, when the document is scrolled, the object remains exactly where it has been placed, with the main document scrolling beneath

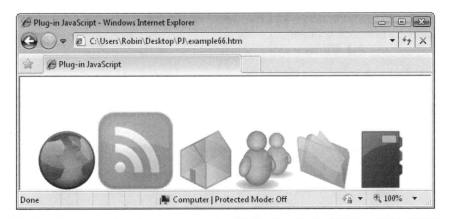

PART I

**FIGURE 2-3**    Creating a simple dock bar using the position property

it—this is a great way to create dock bars and other similar devices. For example, to fix the `object` to the top left corner of the browser window, use the following rules:

```
#object {
   position:fixed;
   top      :0px;
   left     :0px;
}
```

Figure 2-3 shows a simple dock bar created using a value of `fixed` for the `position` property to align the icons at the screen bottom. With a little JavaScript or proprietary CSS transforms, the icons can be made to resize as the mouse passes over them, as is happening to the second icon. See my book *Plug-in JavaScript* (McGraw-Hill Professional, 2010) for this and many other neat JavaScript plug-ins.

## Pseudo Classes

A number of selectors and classes, used only within a style sheet, do not have any matching tags or attributes within any HTML. Their task is to classify elements using characteristics other than their name, attributes, or content that cannot be deduced from the document tree. These include pseudo classes such as `first-line`, `first-child`, and `first-letter`.

Pseudo classes are separated from elements using a : (colon) character. To create a class called `bigfirst` for emphasizing the first letter of an element, you would use a rule such as the following:

```
.bigfirst:first-letter {
   font-size:400%;
   float     :left;
}
```

When the `bigfirst` class is applied to an element, the first letter's display size is much enlarged, with the remaining text (at normal size) neatly flowing around it (due to the `float` property), as if the first letter were an image or other object.

Other pseudo classes include `hover`, `link`, `active`, and `visited`, all of which are mostly useful for applying to anchor elements, as in the following rules, which set the default color of all links to blue, and that of links that have already been visited to light blue:

```
a:link    { color:blue;     }
a:visited { color:lightblue; }
```

The following pair of rules is interesting in that it uses the `hover` pseudo class, meaning they are applied only when the mouse is placed over the element and, in this example, they change the link to white text on a red background, providing a dynamic effect you would normally only expect from using JavaScript code:

```
a:hover {
    color     :white;
    background:red;
}
```

Here I have used the `background` property with a single argument, instead of the longer `background-color` property. The `active` pseudo class is also dynamic in that it effects a change to a link during the time between the mouse button being clicked and released—as with this rule, which changes the link color to dark blue:

```
a:active { color:darkblue; }
```

Another interesting dynamic pseudo class is `focus`, which is applied only when an element is focused by the user selecting it with the keyboard or mouse, as with the following rule, which uses the universal selector to always place a mid-gray, dotted, 2-pixel border around the currently focused object:

```
*:focus { border:2px dotted #888888; }
```

## Shorthand

To save space, groups of related CSS properties can be concatenated into a single shorthand assignment. For example, I have already used the shorthand for creating a border a few times, as in the `focus` rule in the previous section, which is actually a shorthand concatenation of the following rule set:

```
*:focus {
    border-width:2px;
    border-style:dotted;
    border-color:#888888;
}
```

When using a shorthand rule, you need only apply the properties up to the point where you wish to change values. So you could use the following to set only a border's width and style, but not its color:

```
*:focus { border:2px dotted; }
```

## The Box Model

The fundamental CSS properties affecting the layout of a page are based around the box model; a nested set of properties surrounding an element, as shown in Figure 2-4.

Virtually all elements have (or can have) these properties, including the document body, whose margin you can, for example, remove with the following rule:

```
body { margin:0px; }
```

Once you have the hang of the box model, you will be well on your way to creating professionally laid out pages, since these properties alone will make up much of your page styling.

### Margin

The margin is the outermost level of the box model. It separates elements from each other and its use is quite smart. For example, assume you have chosen to give a number of elements a default margin of 10 pixels around them. When placed on top of each other, this would create a gap of 20 pixels due to adding the border widths together.

However, to overcome this potential issue, when two elements with borders are directly one above the other, only the larger of the two margins is used to separate them. If both margins are the same width, just one of the widths is used. This way, you are much more likely to get the result you want. You should note, however, that the margins of absolutely positioned or inline elements do not collapse.

The margins of an element can be changed en-masse with the margin property, or individually with margin-left, margin-top, margin-right, and margin-bottom.

**FIGURE 2-4**
The nested levels of the CSS box model

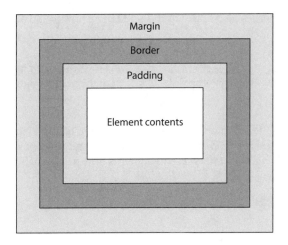

When setting the `margin` property, you can supply one, two, three, or four arguments, which have the effects commented in the following rules:

```
margin:1px;             /* Set all margins to 1 pixel width       */
margin:1px 2px;         /* Set the top and bottom margins to 1 pixel
                           and the left and right to 2 pixels width */
margin:1px 2px 3px;     /* Set the top margin to 1 pixel, the left
                           and right to 2 pixels and the bottom
                           margin to 3 pixels width                */
margin:1px 2px 3px 4px; /* Set the top margin to 1 pixel, the right
                           to 2 pixels, the bottom to 3 pixels and
                           the left margin to 4 pixels width        */
```

## Border

The border level of the box model is similar to the margin except that there is no collapsing. The main properties used to modify borders are `border`, `border-left`, `border-top`, `border-right`, and `border-bottom`, and each of these can have other subproperties added as suffixes, such as `-color`, `-style`, and `-width`.

The four ways of accessing individual property settings used for the `margin` property also apply with the `border-width` property, so all the following are valid rules:

```
border-width:1px;             /* All borders              */
border-width:1px 2px;         /* Top/bottom and left/right */
border-width:1px 2px 3px;     /* Top, left/right and bottom */
border-width:1px 2px 3px 4px; /* Top, right, bottom and left */
```

## Padding

The deepest of the box model levels is the padding, which is applied inside any borders and/or margins. The main properties used to modify padding are `padding`, `padding-left`, `padding-top`, `padding-right`, and `padding-bottom`.

The four ways of accessing individual property settings used for the `margin` and `border` properties also apply to the `padding` property, so all the following are valid rules:

```
padding:1px;             /* All borders              */
padding:1px 2px;         /* Top/bottom and left/right */
padding:1px 2px 3px;     /* Top, left/right and bottom */
padding:1px 2px 3px 4px; /* Top, right, bottom and left */
```

## Content

Deep within the box model levels, at their center, lies an element that can be styled in all the ways discussed in this chapter, and which can (and usually will) contain further subelements. They in turn may contain sub-subelements and so on, each with their own styling and box model settings.

## Summary

Although it has covered only a subset of CSS (there are many, many more aspects to the language than could ever be properly discussed in a single chapter), there is enough here to help you understand all the plug-ins in this book and modify them to your own requirements. You should also find this chapter a handy reference as your skills develop.

# PART II
# The Classes

# CHAPTER 3

## Manipulating Objects

This chapter introduces 19 groups of CSS classes you can use in your web pages to manage the positioning of elements, change text and background colors, add gradient fills and box shadows, alter transparency, and do a whole lot more.

Using the supplied *PC.css* file (available at *plugincss.com*), you can simply add class names to your HTML class declarations to apply any of a wide range of styling to an element, without having to write any CSS yourself.

And because modern browsers support the use of multiple class names in a declaration, you can supply as many classes as you like to style elements exactly how you want then. This means that with over 880 classes to draw on in this chapter alone, you can concentrate on creating great web pages without the hassle of writing and tweaking CSS rules.

## PLUG-IN 1   Positioning

The positioning classes let you decide the type of positioning to use for an object between the four types available (absolute, fixed, relative, and static), each of which changes the way CSS properties will affect objects using them. For example, Figure 3-1 shows two sections of text that have been given vertical offsets of 25 pixels, but because one has absolute positioning and the other is fixed, when the document is scrolled, one of them scrolls and the other remains where it is.

### Classes and Properties

| | |
|---|---|
| `absolute`<br>`abs` | Class to assign absolute positioning to an object, plus a shorthand version to save on typing |
| `fixed`<br>`fix` | Class to assign fixed positioning to an object, plus a shorthand version to save on typing |
| `relative`<br>`rel` | Class to assign relative positioning to an object, plus a shorthand version to save on typing |
| `static`<br>`sta` | Class to assign static positioning to an object, plus a shorthand version to save on typing |
| `position` | Property containing the type of object positioning to use out of absolute, fixed, relative, or static |

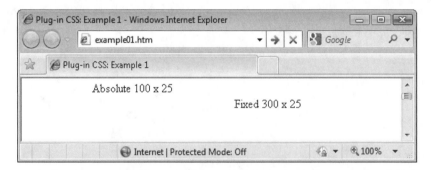

**FIGURE 3-1**   Different positioning types behave in different ways.

## About the Classes

The four classes in this group are `absolute`, `fixed`, `relative`, and `static`, and they have the following effects:

- **`absolute`**  When this position property is assigned to an object, it can be removed from the normal flow of the document to any other part. When it is moved, any other objects that can will move in to occupy the space released. Absolute objects can be placed behind or in front of other objects, and their coordinates are relative to the first parent object that has a position other than static.

- **`fixed`**  This type of positioning is similar to absolute, except that the object's coordinates are based on the browser window, such that if the document is scrolled, any fixed objects remain where they are and do not scroll with it.

- **`relative`**  An object that is given relative positioning has its coordinates based on the location it occupied when the document was fully loaded.

- **`static`**  Static positioning is the default for all elements and indicates that an object is to remain at the position within a document that it first occupied when the document was fully loaded.

## How to Use Them

To use these classes, you reference them from HTML, like this:

```
<span class='absolute'>Example text</span>
```

Here's an example HTML page illustrating use of the `absolute` and `fixed` classes:

```
<!DOCTYPE HTML PUBLIC "-//W3C//DTD HTML 4.01 Transitional//EN"
    "http://www.w3.org/TR/html4/loose.dtd">
<!-- saved from url=(0014)about:internet -->
<html>
    <head>
        <title>Plug-in CSS: Example 1</title>
        <link rel='stylesheet' type='text/css' href='PC.css' />
        <script src='PJ.js'></script><script src='PC.js'></script>
    </head>
    <body>
        <span class='absolute' style='left:100px; top:25px;'>
            Absolute 100 x 25
        </span>
        <span class='fixed'    style='left:300px; top:25px;'>
            Fixed 300 x 25
        </span>
        <br /><br /><br /><br /><br /><br /><br /><br /><br /><br /><br />
        <br /><br /><br /><br /><br /><br /><br /><br /><br /><br /><br />
    </body>
</html>
```

In this example, one span has been made absolute and moved to a position 100 pixels across by 25 down from the document start, while the other is fixed at an offset of 300 pixels across and 25 down from the top left corner of the browser window.

The <br /> tags that follow create 22 blank lines so that if you open this code in a small browser window, it will create a scroll bar at the right side which, if you scroll it, will move the text with absolute positioning, but the fixed text will remain in place.

You probably have noticed the use of inline styles in this example, such as `style='left:100px; top:25px;'`. These are required to assign the coordinates to each element. Later on, you will see how you can use much simpler classes instead of direct CSS rules.

Also, to save on typing, instead of using the longhand class names of `absolute`, `relative`, `fixed`, and `static`, you can use the alternate shorthand names of `abs`, `fix`, `rel`, and `sta` instead (there are handy shorthand versions for many of the more commonly used classes in this book).

---

**NOTE** *Because this is the first example, I have shown you a complete HTML web page including all the lines you need at the start, such as the document type and the "saved from" comment used to stop Internet Explorer from displaying errors when a page is viewed on a local file system. I have also shown the page title and the HTML required to load in the style sheet and JavaScript files. However, in future examples I will show only the main HTML. Don't forget that you can download all the examples in their entirety from the companion web site at plugincss.com.*

### The Classes

```
.absolute,   .abs { position:absolute; }
.fixed,      .fix { position:fixed;    }
.relative,   .rel { position:relative; }
.static,     .sta { position:static;   }
```

## Floating

The float property makes it possible for you to choose to place an object at either the right or left of a section of HTML and have accompanying text flow around it. To enable you to do this without writing any CSS rules, you can use the ready-made ones supplied with this plug-in.

In Figure 3-2, both the `leftfloat` and `rightfloat` classes have been used to display boats on either side of the screen with text flowing around them.

### Classes and Properties

| | |
|---|---|
| leftfloat<br>lf | Class to float an object to the left and make text and other elements flow around it (plus shorthand version) |
| leftfloat_h<br>lf_h | The same as leftfloat, but this style is only applied when the mouse is over the element to which it applies (plus shorthand version) |
| rightfloat<br>rf | Class to float an object to the left and make text and other elements flow around it (plus shorthand version) |
| rightfloat_h<br>rf_h | The same as rightfloat, but this style is only applied when the mouse is over the element to which it applies (plus shorthand version) |
| nofloat<br>nf | Class to unfloat a previously floated object (plus shorthand version) |
| nofloat_h<br>nf_h | The same as nofloat, but this style is applied only when the mouse is over the element to which it applies (plus shorthand version) |
| float | Property to float an object, which accepts the values left, right, or none |

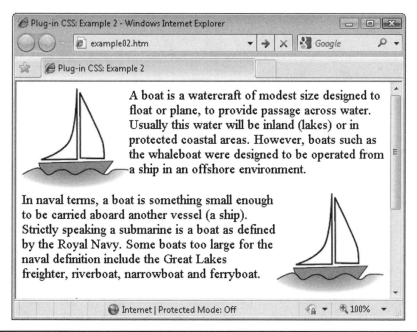

**FIGURE 3-2** Using the leftfloat and rightfloat classes

## About the Classes

This group has three main classes:

- **leftfloat** This class floats an object to the left, with other elements flowing around it. The flowing can be exited by issuing a `<br clear='left'>` tag, which causes all following HTML to appear under the floated object.
- **rightfloat** This class floats an object to the right, with other elements flowing around it. The flowing can be exited by issuing a `<br clear='right'>` tag, which causes all following HTML to appear under the floated object.
- **nofloat** Using this class will unfloat an object that has previously been floated.

As well as the shorthand versions of these class names, there is another group of classes that have the suffix _h appended to their names. This is one of the more powerful features of the plug-ins in this book in that (where it makes logical sense) each class also has an accompanying hover class denoted by the _h suffix. When these hover classes are used, their styles will be applied only when the mouse is over the object to which they refer. This makes it easy for you to apply rollover and other dynamic effects without writing a single line of either CSS or JavaScript.

## How to Use Them

To use these classes, you refer to them from any section of HTML to which you wish them applied. For example, the following HTML creates two floats—one on the left and one on the right—with text flowing around them (as shown in Figure 3-2):

```
<font size='4'>
<img class='lf' src='boat.png'>A boat is a watercraft of modest size
designed to float or plane, to provide passage across water. Usually
this water will be inland (lakes) or in protected coastal areas.
However, boats such as the whaleboat were designed to be operated from
a ship in an offshore environment.<br clear='left'>

<img class='rf' src='boat.png'>In naval terms, a boat is something small
enough to be carried aboard another vessel (a ship). Strictly speaking
a submarine is a boat as defined by the Royal Navy. Some boats too large
for the naval definition include the Great Lakes freighter, riverboat,
narrowboat and ferryboat.<br clear='right'>
```

Note the use of the <br clear='...'> tags to end the floating at specific places in the HTML. As well as these specific tags, if you want to ensure that no floats are applied to a section of text, you can also issue the tag <br clear='all'> to clear any and all left or right floats. You will also see that I have used the lf and rf shorthand versions of the class names, instead of having to type in the longer class names of leftfloat and rightfloat.

---

**NOTE**  *As mentioned in the previous plug-in group, the start and end portions of the HTML file are not shown here since they will usually all be exactly the same as each other. Therefore, only the main HTML is shown in this and all future examples.*

### Using the Hover Classes

To change the float property of an object when the mouse passes over it, you can use one of the class names with the _h suffix, like this:

```
<img class='lf_h' src='boat.png'>This text will display below the boat
image by default. But when the mouse is passed over the boat it will
move up to flow around the image.
```

In the following and in many other plug-in groups, you will see how this feature particularly comes into its own.

---

**NOTE**  *Although it's not likely that you would often want to change the float property of an element when it is hovered over, it is certainly possible that this feature could be required for certain applications and, as it takes only a few extra characters of CSS to support, there's no reason to omit the feature.*

## The Classes

```
.leftfloat,   .leftfloat_h:hover,   .lf,  .lf_h:hover { float:left;  }
.rightfloat,  .rightfloat_h:hover,  .rf,  .rf_h:hover { float:right; }
.nofloat,     .nofloat_h:hover,     .nf,  .nf_h:hover { float:none;  }
```

PLUG-IN

# 3  Background Colors

This group of classes illustrates the power of the plug-ins because they provide six different ways of changing the background color of an object to any of 21 different colors. Figure 3-3 shows six objects, with each using one of the different methods of changing the background color. In the first three, the entire element is modified, while in the second three only links that are contained within the element are affected.

As you hover over and/or click the different links, you will see the color change for the whole element in lines 2 and 3, but only for the link part in lines 5 and 6. As with all the examples, the one used to create this screen grab is downloadable from the companion web site at *plugincss.com*.

## Classes and Properties

| | |
|---|---|
| aqua_b<br>aqua_ba<br>aqua_bh<br>aqua_lb<br>aqua_lba<br>aqua_lbh | Class to change the background color of an object to aqua (aqua_b), plus classes to do so only if the object is actively being clicked (aqua_ba) or hovered over (aqua_bh), and another three classes to change the background of any links within the object (aqua_lb), any links within the object that are actively being clicked (aqua_lba), and any links within the object that are being hovered over (aqua_lbh) |
| black_b (etc...) | Classes – as aqua but for black |
| blue_b (etc...) | Classes – as aqua but for blue |
| brown_b (etc...) | Classes – as aqua but for brown |
| fuchsia_b (etc...) | Classes – as aqua but for fuchsia |
| gold_b (etc...) | Classes – as aqua but for gold |
| gray_b (etc...) | Classes – as aqua but for gray |
| green_b (etc...) | Classes – as aqua but for green |
| khaki_b (etc...) | Classes – as aqua but for khaki |
| lime_b (etc...) | Classes – as aqua but for lime |

**FIGURE 3-3**    This plug-in group offers many different ways of changing background colors.

| | |
|---|---|
| `maroon_b` (etc...) | Classes – as aqua but for maroon |
| `navy_b` (etc...) | Classes – as aqua but for navy |
| `olive_b` (etc...) | Classes – as aqua but for olive |
| `orange_b` (etc...) | Classes – as aqua but for orange |
| `pink_b` (etc...) | Classes – as aqua but for pink |
| `purple_b` (etc...) | Classes – as aqua but for purple |
| `red_b` (etc...) | Classes – as aqua but for red |
| `silver_b` (etc...) | Classes – as aqua but for silver |
| `teal_b` (etc...) | Classes – as aqua but for teal |
| `white_b` (etc...) | Classes – as aqua but for white |
| `yellow_b` (etc...) | Classes – as aqua but for yellow |
| background | Property containing background settings |

## About the Classes

This plug-in group has 21 main classes, with six different types of each that can be selected by choosing the required suffix. The preceding *Classes and Properties* table lists the available colors. Here is what the suffixes do:

- **_b**   Used to refer to a background property.
- **_ba**   Used to refer only to the background property of an object that is active (in other words, that is in the process of being clicked).
- **_bh**   Used to refer only to the background property of an object that the mouse is hovering over.
- **_lb**   Used to refer only to the background property of a link within the object.
- **_lba**   Used to refer only to the background property of a link within the object that is actively being clicked.
- **_lbh**   Used to refer only to the background property of a link within the object over which the mouse is hovering.

## How to Use Them

When you wish to change the background color of an object, first choose the color out of the 21 in the *Classes and Properties* table, and then decide when the color should be applied. So, let's assume you want to change the background color of an object to gold. To do this, you only need to use some simple HTML such as this:

```
<div class='gold_b'>This element has a gold background</div>
```

Or, if you wish the background color to change to orange, but only when the mouse is over it, you might use the following code:

```
<div class='orange_bh'>This element turns orange when moused over</div>
```

Then again, perhaps you would like the background to change color only when it is clicked. In which case, you might use code such as this:

```
<div class='purple_ba'>This element turns purple when clicked</div>
```

Or you can be really creative and combine all three effects into one, like this:

```
<div class='gold_b orange_bh purple_ba'>This element has a gold
background that turns orange when hovered over and purple when
clicked</div>
```

### Changing Links within the Object

Sometimes you won't want to change the background color of an entire object, but may wish to do so for any links it contains, and you can do this using HTML such as the following:

```
<div class='gold_lb'>This element has a plain background.
<a href='#'>And this link has a gold background</a></div>
```

Or all three types of color change can be applied to just the links within an object, like this:

```
<div class='gold_lb orange_lbh purple_lba'>This element has a plain
background. <a href='#'>And this link has a gold background that
turns orange when hovered over and purple when clicked</a></div>
```

Here's the HTML used to create the screen grab in Figure 3-3:

```
<div class='aqua_b'  >This is text. <a href='#'>This is a link</a>.</div>
<div class='aqua_ba' >This is text. <a href='#'>This is a link</a>.</div>
<div class='aqua_bh' >This is text. <a href='#'>This is a link</a>.</div>
<div class='aqua_lb' >This is text. <a href='#'>This is a link</a>.</div>
<div class='aqua_lba'>This is text. <a href='#'>This is a link</a>.</div>
<div class='aqua_lbh'>This is text. <a href='#'>This is a link</a>.</div>
```

As you can see, these classes provide a great deal of interactive functionality, with no need for writing JavaScript programs or creating your own CSS rules.

---

***TIP*** *Try downloading the example file from the companion web site and clicking on (and hovering over) different parts of each element to get a feel for how the different suffixes work.*

## The Classes

```
.aqua_b,       .aqua_ba:active,    .aqua_bh:hover,
.aqua_lb a,    .aqua_lba a:active, .aqua_lbh a:hover   {background:#0ff}
.black_b,      .black_ba:active,   .black_bh:hover,
.black_lb a,   .black_lba a:active,.black_lbh a:hover  {background:#000}
.blue_b,       .blue_ba:active,    .blue_bh:hover,
.blue_lb a,    .blue_lba a:active, .blue_lbh a:hover   {background:#00f}
.brown_b,      .brown_ba:active,   .brown_bh:hover,
.brown_lb a,   .brown_lba a:active,.brown_lbh a:hover  {background:#c44}
.fuchsia_b,    .fuchsia_ba:active, .fuchsia_bh:hover,
.fuchsia_lb a,.fuchsia_lba a:active,.fuchsia_lbh a:hover{background:#f0f}
```

```
.gold_b,            .gold_ba:active,        .gold_bh:hover,
.gold_lb a,         .gold_lba a:active,     .gold_lbh a:hover     {background:#fc0}
.gray_b,            .gray_ba:active,        .gray_bh:hover,
.gray_lb a,         .gray_lba a:active,     .gray_lbh a:hover     {background:#888}
.green_b,           .green_ba:active,       .green_bh:hover,
.green_lb a,        .green_lba a:active,    .green_lbh a:hover    {background:#080}
.khaki_b,           .khaki_ba:active,       .khaki_bh:hover,
.khaki_lb a,        .khaki_lba a:active,    .khaki_lbh a:hover    {background:#cc8}
.lime_b,            .lime_ba:active,        .lime_bh:hover,
.lime_lb a,         .lime_lba a:active,     .lime_lbh a:hover     {background:#0f0}
.maroon_b,          .maroon_ba:active,      .maroon_bh:hover,
.maroon_lb a,       .maroon_lba a:active,   .maroon_lbh a:hover   {background:#800}
.navy_b,            .navy_ba:active,        .navy_bh:hover,
.navy_lb a,         .navy_lba a:active,     .navy_lbh a:hover     {background:#008}
.olive_b,           .olive_ba:active,       .olive_bh:hover,
.olive_lb a,        .olive_lba a:active,    .olive_lbh a:hover    {background:#880}
.orange_b,          .orange_ba:active,      .orange_bh:hover,
.orange_lb a,       .orange_lba a:active,   .orange_lbh a:hover   {background:#f80}
.pink_b,            .pink_ba:active,        .pink_bh:hover,
.pink_lb a,         .pink_lba a:active,     .pink_lbh a:hover     {background:#f88}
.purple_b,          .purple_ba:active,      .purple_bh:hover,
.purple_lb a,       .purple_lba a:active,   .purple_lbh a:hover   {background:#808}
.red_b,             .red_ba:active,         .red_bh:hover,
.red_lb a,          .red_lba a:active,      .red_lbh a:hover      {background:#f00}
.silver_b,          .silver_ba:active,      .silver_bh:hover,
.silver_lb a,       .silver_lba a:active,   .silver_lbh a:hover   {background:#ccc}
.teal_b,            .teal_ba:active,        .teal_bh:hover,
.teal_lb a,         .teal_lba a:active,     .teal_lbh a:hover     {background:#088}
.white_b,           .white_ba:active,       .white_bh:hover,
.white_lb a,        .white_lba a:active,    .white_lbh a:hover    {background:#fff}
.yellow_b,          .yellow_ba:active,      .yellow_bh:hover,
.yellow_lb a,       .yellow_lba a:active,   .yellow_lbh a:hover   {background:#ff0}
```

# Gradients

Most modern browsers already support graduated background fills (with the surprising exception of Opera, which is usually very good at supporting web standards). Therefore, the classes in this group can be used to easily create gradient effects. And even Opera doesn't look too bad as it defaults to a single color average of the gradient.

Figure 3-4 shows a selection of gradients being applied to objects with the same suffixes as used by the solid color background classes (such as aqua_b).

## Classes and Properties

| | |
|---|---|
| carrot1<br>carrot1_a<br>carrot1_h<br>carrot1_l<br>carrot1_la<br>carrot1_lh | Class to change the background gradient of an object to the range of colors you would see in a carrot (carrot1), plus classes to do so only if the object is actively being clicked (carrot1_a) or hovered over (carrot1_h), and another three classes to change the background of any links within the object (carrot1_l), any links within the object that are actively being clicked (carrot1_la), and any links within the object that are being hovered over (carrot1_lh) |

| | |
|---|---|
| chrome1 (etc...) | Classes – as carrot1 but for a range of chrome steel colors |
| coffee1 (etc...) | Classes – as carrot1 but for a range of coffee brown colors |
| dusk1 (etc...) | Classes – as carrot1 but for a range of dusky blue colors |
| earth1 (etc...) | Classes – as carrot1 but for a range of brown earth colors |
| fire1 (etc...) | Classes – as carrot1 but for a range of yellowy orange fire colors |
| grass1 (etc...) | Classes – as carrot1 but for a range of fresh green grass colors |
| iron1 (etc...) | Classes – as carrot1 but for a range of metallic iron colors |
| plum1 (etc...) | Classes – as carrot1 but for a range of purple plum colors |
| rose1 (etc...) | Classes – as carrot1 but for a range of red rose colors |
| sky1 (etc...) | Classes – as carrot1 but for a range of blue sky colors |
| sunset1 (etc...) | Classes – as carrot1 but for a range of orangy sunset colors |
| tin1 (etc...) | Classes – as carrot1 but for a range of metallic tin colors |
| water1 (etc...) | Classes – as carrot1 but for a range of clear blue water colors |
| wine1 (etc...) | Classes – as carrot1 but for a range of deep red wine colors |
| background | Property to which the gradient (or solid color) is applied |
| filter | Property used by Internet Explorer for creating gradients and other effects |

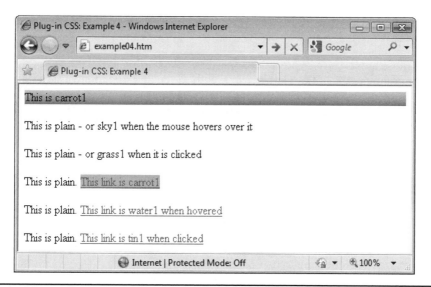

**Figure 3-4**   Applying gradient backgrounds is easy with these classes.

## About the Classes

This plug-in group has 15 main classes, with six different types of each that can be selected by choosing the required suffix. The preceding *Classes and Properties* table lists the available gradients. Here is what the suffixes do:

- **(no suffix)** Without a suffix, the object's background gradient will be set to the color supplied.
- **_a** This suffix is used to refer only to the background gradient of an object that is active (in other words, that is in the process of being clicked).
- **_h** This suffix is used to refer only to the background gradient of an object that the mouse is hovering over.
- **_l** This suffix is used to refer only to the background gradient of a link within the object.
- **_la** This suffix is used to refer only to the background gradient of a link within the object that is actively being clicked.
- **_lh** This suffix is used to refer only to the background gradient of a link within the object over which the mouse is hovering.

There is no _b suffix since gradients are background-only properties anyway. Therefore, all the other suffixes are a little shorter than those used for the solid colors in the previous plug-in group.

The property used to achieve the gradient (or solid fallback color) background is the background property. In the case of the Apple Safari and Google Chrome browsers, it is passed a string that looks like this:

```
background:-webkit-gradient(linear, left top, left bottom,
   from(#f44), to(#922));
```

This tells those browsers to create a linear gradient fill, starting at the top left of the object and continuing to the bottom left, starting with the color #f44, slowly graduating to the color #922.

Firefox and other Mozilla-based browsers require the following string format to be applied to the property:

```
background:-moz-linear-gradient(top, #f44, #922);
```

While all other browsers (and all future browsers once it is made the international standard) should send a string such as this:

```
background:linear-gradient(left top, #f44, #922);
```

Microsoft, often the odd one out, takes quite a different approach, so it is necessary to pass a string such as the following to its filter property:

```
filter:progid:DXImageTransform.Microsoft.Gradient(
   startColorstr='#f04040', endColorstr='#902020');
```

Also, for those browsers that do not support gradients, a simple solid color string such as #d33 is provided before any of the preceding lines, so that if all the gradient rules fail, at least the simple color setting will remain active.

The downside of all this, as you will often see as you progress through this book, is that all the browsers have to be catered to and, therefore, all the different strings must be applied for each gradient. This means that the CSS rules end up quite large. But then again, because all the work has already been done for you, all you need to do is include the CSS file and use simple class names in your HTML—you can forget about how cumbersome some of the rules are.

## How to Use Them

You apply a gradient in much the same way as a solid background color. For example, to set the background gradient of an object to the water1 gradient, you might use HTML such as this:

```
<div class='water1'>This is the water1 gradient</div>
```

As with the solid-colored backgrounds, you can also choose when a gradient is to be applied according to whether an object is moused over or clicked, and also whether the object contains any links that should have their gradients changed.

Here's the HTML code used to create the screen grab in Figure 3-4:

```
<div class='carrot1'>This is carrot1</div><br />

<div class='sky1_h'>This is plain - or sky1 when the mouse hovers over
it</div><br />

<div class='grass1_a'>This is plain - or grass1 when it is
clicked</div><br />

<div class='carrot1_l'>This is plain. <a href='#'>This link is
carrot1</a></div><br />

<div class='water1_lh'>This is plain. <a href='#'>This link is
water1 when hovered</a></div><br />

<div class='tin1_la'>This is plain. <a href='#'>This link is
tin1 when clicked</a></div>
```

It is very similar to the example in the previous plug-in group, in that the first three objects have their entire background gradient set, while the second three have only the links contained within them changed.

Incidentally, if you are wondering why all these class names end with the number 1, it's because there's a complementary set of gradients that fade in the other vertical direction, in the following plug-in group.

---

**NOTE**  *These classes degrade gracefully, so older browsers that do not support gradient backgrounds, and the current version of Opera (10.6 as I write) will simply show a solid background representative of the average gradient color when you use them. Hopefully, Opera will support this feature soon.*

PART II

## The Classes

```
.carrot1,      .carrot1_a:active,    .carrot1_h:hover,
.carrot1_l a, .carrot1_la a:active, .carrot1_lh a:hover {
   background:#ea4;
   background:-webkit-gradient(linear, left top, left bottom,
             from(#fd8), to(#c60));
   background:-moz-linear-gradient(top, #fd8, #c60);
   background:linear-gradient(left top, #fd8, #c60);
   filter    :progid:DXImageTransform.Microsoft.Gradient(
             startColorstr='#f0d080', endColorstr='#c06000');
}
.chrome1,      .chrome1_a:active,    .chrome1_h:hover,
.chrome1_l a, .chrome1_la a:active, .chrome1_lh a:hover {
   background:#ddd;
   background:-webkit-gradient(linear, left top, left bottom,
             from(#fff), to(#aaa));
   background:-moz-linear-gradient(top, #fff, #aaa);
   background:linear-gradient(left top, #fff, #aaa);
   filter    :progid:DXImageTransform.Microsoft.Gradient(
             startColorstr='#f0f0f0', endColorstr='#a0a0a0');
}
.coffee1,      .coffee1_a:active,    .coffee1_h:hover,
.coffee1_l a, .coffee1_la a:active, .coffee1_lh a:hover {
   background:#c94;
   background:-webkit-gradient(linear, left top, left bottom,
             from(#fc6), to(#752));
   background:-moz-linear-gradient(top, #fc6, #752);
   background:linear-gradient(left top, #fc6, #752);
   filter    :progid:DXImageTransform.Microsoft.Gradient(
             startColorstr='#f0c060', endColorstr='#705020');
}
.dusk1,      .dusk1_a:active,    .dusk1_h:hover,
.dusk1_l a, .dusk1_la a:active, .dusk1_lh a:hover {
   background:#79c;
   background:-webkit-gradient(linear, left top, left bottom,
             from(#8ad), to(#357));
   background:-moz-linear-gradient(top, #8ad, #357);
   background:linear-gradient(left top, #8ad, #357);
   filter    :progid:DXImageTransform.Microsoft.Gradient(
             startColorstr='#80a0d0', endColorstr='#305070');
}
.earth1,      .earth1_a:active,    .earth1_h:hover,
.earth1_l a, .earth1_la a:active, .earth1_lh a:hover {
   background:#a86;
   background:-webkit-gradient(linear, left top, left bottom,
             from(#db8), to(#532));
   background:-moz-linear-gradient(top, #db8, #532);
   background:linear-gradient(left top, #db8, #532);
   filter    :progid:DXImageTransform.Microsoft.Gradient(
             startColorstr='#d0b080', endColorstr='#503020');
}
.fire1,      .fire1_a:active,    .fire1_h:hover,
.fire1_l a, .fire1_la a:active, .fire1_lh a:hover {
   background:#db3;
```

```
    background:-webkit-gradient(linear, left top, left bottom,
              from(#ef5), to(#b40));
    background:-moz-linear-gradient(top, #ef5, #b40);
    background:linear-gradient(left top, #ef5, #b40);
    filter   :progid:DXImageTransform.Microsoft.Gradient(
              startColorstr='#e0f050', endColorstr='#b04000');
}
.grass1,       .grass1_a:active,    .grass1_h:hover,
.grass1_l a,   .grass1_la a:active, .grass1_lh a:hover {
    background:#7b6;
    background:-webkit-gradient(linear, left top, left bottom,
              from(#ae9), to(#160));
    background:-moz-linear-gradient(top, #ae9, #160);
    background:linear-gradient(left top, #ae9, #160);
    filter   :progid:DXImageTransform.Microsoft.Gradient(
              startColorstr='#a0e090', endColorstr='#106000');
}
.iron1,        .iron1_a:active,     .iron1_h:hover,
.iron1_l a,    .iron1_la a:active,  .iron1_lh a:hover {
    background:#777;
    background:-webkit-gradient(linear, left top, left bottom,
              from(#999), to(#333));
    background:-moz-linear-gradient(top, #999, #333);
    background:linear-gradient(left top, #999, #333);
    filter   :progid:DXImageTransform.Microsoft.Gradient(
              startColorstr='#909090', endColorstr='#303030');
}
.plum1,        .plum1_a:active,     .plum1_h:hover,
.plum1_l a,    .plum1_la a:active,  .plum1_lh a:hover {
    background:#969;
    background:-webkit-gradient(linear, left top, left bottom,
              from(#b8a), to(#636));
    background:-moz-linear-gradient(top, #b8a, #636);
    background:linear-gradient(left top, #b8a, #636);
    filter   :progid:DXImageTransform.Microsoft.Gradient(
              startColorstr='#b080a0', endColorstr='#603060');
}
.rose1,        .rose1_a:active,     .rose1_h:hover,
.rose1_l a,    .rose1_la a:active,  .rose1_lh a:hover {
    background:#e45;
    background:-webkit-gradient(linear, left top, left bottom,
              from(#f67), to(#b12));
    background:-moz-linear-gradient(top, #f67, #b12);
    background:linear-gradient(top, #f67, #b12);
    filter   :progid:DXImageTransform.Microsoft.Gradient(
              startColorstr='#f06070', endColorstr='#b01020');
}
.sky1,         .sky1_a:active,      .sky1_h:hover,
.sky1_l a,     .sky1_la a:active,   .sky1_lh a:hover {
    background:#abe;
    background:-webkit-gradient(linear, left top, left bottom,
              from(#cdf), to(#68c));
    background:-moz-linear-gradient(top, #cdf, #68c);
    background:linear-gradient(left top, #cdf, #68c);
```

```
    filter    :progid:DXImageTransform.Microsoft.Gradient(
               startColorstr='#c0d0f0', endColorstr='#6080c0');
}
.sunset1,      .sunset1_a:active,     .sunset1_h:hover,
.sunset1_l a, .sunset1_la a:active,  .sunset1_lh a:hover {
   background:#ed3;
   background:-webkit-gradient(linear, left top, left bottom,
              from(#fe4), to(#ca0));
   background:-moz-linear-gradient(top, #fe4, #ca0);
   background:linear-gradient(left top, #fe4, #ca0);
   filter    :progid:DXImageTransform.Microsoft.Gradient(
              startColorstr='#f0e040', endColorstr='#c0a000');
}
.tin1,        .tin1_a:active,     .tin1_h:hover,
.tin1_l a,    .tin1_la a:active,  .tin1_lh a:hover {
   background:#aaa;
   background:-webkit-gradient(linear, left top, left bottom,
              from(#bbb), to(#777));
   background:-moz-linear-gradient(top, #bbb, #777);
   background:linear-gradient(left top, #bbb, #777);
   filter    :progid:DXImageTransform.Microsoft.Gradient(
              startColorstr='#b0b0b0', endColorstr='#707070');
}
.water1,      .water1_a:active,     .water1_h:hover,
.water1_l a,  .water1_la a:active,  .water1_lh a:hover {
   background:#ace;
   background:-webkit-gradient(linear, left top, left bottom,
              from(#eff), to(#58c));
   background:-moz-linear-gradient(top, #eff, #58c);
   background:linear-gradient(left top, #eff, #58c);
   filter    :progid:DXImageTransform.Microsoft.Gradient(
              startColorstr='#e0f0f0', endColorstr='#5080c0');
}
.wine1,       .wine1_a:active,     .wine1_h:hover,
.wine1_l a,   .wine1_la a:active,  .wine1_lh a:hover {
   background:#d33;
   background:-webkit-gradient(linear, left top, left bottom,
              from(#f44), to(#922));
   background:-moz-linear-gradient(top, #f44, #922);
   background:linear-gradient(left top, #f44, #922);
   filter    :progid:DXImageTransform.Microsoft.Gradient(
              startColorstr='#f04040', endColorstr='#902020');
}
```

**PLUG-IN 5**

## Inverse Gradients

The classes in this plug-in group are the inverse of the ones in the previous section in that they create background gradient fills that look as if the previous fills were flipped from top to bottom. They are particularly useful as mouseover or button click effects as can be seen in Figure 3-5, which is an updated version of the example in the previous plug-in group that now alternates gradients when clicked and/or hovered over.

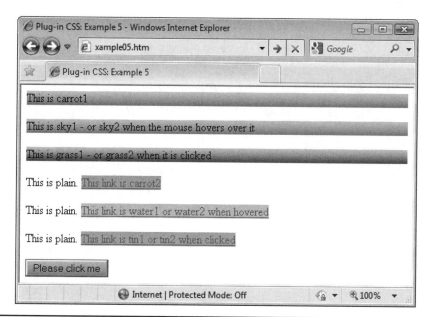

**FIGURE 3-5**    Using complementary gradient pairs for link and hover effects

Notice how the second set of links does not show any gradients. This is due to an unfortunate bug in Internet Explorer (the browser used for the screen grab), and serves to illustrate how these classes will degrade gracefully when they cannot be applied to their fullest effect. In any case, with a little extra HTML, it is easy to work around this IE bug by using only the first three types of class that assign gradients to an entire object—then Opera will be the only browser unable to show them (but it will at least still display a solid color representative of the gradient).

## Classes and Properties

| | |
|---|---|
| carrot2 (etc...) | Classes – as carrot1 but reversed from top to bottom |
| chrome2 (etc...) | Classes – as chrome1 but reversed from top to bottom |
| coffee2 (etc...) | Classes – as coffee1 but reversed from top to bottom |
| dusk2 (etc...) | Classes – as dusk1 but reversed from top to bottom |
| earth2 (etc...) | Classes – as earth1 but reversed from top to bottom |
| fire2 (etc...) | Classes – as fire1 but reversed from top to bottom |
| grass2 (etc...) | Classes – as grass1 but reversed from top to bottom |
| iron2 (etc...) | Classes – as iron1 but reversed from top to bottom |

| | |
|---|---|
| plum2 (etc...) | Classes – as plum1 but reversed from top to bottom |
| rose2 (etc...) | Classes – as rose1 but reversed from top to bottom |
| sky2 (etc...) | Classes – as sky1 but reversed from top to bottom |
| sunset2 (etc...) | Classes – as sunset1 but reversed from top to bottom |
| tin2 (etc...) | Classes – as tin1 but reversed from top to bottom |
| water2 (etc...) | Classes – as water1 but reversed from top to bottom |
| wine2 (etc...) | Classes – as wine1 but reversed from top to bottom |
| background | Property to which the gradient (or solid color) is applied |
| filter | Property used by Internet Explorer for creating gradients and other effects |

## About the Classes

These classes are almost identical to those in the previous plug-in group except that they have a number 2 in them instead of a 1, and they display gradients that are the inverse from top to bottom.

## How to Use Them

You can use these classes in the same way as the first set of gradients, or use them to make cool mouseover effects like in the following example, which is an extension of the one in the previous plug-in group that swaps the gradients when moused over and/or clicked:

```
<div class='carrot2'>This is carrot2</div><br />

<div class='sky1 sky2_h'>This is sky1 - or sky2 when the mouse hovers
over it</div><br />

<div class='grass1 grass2_a'>This is grass1 - or grass2 when it is
clicked</div><br />

<div class='carrot2_l'>This is plain. <a href='#'>This link is
carrot2</a></div><br />

<div class='water1_l water2_lh'>This is plain. <a href='#'>This link is
water1 or water2 when hovered</a></div><br />

<div class='tin1_l tin2_la'>This is plain. <a href='#'>This link is
tin1 or tin2 when clicked</a></div>
```

Already, these are some quite impressive effects, but now take a look at what you can do with the HTML <button> tag:

```
<button class='sky1 sky2_a'>Please click me</button>
```

When you click buttons that use gradient classes in this way, they appear to depress even more than normal and produce a highly professional looking effect.

***Caution*** *Unfortunately, Microsoft Internet Explorer has a bug—one of many in fact—such that the second set of three objects in the example (in which links within an object are addressed) will not show as gradients. For some reason, Internet Explorer balks at CSS rules like* .classname a { filter:…; }, *and refuses to apply the filter (although it will apply other styles), so only the background solid color will be applied for these objects. Curiously, IE works fine with rules such as* .classname { filter:…; }—*hopefully this will be addressed in version 9. Anyway, until it is corrected, this is one example of how the classes sometimes have to gracefully degrade in certain situations.*

## The Classes

```
.carrot2,      .carrot2_a:active,     .carrot2_h:hover,
.carrot2_l a, .carrot2_la a:active, .carrot2_lh a:hover {
   background:#d93;
   background:linear-gradient(left top, #c60, #fd8);
   background:-webkit-gradient(linear, left top, left bottom,
             from(#c60), to(#fd8));
   background:-moz-linear-gradient(top, #c60, #fd8);
   filter    :progid:DXImageTransform.Microsoft.Gradient(
             startColorstr='#c06000', endColorstr='#f0d080');
}
.chrome2,      .chrome2_a:active,     .chrome2_h:hover,
.chrome2_l a, .chrome2_la a:active, .chrome2_lh a:hover {
   background:#ccc;
   background:linear-gradient(left top, #aaa, #fff);
   background:-webkit-gradient(linear, left top, left bottom,
             from(#aaa), to(#fff));
   background:-moz-linear-gradient(top, #aaa, #fff);
   filter    :progid:DXImageTransform.Microsoft.Gradient(
             startColorstr='#a0a0a0', endColorstr='#f0f0f0');
}
.coffee2,      .coffee2_a:active,     .coffee2_h:hover,
.coffee2_l a, .coffee2_la a:active, .coffee2_lh a:hover {
   background:#b83;
   background:linear-gradient(left top, #752, #fc6);
   background:-webkit-gradient(linear, left top, left bottom,
             from(#752), to(#fc6));
   background:-moz-linear-gradient(top, #752, #fc6);
   filter    :progid:DXImageTransform.Microsoft.Gradient(
             startColorstr='#705020', endColorstr='#f0c060');
}
.dusk2,       .dusk2_a:active,      .dusk2_h:hover,
.dusk2_l a,   .dusk2_la a:active,   .dusk2_lh a:hover {
   background:#68b;
   background:linear-gradient(left top, #357, #8ad);
   background:-webkit-gradient(linear, left top, left bottom,
             from(#357), to(#8ad));
   background:-moz-linear-gradient(top, #357, #8ad);
   filter    :progid:DXImageTransform.Microsoft.Gradient(
             startColorstr='#305070', endColorstr='#80a0d0');
}
```

```
.earth2,          .earth2_a:active,      .earth2_h:hover,
.earth2_l a,    .earth2_la a:active,    .earth2_lh a:hover {
   background:#975;
   background:linear-gradient(left top, #532, #db8);
   background:-webkit-gradient(linear, left top, left bottom,
            from(#532), to(#db8));
   background:-moz-linear-gradient(top, #532, #db8);
   filter    :progid:DXImageTransform.Microsoft.Gradient(
            startColorstr='#503020', endColorstr='#d0b080');
}
.fire2,          .fire2_a:active,      .fire2_h:hover,
.fire2_l a,    .fire2_la a:active,    .fire2_lh a:hover {
   background:#ca2;
   background:linear-gradient(left top, #b40, #ef5);
   background:-webkit-gradient(linear, left top, left bottom,
            from(#b40), to(#ef5));
   background:-moz-linear-gradient(top, #b40, #ef5);
   filter    :progid:DXImageTransform.Microsoft.Gradient(
            startColorstr='#b04000', endColorstr='#e0f050');
}
.grass2,          .grass2_a:active,      .grass2_h:hover,
.grass2_l a,    .grass2_la a:active,    .grass2_lh a:hover {
   background:#6a5;
   background:linear-gradient(left top, #160, #ae9);
   background:-webkit-gradient(linear, left top, left bottom,
            from(#160), to(#ae9));
   background:-moz-linear-gradient(top, #160, #ae9);
   filter    :progid:DXImageTransform.Microsoft.Gradient(
            startColorstr='#106000', endColorstr='#aaee99');
}
.iron2,          .iron2_a:active,      .iron2_h:hover,
.iron2_l a,    .iron2_la a:active,    .iron2_lh a:hover {
   background:#666;
   background:linear-gradient(left top, #333, #999);
   background:-webkit-gradient(linear, left top, left bottom,
            from(#333), to(#999));
   background:-moz-linear-gradient(top, #333, #999);
   filter    :progid:DXImageTransform.Microsoft.Gradient(
            startColorstr='#303030', endColorstr='#909090');
}
.plum2,          .plum2_a:active,      .plum2_h:hover,
.plum2_l a,    .plum2_la a:active,    .plum2_lh a:hover {
   background:#858;
   background:linear-gradient(left top, #636, #b8a);
   background:-webkit-gradient(linear, left top, left bottom,
            from(#636), to(#b8a));
   background:-moz-linear-gradient(top, #636, #b8a);
   filter    :progid:DXImageTransform.Microsoft.Gradient(
            startColorstr='#603060', endColorstr='#b080a0');
}
.rose2,          .rose2_a:active,      .rose2_h:hover,
.rose2_l a,    .rose2_la a:active,    .rose2_lh a:hover {
   background:#d34;
   background:linear-gradient(left top, #b12, #f67);
   background:-webkit-gradient(linear, left top, left bottom,
            from(#b12), to(#f67));
```

```
    background:-moz-linear-gradient(top, #b12, #f67);
    filter    :progid:DXImageTransform.Microsoft.Gradient(
               startColorstr='#b01020', endColorstr='#f06070');
}
.sky2,        .sky2_a:active,       .sky2_h:hover,
.sky2_l a,    .sky2_la a:active,    .sky2_lh a:hover {
    background:#9ad;
    background:linear-gradient(left top, #68c, #cdf);
    background:-webkit-gradient(linear, left top, left bottom,
               from(#68c), to(#cdf));
    background:-moz-linear-gradient(top, #68c, #cdf);
    filter    :progid:DXImageTransform.Microsoft.Gradient(
               startColorstr='#6080c0', endColorstr='#c0d0f0');
}
.sunset2,     .sunset2_a:active,    .sunset2_h:hover,
.sunset2_l a, .sunset2_la a:active, .sunset2_lh a:hover {
    background:#dc2;
    background:linear-gradient(left top, #ca0, #fe4);
    background:-webkit-gradient(linear, left top, left bottom,
               from(#ca0), to(#fe4));
    background:-moz-linear-gradient(top, #ca0, #fe4);
    filter    :progid:DXImageTransform.Microsoft.Gradient(
               startColorstr='#c0a000', endColorstr='#f0e040');
}
.tin2,        .tin2_a:active,       .tin2_h:hover,
.tin2_l a,    .tin2_la a:active,    .tin2_lh a:hover {
    background:#999;
    background:linear-gradient(left top, #777, #bbb);
    background:-webkit-gradient(linear, left top, left bottom,
               from(#777), to(#bbb));
    background:-moz-linear-gradient(top, #777, #bbb);
    filter    :progid:DXImageTransform.Microsoft.Gradient(
               startColorstr='#707070', endColorstr='#b0b0b0');
}
.water2,      .water2_a:active,     .water2_h:hover,
.water2_l a,  .water2_la a:active,  .water2_lh a:hover {
    background:#9bd;
    background:linear-gradient(left top, #58c, #eff);
    background:-webkit-gradient(linear, left top, left bottom,
               from(#58c), to(#eff));
    background:-moz-linear-gradient(top, #58c, #eff);
    filter    :progid:DXImageTransform.Microsoft.Gradient(
               startColorstr='#5080c0', endColorstr='#e0f0f0');
}
.wine2,       .wine2_a:active,      .wine2_h:hover,
.wine2_l a,   .wine2_la a:active,   .wine2_lh a:hover {
    background:#c22;
    background:linear-gradient(left top, #922, #f44);
    background:-webkit-gradient(linear, left top, left bottom,
               from(#922), to(#f44));
    background:-moz-linear-gradient(top, #922, #f44);
    filter    :progid:DXImageTransform.Microsoft.Gradient(
               startColorstr='#902020', endColorstr='#f04040');
}
```

PART II

## Box Shadows

Adding a shadow effect underneath images and other objects helps them stand out. Using the classes in this plug-in group, you can add box shadows of five different shades in six different ways.

Figure 3-6 shows a photograph repeated six times. The first copy has no box shadow, while the other five range from the lightest to the darkest box shadow. This screen grab was taken using Internet Explorer, which doesn't support blurring. All other browsers blur and round the edges of box shadows, providing a smoother effect.

### Classes and Properties

| | |
|---|---|
| boxshadow<br>boxshadow_a<br>boxshadow_h<br>boxshadow_l<br>boxshadow_la<br>boxshadow_lh | Class to add a box shadow to an object (boxshadow), plus classes to do so only if the object is actively being clicked (boxshadow_a) or hovered over (boxshadow_h), and another three classes to add a box shadow only to any links within the object (boxshadow_l), any links within the object that are actively being clicked (boxshadow_la), and any links within the object that are being hovered over (boxshadow_lh) |
| lightestboxshadow (etc...) | Class – as boxshadow but with the lightest shadow |
| lightboxshadow (etc...) | Class – as boxshadow but with a lighter shadow |
| darkboxshadow (etc...) | Class – as boxshadow but with a darker shadow |
| darkestboxshadow (etc...) | Class – as boxshadow but with the darkest shadow |
| -moz-box-shadow | Property to create a box shadow on Firefox and other Mozilla browsers |
| -webkit-box-shadow | Property to create a box shadow on Safari and Chrome |
| filter | Property to create box shadows and other effects on Internet Explorer |
| box-shadow | Property to create a box shadow on all other browsers |

### About the Classes

This group has five classes, each of which is supplied with the standard suffixes used to change the way they act: _a for active, _h for hover, _l for a link, _la for an active link, and _lh for a hovered link.

The box shadow is applied using the box-shadow CSS property, or –moz-box-shadow for Mozilla-based browsers such as Firefox, or –webkit-box-shadow for Safari and Chrome. In all cases, the values passed are the shadow color, its vertical and horizontal offset from the object, and the amount of blurring to use. So a typical box shadow rule looks like this:

```
box-shadow:#444444 4px 4px 6px;
```

On Internet Explorer, box shadowing is handled by the filter property and the equivalent CSS rule is as follows:

```
filter:progid:DXImageTransform.Microsoft.Shadow(color='#444444',
Direction=135, Strength=6);
```

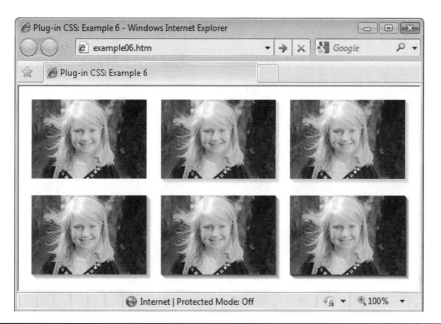

**FIGURE 3-6** Adding box shadows makes objects stand out from the page.

***TIP*** *If you are interested in tweaking the* PC.css *file, there is also a* DropShadow *filter argument available in Internet Explorer that provides a different effect and which is identical in use to the* Shadow *argument, except for the extra four letters preceding the word* Shadow. *You could therefore use it in the following way:*

```
filter:progid:DXImageTransform.Microsoft.DropShadow(color='#444444',
Direction=135, Strength=6);
```

## How to Use Them

To add a box shadow to an object, enter its class name into some HTML, like this:

```
<img class='boxshadow' src='photo1.jpg' />
```

You can also choose any of the four lighter or darker variants, or add one of the action suffixes to change the way the box shadow is implemented. For example, to add a darker box shadow to an object when it is being hovered over, you might do this:

```
<img class='darkboxshadow_h' src='photo1.jpg' />
```

Or you could combine the two to give an object a lighter box shadow that changes to a darker one when hovered over, like this:

```
<img class='lightboxshadow darkboxshadow_h ' src='photo1.jpg' />
```

Here is the HTML that was used to create the screen grab in Figure 3-6:

```
<div class='black_bh' style='padding:10px;'>
    <img                              src='photo1.jpg' />    
    <img class='lightestboxshadow' src='photo1.jpg' />    
    <img class='lightboxshadow'    src='photo1.jpg' /> <br /><br />
    <img class='boxshadow'         src='photo1.jpg' />    
    <img class='darkboxshadow'     src='photo1.jpg' />    
    <img class='darkestboxshadow'  src='photo1.jpg' />
</div>
```

In this example, there are six instances of a photo: one with no box shadow, and five more with shadows of varying shades. A few   and <br /> tags are used to neatly space them out.

Enclosing these photos is a <div> tag that has been set to change its background color to black when hovered over (using the black_bh class), so you can pass the mouse over it and see the effect of the lighter shadows when used on a dark background.

## The Classes

```
.boxshadow,                    .boxshadow_a:active,
.boxshadow_h:hover,            .boxshadow_l a,
.boxshadow_la a:active,        .boxshadow_lh a:hover {
    -moz-box-shadow    :#888888 4px 4px 6px;
    -webkit-box-shadow:#888888 4px 4px 6px;
    box-shadow         :#888888 4px 4px 6px;
    filter             :progid:DXImageTransform.Microsoft.Shadow(
                        color='#888888', Direction=135, Strength=6);
}
.lightestboxshadow,            .lightestboxshadow_a:active,
.lightestboxshadow_h:hover,    .lightestboxshadow_l a,
.lightestboxshadow_la a:active, .lightestboxshadow_lh a:hover {
    -moz-box-shadow    :#ffffff 4px 4px 6px;
    -webkit-box-shadow:#ffffff 4px 4px 6px;
    box-shadow         :#ffffff 4px 4px 6px;
    filter             :progid:DXImageTransform.Microsoft.Shadow(
                        color='#cccccc', Direction=135, Strength=6);
}
.lightboxshadow,               .lightboxshadow_a:active,
.lightboxshadow_h:hover,       .lightboxshadow_l a,
.lightboxshadow_la a:active,   .lightboxshadow_lh a:hover {
    -moz-box-shadow    :#cccccc 4px 4px 6px;
    -webkit-box-shadow:#cccccc 4px 4px 6px;
    box-shadow         :#cccccc 4px 4px 6px;
    filter             :progid:DXImageTransform.Microsoft.Shadow(
                        color='#cccccc', Direction=135, Strength=6);
}
.darkboxshadow,                .darkboxshadow_a:active,
.darkboxshadow_h:hover,        .darkboxshadow_l a,
.darkboxshadow_la a:active,    .darkboxshadow_lh a:hover {
    box-shadow         :#444444 4px 4px 6px;
    -moz-box-shadow    :#444444 4px 4px 6px;
```

```
    -webkit-box-shadow:#444444 4px 4px 6px;
    filter             :progid:DXImageTransform.Microsoft.Shadow(
                        color='#444444', Direction=135, Strength=6);
}
.darkestboxshadow,              .darkestboxshadow_a:active,
.darkestboxshadow_h:hover,      .darkestboxshadow_l a,
.darkestboxshadow_la a:active,  .darkestboxshadow_lh a:hover {
    -moz-box-shadow    :#000000 4px 4px 6px;
    -webkit-box-shadow:#000000 4px 4px 6px;
    box-shadow         :#000000 4px 4px 6px;
    filter             :progid:DXImageTransform.Microsoft.Shadow(
                        color='#000000', Direction=135, Strength=6);
}
```

## Padding

**PLUG-IN 7**

When you need to quickly add some padding around an object, as long as you're happy to use values of 2, 5, 8, 11, or 15 pixels, you can simply drop one of the class names in this group into your HTML.

For example, Figure 3-7 shows the example from the previous plug-in group modified so that each picture has a different amount of padding. A border has been added to each to make it clear how much padding has been applied.

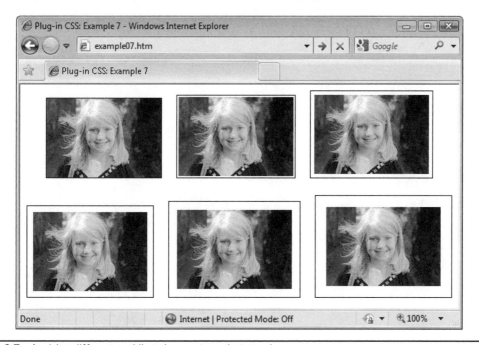

**FIGURE 3-7**  Applying different padding classes to a photograph

## Classes and Properties

| | |
|---|---|
| padding<br>padding_a<br>padding_h<br>padding_l<br>padding_la<br>padding_lh | Class to add 8 pixels of padding around an object (padding), plus classes to do so only if the object is actively being clicked (padding_a) or hovered over (padding_h), and another three classes to add padding only to any links within the object (padding_l), any links within the object that are actively being clicked (padding_la), and any links within the object that are being hovered over (padding_lh) |
| smallestpadding<br>(etc…) | Class – as padding but with 2 pixels of padding |
| smallpadding<br>(etc…) | Class – as padding but with 5 pixels of padding |
| largepadding<br>(etc…) | Class – as padding but with 11 pixels of padding |
| largestpadding<br>(etc…) | Class – as padding but with 15 pixels of padding |
| padding | Property to set an object's padding |

## About the Classes

This group has five classes, and each is supplied with the standard suffixes used to change the way they act: _a for active, _h for hover, _l for a link, _la for an active link, and _lh for a hovered link. Padding is applied using the padding CSS property, with values of 2px, 5px, 8px, 11px, or 15px, like this:

**padding**:8px;

## How to Use Them

Using the padding classes is as easy as choosing the size you need and using that classname in a class='…' argument, like this:

```
<img class='padding' src='photo1.jpg' />
```

You can add padding to most objects, not just images. You can also choose to use any of the dynamic versions of these classes. For example, to give an object a small padding and then enlarge it when the mouse hovers over it, you could use code such as this:

```
<img class='smallpadding largepadding_h' src='photo1.jpg' />
```

Or to change the padding only when the object is clicked, you could use:

```
<img class='smallpadding largepadding_a' src='photo1.jpg' />
```

And, of course, there are also the classes for modifying only links within an object, like the following, which applies a small padding to any such links, and which changes to a larger padding when the link is hovered over:

```
<img class='smallpadding_l largepadding_lh' src='photo1.jpg' />
```

Here is the HTML used to create the page shown in Figure 3-7:

```
<img border='1'                        src='photo1.jpg' />    
<img border='1' class='smallestpadding' src='photo1.jpg' />    
<img border='1' class='smallpadding'    src='photo1.jpg' /> <br /><br />
<img border='1' class='padding'         src='photo1.jpg' />    
<img border='1' class='largepadding'    src='photo1.jpg' />    
<img border='1' class='largestpadding'  src='photo1.jpg' />
```

## The Classes

```
.padding,                        .padding_a:active,
.padding_h:hover,                .padding_l a,
.padding_la a:active,            .padding_lh a:hover
   { padding:8px;   }
.smallestpadding,                .smallestpadding_a:active,
.smallestpadding_h:hover,        .smallestpadding_l a,
.smallestpadding_la a:active,    .smallestpadding_lh a:hover
   { padding:2px;   }
.smallpadding,                   .smallpadding_a:active,
.smallpadding_h:hover,           .smallpadding_l a,
.smallpadding_la a:active,       .smallpadding_lh a:hover
   { padding:5px;   }
.largepadding,                   .largepadding_a:active,
.largepadding_h:hover,           .largepadding_l a,
.largepadding_la a:active,       .largepadding_lh a:hover
   { padding:11px; }
.largestpadding,                 .largestpadding_a:active,
.largestpadding_h:hover,         .largestpadding_l a,
.largestpadding_la a:active,     .largestpadding_lh a:hover
   { padding:15px; }
```

## Rounded Borders

You can create rounded borders in many ways, from using images and image parts, to table cells, nested elements, and so on. Generally, they are quite complicated to use, but thankfully the new CSS 3 border-radius command is supported on all browsers except Internet Explorer, and even that browser can handle them from version 9 on, as can be seen in Figure 3-8, which shows a screen grab from the IE 9 Platform Preview.

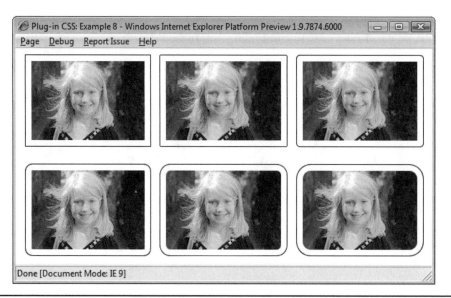

FIGURE 3-8    These rounded borders work on all modern browsers, including IE 9.

## Classes and Properties

| | |
|---|---|
| round<br>round_a<br>round_h<br>round_l<br>round_la<br>round_lh | Class to add a 10-pixel rounded border radius to an object (round), plus classes to do so only if the object is actively being clicked (round_a) or hovered over (round_h), and another three classes to add the border only to any links within the object (round_l), any links within the object that are actively being clicked (round_la), and any links within the object that are being hovered over (round_lh) |
| smallestround (etc...) | Class – as round but creates a 2-pixel radius rounded border |
| smallround (etc...) | Class – as round but creates a 5-pixel radius rounded border |
| largeround (etc...) | Class – as round but creates a 15-pixel radius rounded border |
| largestround (etc...) | Class – as round but creates a 20-pixel radius rounded border |
| -moz-border-radius | Property to create a rounded border on Firefox and other Mozilla browsers |
| -webkit-border-radius | Property to create a rounded border on Safari and Chrome |
| border-radius | Property to create a rounded border on all other browsers |

## About the Classes

This group has five classes, each of which is supplied with the standard suffixes used to change the way they act: _a for active, _h for hover, _l for a link, _la for an active link, and _lh for a hovered link.

The rounded border is applied using the `border-radius` CSS property, or `-moz-border-radius` for Mozilla-based browsers such as Firefox, or `-webkit-border-radius` for Safari and Chrome. In all cases, a pixel value is passed, like this CSS rule:

```
border-radius:10px;
```

Interestingly, Internet Explorer was late to the game in supporting rounded borders, but today it actually does a better job than the other browsers because if the object is an image it also gets slightly rounded at the corners, whereas other browsers leave the images untouched. I suppose it could be argued that this is a case of Microsoft doing things in a nonstandard way again, but I like their approach to this feature.

## How to Use Them

To add a rounded border to an object, you must first ensure that a border has been enabled. This can be done the old-fashioned way in images with an argument such as `border='1'`, or via CSS such as `border:1px solid;` (or using the border classes later in this chapter).

Once a border is visible, you can round it off by including one of the classes, like this:

```
<img border='1' class='round padding' src='photo1.jpg' />
```

This will add a rounded border with a radius of 10 pixels. You can choose smaller or larger radii and also use the various standard suffixes to change the border only when clicked or hovered over, or only when it is part of a link within the current object.

Here is the HTML used to create Figure 3-8:

```
<img border='1' class='padding'             src='photo1.jpg' />  
<img border='1' class='smallestround padding' src='photo1.jpg' />  
<img border='1' class='smallround padding'   src='photo1.jpg' />
<br /><br />
<img border='1' class='round padding'        src='photo1.jpg' />  
<img border='1' class='largeround padding'   src='photo1.jpg' />  
<img border='1' class='largestround padding' src='photo1.jpg' />
```

## The Classes

```
.round,                     .round_a:active,
.round_h:hover,             .round_l a,
.round_la a:active,         .round_lh a:hover {
   border-radius        :10px;
   -moz-border-radius   :10px;
   -webkit-border-radius:10px;
}
.smallestround,             .smallestround_a:active,
.smallestround_h:hover,     .smallestround_l a,
.smallestround_la a:active, .smallestround_lh a:hover {
   border-radius        :2px;
   -moz-border-radius   :2px;
   -webkit-border-radius:2px;
}
.smallround,                .smallround_a:active,
.smallround_h:hover,        .smallround_l a,
.smallround_la a:active,    .smallround_lh a:hover {
```

```
    border-radius        :5px;
    -moz-border-radius   :5px;
    -webkit-border-radius:5px;
}
.largeround,                .largeround_a:active,
.largeround_h:hover,        .largeround_l a,
.largeround_la a:active,    .largeround_lh a:hover {
    border-radius        :15px;
    -moz-border-radius   :15px;
    -webkit-border-radius:15px;
}
.largestround,              .largestround_a:active,
.largestround_h:hover,      .largestround_l a,
.largestround_la a:active,  .largestround_lh a:hover {
    border-radius        :20px;
    -moz-border-radius   :20px;
    -webkit-border-radius:20px;
}
```

## PLUG-IN 9 Transparency

The ability to change the transparency of an object opens up a wide range of professional effects, and the classes in this plug-in group make doing so very easy. For example, Figure 3-9 shows a photograph displayed at 11 different levels of transparency.

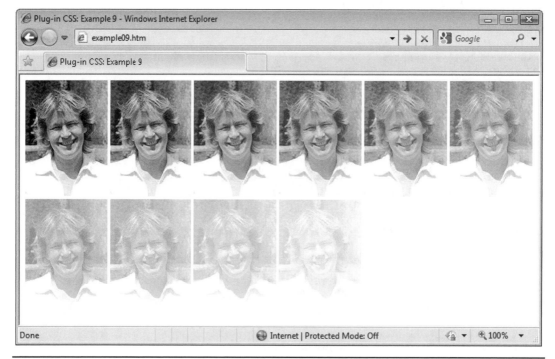

FIGURE 3-9   You can vary the transparency of objects with these classes.

## Classes and Properties

| | |
|---|---|
| `trans00`<br>`trans00_a`<br>`trans00_h`<br>`trans00_l`<br>`trans00_la`<br>`trans00_lh` | Class to set the transparency of an object to 0%, or no transparency (`trans00`), plus classes to do so only if the object is actively being clicked (`trans00_a`) or hovered over (`trans00_h`), and another three classes to set the transparency only for any links within the object (`trans00_l`), any links within the object that are actively being clicked (`trans00_la`), and any links within the object that are being hovered over (`trans00_lh`) |
| `trans01`-`trans10` (etc...) | Classes to change the transparency of an object in steps of 10 percent, including `_a`, `_h`, `_l`, `_la`, and `_lh` suffixes for each |
| `opacity` | Property used by all modern browsers for changing the opacity (and therefore the transparency) of an object |
| `filter` | Property used by Internet Explorer for opacity and other features |

## About the Classes

Transparency, or more precisely the inverse of it, opacity, is one area that most of the browser developers caught up with a while ago, so there is no need to use property names such as `-moz-opacity` or `-webkit-opacity`. Instead, the single property `opacity` is all that is required, as in the following CSS rule, which sets the opacity of an object to 50 percent:

```
opacity:0.5;
```

Of course, Microsoft always likes to be different, so Internet Explorer uses the `filter` property instead, like this (with a value between 0 and 100, rather than 0 and 1):

```
filter:alpha(opacity = '50');
```

## How to Use Them

You can change the opacity of an object by selecting the class name you want out of the 11 levels between 0 and 100 percent. Then, you can optionally choose a suffix to determine how the change should be made, as with the following code, which sets the transparency of a photograph to 50 percent:

```
<img class='trans05' src='photo2.jpg' />
```

A neat trick you can utilize for highlighting photos is to also provide a different level of transparency when a picture is hovered over, as with the following example, which changes the transparency of the photo to zero percent (or solid) when the mouse passes over it:

```
<img class='trans05 trans00_h' src='photo2.jpg' />
```

You can also use the other standard suffixes to change the transparency when an object is clicked, or only for links within an object.

Here is the HTML used to create Figure 3-9:

```
<img class='trans00'            src='photo2.jpg' />
<img class='trans01 trans00_h' src='photo2.jpg' />
<img class='trans02 trans01_h' src='photo2.jpg' />
<img class='trans03 trans02_h' src='photo2.jpg' />
<img class='trans04 trans03_h' src='photo2.jpg' />
<img class='trans05 trans04_h' src='photo2.jpg' />
<img class='trans06 trans05_h' src='photo2.jpg' />
<img class='trans07 trans06_h' src='photo2.jpg' />
<img class='trans08 trans07_h' src='photo2.jpg' />
<img class='trans09 trans08_h' src='photo2.jpg' />
<img class='trans10 trans09_h' src='photo2.jpg' />
```

With the exception of the first, when you pass the mouse over the pictures, they darken by 10 percent.

## The Classes

```
.trans00,       .trans00_a:active,     .trans00_h:hover,
.trans00_l a, .trans00_la a:active, .trans00_lh a:hover {
   opacity:1;
   filter :alpha(opacity = '100');
}
.trans01,       .trans01_a:active,     .trans01_h:hover,
.trans01_l a, .trans01_la a:active, .trans01_lh a:hover {
   opacity:0.9;
   filter :alpha(opacity = '90');
}
.trans02,       .trans02_a:active,     .trans02_h:hover,
.trans02_l a, .trans02_la a:active, .trans02_lh a:hover {
   opacity:0.8;
   filter :alpha(opacity = '80');
}
.trans03,       .trans03_a:active,     .trans03_h:hover,
.trans03_l a, .trans03_la a:active, .trans03_lh a:hover {
   opacity:0.7;
   filter :alpha(opacity = '70');
}
.trans04,       .trans04_a:active,     .trans04_h:hover,
.trans04_l a, .trans04_la a:active, .trans04_lh a:hover {
   opacity:0.6;
   filter :alpha(opacity = '60');
}
.trans05,       .trans05_a:active,     .trans05_h:hover,
.trans05_l a, .trans05_la a:active, .trans05_lh a:hover {
   opacity:0.5;
   filter :alpha(opacity = '50');
}
.trans06,       .trans06_a:active,     .trans06_h:hover,
.trans06_l a, .trans06_la a:active, .trans06_lh a:hover {
   opacity:0.4;
   filter :alpha(opacity = '40');
}
```

```
.trans07,       .trans07_a:active,     .trans07_h:hover,
.trans07_l a, .trans07_la a:active, .trans07_lh a:hover {
   opacity:0.3;
   filter :alpha(opacity = '30');
}
.trans08,       .trans08_a:active,     .trans08_h:hover,
.trans08_l a, .trans08_la a:active, .trans08_lh a:hover {
   opacity:0.2;
   filter :alpha(opacity = '20');
}
.trans09,       .trans09_a:active,     .trans09_h:hover,
.trans09_l a, .trans09_la a:active, .  a:hover {
   opacity:0.1;
   filter :alpha(opacity = '10');
}
.trans10,       .trans10_a:active,     .trans10_h:hover,
.trans10_l a, .trans10_la a:active, .trans10_lh a:hover {
   opacity:0;
   filter :alpha(opacity = '0');
}
```

## PLUG-IN 10  Visibility and Display

The classes in this plug-in group provide different ways of presenting objects, including making them visible or invisible, hidden (a different type of invisible), or positioning them either inline or as a block.

Figure 3-10 shows three images in which the first is presented normally using the visible class (which is the default for all objects). The second uses the invisible class, which retains its dimensions, as can be seen by the caption still in the correct place. The third image uses the hidden class, so it has been completely removed from display, as can be seen by the caption which has collapsed in to occupy the space released.

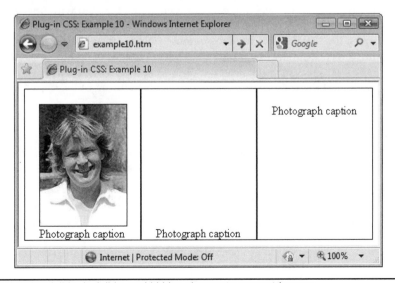

**Figure 3-10**   Using the visible, invisible, and hidden classes to present images

## Classes and Properties

| | |
|---|---|
| `visible` | Class to make an object visible |
| `invisible` | Class to make an object invisible but retain its dimensions |
| `hidden` | Class to hide an object, reducing its dimensions to zero |
| `block` | Class to make an object visible and to give it the properties of a `<div>` element—it will display underneath the preceding object and force following objects to display under it |
| `inline` | Class to make an object visible and to give it the properties of a `<span>` element—it will display to the right of the preceding object (if there's room) and following objects will display to the right of it (if there's room) |
| `table-cell` | Class to give an object the attributes of a table cell |
| `valigntop` | Class to vertically align an object to the top of the containing object (used mainly for `tablecell` classes) |
| `valignmid` | Class to vertically align an object to the middle of the containing object (used mainly for `tablecell` classes) |
| `valignbot` | Class to vertically align an object to the bottom of the containing object (used mainly for `tablecell` classes) |
| `visibility` | Property to set the visibility and invisibility of an object |
| `display` | Property to set the hidden, block, and inline display of an object |

## About the Classes

Unlike the transparency class of `trans10` (which makes an object totally transparent but keeps its position and dimensions), when an object uses either the `invisible` or `hidden` classes, it also has no associated actions and therefore cannot be hovered over or clicked. If you try to do these things on an invisible object, the browser will ignore them. As for hidden objects, they are removed from the web page so other elements that can will move in to occupy the space released.

Therefore, none of the usual suffix versions of these classes are available. If they were, they would be completely useless. For example, if a hover class were created for hiding an object, as soon as the object disappeared a mouse out event would trigger and the object would reappear again and the process would start all over, resulting in the object appearing to flicker.

## How to Use Them

The `visible`, `invisible`, and `hidden` classes are mostly of use for assigning initial settings to objects that you may change later using JavaScript. For example, you may wish to hide an element that should display only at the correct time, or when a certain action is performed.

Here's some HTML that shows the effects of using the different classes:

```
<div style='padding:20px; border:1px solid; width:120px; height:164px;'
   class='leftfloat'>
   <img border='1' class='visible' src='photo2.jpg' />Photograph caption
</div>
```

```
<div style='padding:20px; border:1px solid; width:120px; height:164px;'
   class='leftfloat'>
   <img border='1' class='invisible' src='photo2.jpg'/>Photograph caption
</div>
<div style='padding:20px; border:1px solid; width:120px; height:164px;'
   class='leftfloat'>
   <img border='1' class='hidden' src='photo2.jpg' />Photograph caption
</div>
```

Each image is embedded within a <div> that has 20 pixels of padding, a solid border, and is floated to the left. These act as placeholders. Then, within each <div> there is one instance each of a `visible`, `invisible`, and `hidden` class, each followed by a picture caption. The result is the screen grab in Figure 3-10.

### Using the `block` and `inline` Classes

The other two classes in this group have the effect of giving an object either the positioning properties of a <div>, for the `block` class, or those of a <span> for the `inline` class.

Objects with a `block` display property start on a new line, and objects that follow them also start on a new line. Objects with an `inline` display property follow on from the right of the previous object, only dropping to the next line if they would extend past the right margin. Also, if there's room, objects following after an inline object will also display to the right of it.

### The `tablecell` and `valign` Classes

Sometimes it can be helpful to give an object the properties of a table cell. For example, when used in a table cell, the `vertical-align` property mimics the deprecated HTML `valign` property, so it can be used to vertically center objects inside other objects, like this:

```
<div class='tablecell valignmid'>
   This text is vertically centered
</div>
```

You can also use the `valigntop` and `valignbot` classes in table cells.

### The Classes

```
.visible    { visibility:visible;   }
.invisible  { visibility:hidden;     }
.hidden     { display     :none;     }
.block      { display     :block;    }
.inline     { display     :inline;   }
.tablecell  { display     :table-cell; }
.valigntop  { vertical-align:top;    }
.valignmid  { vertical-align:middle; }
.valignbot  { vertical-align:bottom; }
```

## PLUG-IN 11  Scroll Bars

Using the plug-ins in this group, you can decide whether and how to display scroll bars on an object that supports them. In Figure 3-11, an excerpt from a poem by William Blake is displayed in three different ways. The first instance uses forced vertical and horizontal scroll bars, the second uses no scroll bars, and the third uses automatic scroll bars—therefore, only the vertical scroll bar is visible.

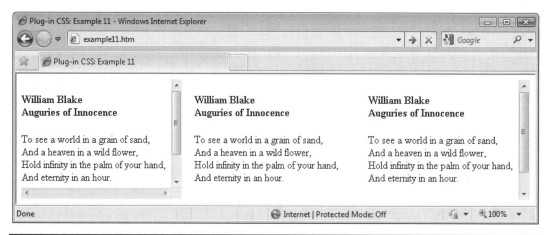

**FIGURE 3-11** Use these classes to choose the types of scroll bars you want.

## Classes and Properties

| | |
|---|---|
| scroll<br>scroll_a<br>scroll_h<br>scroll_l<br>scroll_la<br>scroll_lh<br>scroll_f | Class to set the overflow property (and hence the scrolling) of an object (scroll), plus classes to do so only if the object is actively being clicked (scroll_a) or hovered over (scroll_h), and another three classes to set the scroll bars only for any links within the object (scroll_l), any links within the object that are actively being clicked (scroll_la), and any links within the object that are being hovered over (scroll_lh), or when the object has focus (scroll_f) |
| noscroll (etc...) | Class to set the overflow property of an object to hidden, and therefore remove any scroll bars |
| nooverflow (etc...) | Class that is an alias of noscroll, and does exactly the same |
| autoscroll (etc...) | Class to set the overflow property of an object to auto, and therefore show only those scroll bars needed to view the object's contents |
| overflow (etc...) | Class that is an alias of autoscroll, and does exactly the same |
| overflow | Property of an object to specify whether contents are allowed to overflow, and if so, how |

## About the Classes

These classes let you specify what to do with any content that would otherwise overflow the bounds of its containing object. You can choose to force the display of both vertical and horizontal scroll bars with the scroll class, to hide any overflow with the noscroll (or nooverflow) class, or to let the browser choose whether and which scroll bars to use with the autoscroll (or overflow) class.

The standard suffixes of _a, _h, _l, _la, and _lh are also supported to apply the change only when the mouse is hovering over an object or it is being clicked, or to apply the setting only to links within the object. There is also a new suffix available that hasn't been seen before, _f, which is available on classes such as this that may apply to input elements. With it, you can apply the setting only to an element that has focus, such as an <input> or <textarea> that has been clicked.

## How to Use Them

There are three different types of scroll bar classes: scroll, noscroll (also called nooverflow), and autoscroll (also called overflow). Once you have decided which to apply to an object and (optionally) whether to use any suffix to control the way the setting is applied, simply embed the class name as an argument in the class='...' section of the object declaration, like this:

```
<div class='autoscroll'>
   The contents goes here
</div>
```

Alternatively, scroll bars are actually only required on an object when you want to scroll it, so you could choose to only display them when the mouse passes over scrollable text, like this:

```
<div class='autoscroll_h'>
   The contents goes here
</div>
```

Or maybe you have created a <textarea> field and only want scroll bars to appear when the user clicks into it to begin typing, which you can do using the _f suffix, like this:

```
<textarea rows='5' cols='50' class='noscroll autoscroll_f'>
   The contents goes here
</textarea>
```

In this case, it's important that the noscroll class is used in conjunction with autoscroll_f so that the scroll bars will disappear when the object no longer has focus.

Here's the HTML that was used to produce the screen grab in Figure 3-11:

```
<div class='scroll leftfloat' style='width:250px; height:180px;'>
   <h4>William Blake<br />Auguries of Innocence</h4>
   To see a world in a grain of sand,<br />
   And a heaven in a wild flower,<br />
   Hold infinity in the palm of your hand,<br />
   And eternity in an hour.<br /><br />
   A robin redbreast in a cage<br />
   Puts all heaven in a rage.
</div>

<div class='noscroll autoscroll_h leftfloat'
   style='width:250px; height:180px; padding-left:20px'>
   <h4>William Blake<br />Auguries of Innocence</h4>
```

```
        To see a world in a grain of sand,<br />
        And a heaven in a wild flower,<br />
        Hold infinity in the palm of your hand,<br />
        And eternity in an hour.<br /><br />
        A robin redbreast in a cage<br />
        Puts all heaven in a rage.
</div>

<div class='autoscroll'
     style='width:250px; height:180px; padding-left:20px'>
        <h4>William Blake<br />Auguries of Innocence</h4>
        To see a world in a grain of sand,<br />
        And a heaven in a wild flower,<br />
        Hold infinity in the palm of your hand,<br />
        And eternity in an hour.<br /><br />
        A robin redbreast in a cage<br />
        Puts all heaven in a rage.
</div>
```

The first instance of the poem has forced scroll bars, the second has none (but if the mouse is passed over it, an automatic vertical scroll bar will appear), and the third has an automatic vertical scroll bar.

## The Classes

```
.scroll,                .scroll_a:active,        .scroll_h:hover,
.scroll_l a,            .scroll_la a:active,     .scroll_lh a:hover,
.scroll_f:focus
    { overflow:scroll; }
.noscroll,              .noscroll_a:active,      .noscroll_h:hover,
.noscroll_l a,          .noscroll_la a:active,   .noscroll_lh a:hover,
.nooverflow,            .nooverflow_a:active,    .nooverflow_h:hover,
.nooverflow_l a,        .nooverflow_la a:active, .nooverflow_lh a:hover,
.noscroll_f:focus,      .nooverflow_f:focus
    { overflow:hidden; }
.autoscroll,            .autoscroll_a:active,    .autoscroll_h:hover,
.autoscroll_l a,        .autoscroll_la a:active, .autoscroll_lh a:hover,
.overflow,              .overflow_a:active,      .overflow_h:hover,
.overflow_l a,          .overflow_la a:active,   .overflow_lh a:hover,
.autoscroll_f:focus, .overflow_f:focus
    { overflow:auto;    }
```

## PLUG-IN 12   Maximum Sizes

Using these classes, you can resize an object to better fill the amount of space allocated to it by its containing object. For example, in Figure 3-12 a 250 × 167 pixel photograph is displayed in four different ways within a 500 × 100 pixel boundary, using the nooverflow class to prevent any part of the image from leaking outside of the boundary.

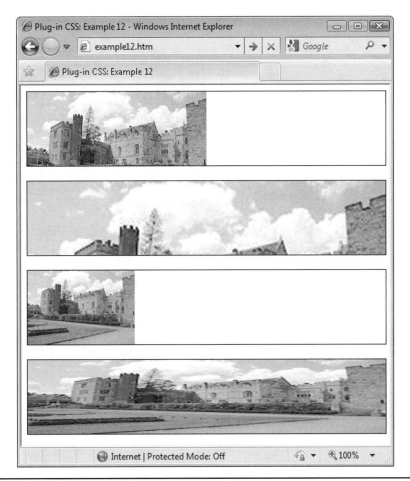

**FIGURE 3-12**    Setting an image's dimensions to various maximum values

The first image is displayed using its default dimensions, but as it is taller than 100 pixels, the bottom half is cut off.

The second image has had its width increased to that of the containing object and, because no new size was specified for its height, the image has also been resized vertically by the browser to retain the same relative dimensions. This time most of the image is now missing.

The third image has had its height set to that of the containing object and its width has been accordingly reduced by the browser. Since the photo's width is less than the width of the containing object, the entire image is visible.

Lastly, the final image has been resized to the width and height of the containing object and, while the whole image is in view, it has been horizontally stretched.

## Classes and Properties

| | |
|---|---|
| maxwidth<br>maxwidth_a<br>maxwidth_h<br>maxwidth_l<br>maxwidth_la<br>maxwidth_lh | Class to set an object's width to that of its containing object (maxwidth), plus classes to do so only if the object is actively being clicked (maxwidth_a) or hovered over (maxwidth_h), and another three classes to set the width only for any links within the object (maxwidth_l), any links within the object that are actively being clicked (maxwidth_la), and any links within the object that are being hovered over (maxwidth_lh) |
| maxheight (etc...) | Class to set an object's height to that of its containing object |
| maxsize (etc...) | Class to set both an object's width and height to those of its containing object |
| width | Property for changing the width of an object |
| height | Property for changing the height of an object |

## About the Classes

These classes apply a value of 100 percent to whichever property they refer, allowing you to set the width, height, or both dimensions to those of the containing object. Where the object being resized is an image, if only one dimension is resized the other will be automatically resized by the browser to retain the same aspect ratio.

The CSS rules used are either or both of the following:

```
width:100%;
height:100%;
```

You can also use the standard suffixes to apply the change only when an object is hovered over or clicked, or only to links within an object.

## How to Use Them

To change any dimensions of an object to those of its containing object, use one of the maxwidth, maxheight, or maxsize classes, like this:

```
<img src='photo3.jpg' class='maxwidth' />
```

Or, for example, if you want the object to change only its height when hovered over, you would use code such as this:

```
<img src='photo3.jpg' class='maxheight_h' />
```

To change both dimensions at once, you would use the maxsize class, like this:

```
<img src='photo3.jpg' class='maxsize' />
```

Here's the HTML used to create Figure 3-12:

```
<div class='nooverflow' style='width:500px; height:100px;
   border:1px solid;'>
   <img src='photo3.jpg' />
</div><br />
```

```
<div class='nooverflow' style='width:500px; height:100px;
    border:1px solid;'>
    <img src='photo3.jpg' class='maxwidth' />
</div><br />

<div class='nooverflow' style='width:500px; height:100px;
    border:1px solid;'>
    <img src='photo3.jpg' class='maxheight' />
</div><br />

<div class='nooverflow' style='width:500px; height:100px;
    border:1px solid;'>
    <img src='photo3.jpg' class='maxsize' />
</div>
```

As always, this example file and its images are available for download from the companion web site at *plugincss.com*.

## The Classes

```
.maxwidth,          .maxwidth_a:active,    .maxwidth_h:hover,
.maxwidth_l a,   .maxwidth_la a:active,    .maxwidth_lh a:hover
    { width :100%; }
.maxheight,         .maxheight_a:active,   .maxheight_h:hover
.maxheight_l a, .maxheight_la a:active,  .maxheight_lh a:hover
    { height:100%; }
.maxsize,           .maxsize_a:active,     .maxsize_h:hover,
.maxsize_l a,    .maxsize_la a:active,     .maxsize_lh a:hover
    { height:100%; width:100%; }
```

## PLUG-IN 13  Location

The classes in plug-in group 13 offer a variety of absolute and relative positioning functions. For example, in Figure 3-13 the totop, tobottom, toleft, and toright classes have been used to place four images in the corners of their containing object.

### Classes and Properties

| | |
|---|---|
| totop | Class to move an object to the top edge of its container |
| tobottom | Class to move an object to the bottom edge of its container |
| toleft | Class to move an object to the left edge of its container |
| toright | Class to move an object to the right edge of its container |
| leftby0<br>leftby0_h | Class to move an object left by 0 pixels (or move it to the left edge of the containing object), the _h suffix is used for applying the property only when it is hovered over |
| leftby5 – leftby100<br>(etc...) | Classes to move an object left by a value of 5 or from 10 through 100 pixels in steps of 10, the _h suffix is used for applying the property only when it is hovered over |

| rightby0 – rightby100 (etc...) | Classes – as the `leftby`... classes but moves the object right |
|---|---|
| upby0 – upby100 (etc...) | Classes – as the `leftby`... classes but moves the object up |
| downby0 – downby100 (etc...) | Classes – as the `leftby`... classes but moves the object down |
| `top` | Property for changing the vertical distance of an object from the top of its container, or for moving an object by relative vertical amounts |
| `bottom` | Property for changing the vertical distance of an object from the bottom of its container, or for moving an object by relative vertical amounts |
| `left` | Property for changing the horizontal distance of an object from the left of its container, or for moving an object by relative horizontal amounts |
| `right` | Property for changing the horizontal distance of an object from the right of its container, or for moving an object by relative horizontal amounts |

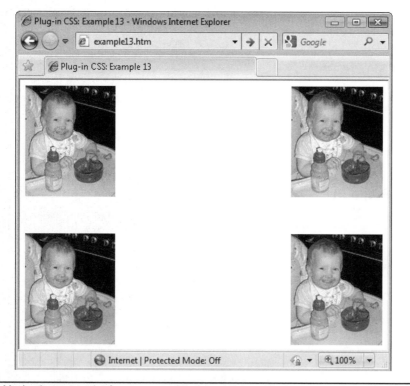

**FIGURE 3-13**    Moving images to the four corners of their containing object

## About the Classes

These classes access the `top`, `bottom`, `left`, and `right` properties of an object to either place it in an absolute position or move it by a relative amount. The _h suffix of the class names is supported to apply the change only when an object is hovered over, while the other suffixes are not supported, since it is unlikely they would ever be used.

Some of the CSS rules used are similar to the following examples:

```
top:20px;
left:-5px;
right:0px;
bottom:50px;
```

## How to Use Them

To position an object against one or more edges of its containing object, you can use code such as the following, which was used to create Figure 3-13:

```
<div class='relative' style='width:500px; height:350px;'>
   <img class='absolute toleft totop'     src='photo4.jpg' />
   <img class='absolute toright totop'    src='photo4.jpg' />
   <img class='absolute toleft tobottom'  src='photo4.jpg' />
   <img class='absolute toright tobottom' src='photo4.jpg' />
</div>
```

This example creates a container out of a `<div>`, which is given a position property of relative so it is no longer static (the default). Therefore, all the absolute objects within it will place themselves relative to it.

Inside the `<div>`, the classes are used in pairs to place each of the photographs in the four corners of the parent object.

### Moving Objects by Relative Amounts

You can also move objects relative to their current position by 5 pixels, or any amount between 10 and 100 pixels in steps of 10, like this:

```
<img class='rightby50 downby50' src='image.jpg' />
```

This example moves the object down and to the right by 50 pixels. If the object doesn't already have a position, it will be placed 50 pixels down from the top and in from the left edge of its containing object.

## The Classes

```
.totop,     .totop_h:hover    { top    :0px; }
.tobottom,  .tobottom_h:hover { bottom:0px; }
.toleft,    .toleft_h:hover   { left   :0px; }
.toright,   .toright_h:hover  { right  :0px; }

.leftby0,   .leftby0_h:hover,
.rightby0,  .rightby0_h:hover { left:0px;    }
.leftby5,   .leftby5_h:hover  { left:-5px;   }
.leftby10,  .leftby10_h:hover { left:-10px;  }
```

```
.leftby20,    .leftby20_h:hover    { left:-20px;   }
.leftby30,    .leftby30_h:hover    { left:-30px;   }
.leftby40,    .leftby40_h:hover    { left:-40px;   }
.leftby50,    .leftby50_h:hover    { left:-50px;   }
.leftby60,    .leftby60_h:hover    { left:-60px;   }
.leftby70,    .leftby70_h:hover    { left:-70px;   }
.leftby80,    .leftby80_h:hover    { left:-80px;   }
.leftby90,    .leftby90_h:hover    { left:-90px;   }
.leftby100,   .leftby100_h:hover   { left:-100px;  }

.rightby5,    .rightby5_h:hover    { left:5px;     }
.rightby10,   .rightby10_h:hover   { left:10px;    }
.rightby20,   .rightby20_h:hover   { left:20px;    }
.rightby30,   .rightby30_h:hover   { left:30px;    }
.rightby40,   .rightby40_h:hover   { left:40px;    }
.rightby50,   .rightby50_h:hover   { left:50px;    }
.rightby60,   .rightby60_h:hover   { left:60px;    }
.rightby70,   .rightby70_h:hover   { left:70px;    }
.rightby80,   .rightby80_h:hover   { left:80px;    }
.rightby90,   .rightby90_h:hover   { left:90px;    }
.rightby100,  .rightby100_h:hover  { left:100px;   }

.upby0,       .upby0_h:hover,
.downby0,     .downby0_h:hover     { top:0px;      }
.upby5,       .upby5_h:hover       { top:-5px;     }
.upby10,      .upby10_h:hover      { top:-10px;    }
.upby20,      .upby20_h:hover      { top:-20px;    }
.upby30,      .upby30_h:hover      { top:-30px;    }
.upby40,      .upby40_h:hover      { top:-40px;    }
.upby50,      .upby50_h:hover      { top:-50px;    }
.upby60,      .upby60_h:hover      { top:-60px;    }
.upby70,      .upby70_h:hover      { top:-70px;    }
.upby80,      .upby80_h:hover      { top:-80px;    }
.upby90,      .upby90_h:hover      { top:-90px;    }
.upby100,     .upby100_h:hover     { top:-100px;   }

.downby5,     .downby5_h:hover     { top:5px;      }
.downby10,    .downby10_h:hover    { top:10px;     }
.downby20,    .downby20_h:hover    { top:20px;     }
.downby30,    .downby30_h:hover    { top:30px;     }
.downby40,    .downby40_h:hover    { top:40px;     }
.downby50,    .downby50_h:hover    { top:50px;     }
.downby60,    .downby60_h:hover    { top:60px;     }
.downby70,    .downby70_h:hover    { top:70px;     }
.downby80,    .downby80_h:hover    { top:80px;     }
.downby90,    .downby90_h:hover    { top:90px;     }
.downby100,   .downby100_h:hover   { top:100px;    }
```

## PLUG-IN 14    Selective Margins

Using the classes in this group of plug-ins, you can specify or change any of the four margins of an object by 5 pixels, or by any amount between 10 and 100 pixels, in steps of 10. In Figure 3-14, eleven <div> tags have been created, each one resting on the left edge

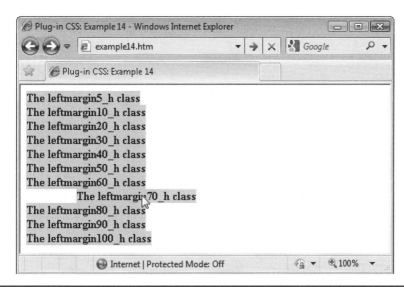

**FIGURE 3-14**   A collection of objects set to indent by differing amounts when hovered over

of the browser, but using classes of `leftmargin5_h` through `leftmargin100_h` to indent them by the specified amount when the mouse passes over. In the screen grab, the mouse is currently over the `<div>` using the `leftmargin70_h` class.

## Classes and Properties

| | |
|---|---|
| `leftmargin0`<br>`leftmargin0_h` | Class to set the left margin of an object to zero pixels, the `_h` suffix is used for applying the property only when it is hovered over |
| `leftmargin5 –`<br>`lefmargin100 (etc...)` | Classes to set the left margin of an object to 5 pixels, or from 10 through 100 pixels in steps of 10 |
| `rightmargin0 (etc...)` | Class – as `leftmargin0` but for the right margin |
| `topmargin0 (etc...)` | Class – as `leftmargin0` but for the top margin |
| `bottommargin0 (etc...)` | Class – as `leftmargin0` but for the bottom margin |
| `margin-left` | Property to change an object's left margin |
| `margin-right` | Property to change an object's right margin |
| `margin-top` | Property to change an object's top margin |
| `margin-bottom` | Property to change an object's bottom margin |

## About the Classes

With these classes, you can change the margins of an object by amounts between 0 and 100 pixels, in steps of 10, and also by 5 pixels. The `_h` suffix for the classes is supported to change a property only when it is being hovered over. The other standard suffixes are not available since they are highly unlikely to be used.

Some of the CSS rules used are similar to the following examples:

```
margin-left:10px;
margin-right:-10px;
margin-top:20px;
margin-bottom:0px;
```

## How to Use Them

To use these classes, refer to the one you need by placing its name in the class='...' argument of an HTML tag, like this:

```
<div class='leftmargin30'>This text is indented by 30 pixels</div>
```

You can also apply the hover versions of these classes, for example enabling you to create professional looking animations for menus, like this:

```
<div class='leftmargin10 leftmargin20_h'>Menu Item 1</div>
<div class='leftmargin10 leftmargin20_h'>Menu Item 2</div>
<div class='leftmargin10 leftmargin20_h'>Menu Item 3</div>
```

Following is the code used to create the screen shown in Figure 3-14:

```
<span class='leftmargin5_h lime_b'>The leftmargin5_h class</span><br />
<span class='leftmargin10_h lime_b'>The leftmargin10_h class</span><br />
<span class='leftmargin20_h lime_b'>The leftmargin20_h class</span><br />
<span class='leftmargin30_h lime_b'>The leftmargin30_h class</span><br />
<span class='leftmargin40_h lime_b'>The leftmargin40_h class</span><br />
<span class='leftmargin50_h lime_b'>The leftmargin50_h class</span><br />
<span class='leftmargin60_h lime_b'>The leftmargin60_h class</span><br />
<span class='leftmargin70_h lime_b'>The leftmargin70_h class</span><br />
<span class='leftmargin80_h lime_b'>The leftmargin80_h class</span><br />
<span class='leftmargin90_h lime_b'>The leftmargin90_h class</span><br />
<span class='leftmargin100_h lime_b'>The leftmargin100_h class</span>
```

Each item has a background fill color of lime green, is aligned with the left side of the browser, and indents by the number of pixels specified in the class name it uses when the mouse passes over it.

Margins are external to objects and are therefore invisible, as can be seen in Figure 3-14, where the lime green background color has not been apportioned to the margin area of the hovered element.

## The Classes

```
.leftmargin0,    .leftmargin0_h:hover   { margin-left:0px;   }
.leftmargin5,    .leftmargin5_h:hover   { margin-left:5px;   }
.leftmargin10,   .leftmargin10_h:hover  { margin-left:10px;  }
.leftmargin20,   .leftmargin20_h:hover  { margin-left:20px;  }
.leftmargin30,   .leftmargin30_h:hover  { margin-left:30px;  }
.leftmargin40,   .leftmargin40_h:hover  { margin-left:40px;  }
.leftmargin50,   .leftmargin50_h:hover  { margin-left:50px;  }
```

```
.leftmargin60,    .leftmargin60_h:hover  { margin-left:60px;  }
.leftmargin70,    .leftmargin70_h:hover  { margin-left:70px;  }
.leftmargin80,    .leftmargin80_h:hover  { margin-left:80px;  }
.leftmargin90,    .leftmargin90_h:hover  { margin-left:90px;  }
.leftmargin100,   .leftmargin100_h:hover { margin-left:100px; }

.rightmargin0,    .rightmargin0_h:hover    { margin-right:0px;   }
.rightmargin5,    .rightmargin5_h:hover    { margin-right:5px;   }
.rightmargin10,   .rightmargin10_h:hover   { margin-right:10px;  }
.rightmargin20,   .rightmargin20_h:hover   { margin-right:20px;  }
.rightmargin30,   .rightmargin30_h:hover   { margin-right:30px;  }
.rightmargin40,   .rightmargin40_h:hover   { margin-right:40px;  }
.rightmargin50,   .rightmargin50_h:hover   { margin-right:50px;  }
.rightmargin60,   .rightmargin60_h:hover   { margin-right:60px;  }
.rightmargin70,   .rightmargin70_h:hover   { margin-right:70px;  }
.rightmargin80,   .rightmargin80_h:hover   { margin-right:80px;  }
.rightmargin90,   .rightmargin90_h:hover   { margin-right:90px;  }
.rightmargin100,  .rightmargin100_h:hover  { margin-right:100px; }

.topmargin0,    .topmargin0_h:hover    { margin-top:0px;   }
.topmargin5,    .topmargin5_h:hover    { margin-top:5px;   }
.topmargin10,   .topmargin10_h:hover   { margin-top:10px;  }
.topmargin20,   .topmargin20_h:hover   { margin-top:20px;  }
.topmargin30,   .topmargin30_h:hover   { margin-top:30px;  }
.topmargin40,   .topmargin40_h:hover   { margin-top:40px;  }
.topmargin50,   .topmargin50_h:hover   { margin-top:50px;  }
.topmargin60,   .topmargin60_h:hover   { margin-top:60px;  }
.topmargin70,   .topmargin70_h:hover   { margin-top:70px;  }
.topmargin80,   .topmargin80_h:hover   { margin-top:80px;  }
.topmargin90,   .topmargin90_h:hover   { margin-top:90px;  }
.topmargin100,  .topmargin100_h:hover  { margin-top:100px; }

.bottommargin0,    .bottommargin0_h:hover    { margin-bottom:0px;   }
.bottommargin5,    .bottommargin5_h:hover    { margin-bottom:5px;   }
.bottommargin10,   .bottommargin10_h:hover   { margin-bottom:10px;  }
.bottommargin20,   .bottommargin20_h:hover   { margin-bottom:20px;  }
.bottommargin30,   .bottommargin30_h:hover   { margin-bottom:30px;  }
.bottommargin40,   .bottommargin40_h:hover   { margin-bottom:40px;  }
.bottommargin50,   .bottommargin50_h:hover   { margin-bottom:50px;  }
.bottommargin60,   .bottommargin60_h:hover   { margin-bottom:60px;  }
.bottommargin70,   .bottommargin70_h:hover   { margin-bottom:70px;  }
.bottommargin80,   .bottommargin80_h:hover   { margin-bottom:80px;  }
.bottommargin90,   .bottommargin90_h:hover   { margin-bottom:90px;  }
.bottommargin100,  .bottommargin100_h:hover  { margin-bottom:100px; }
```

## PLUG-IN 15  Selective Padding

You've already seen the basic padding classes provided in plug-in group 9. You can also use this collection of classes to give you even greater control over which edges to pad and by how much.

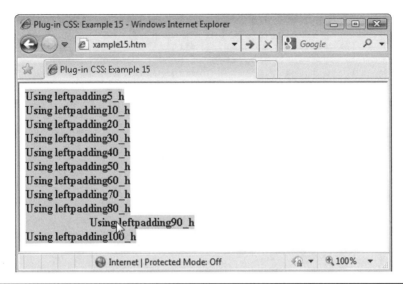

FIGURE **3-15**    The left padding of these objects is set to differing amounts when hovered over

In Figure 3-15, a collection of <span> objects have been given varying leftpadding.._h properties. The mouse is currently over the one assigned a value of 90 pixels, which has therefore been indented by that amount.

## Classes and Properties

| | |
|---|---|
| leftpadding0<br>leftpadding0_h | Class to set the left padding of an object to zero pixels, the _h suffix is used for applying the property only when it is hovered over |
| leftpadding5 –<br>lefpadding100 (etc...) | Classes to set the left padding of an object to 5 pixels, or from 10 through 100 pixels in steps of 10 |
| rightpadding0 (etc...) | Class – as leftpadding0 but for the right padding |
| toppadding0 (etc...) | Class – as leftpadding0 but for the top padding |
| bottompadding0 (etc...) | Class – as leftpadding0 but for the bottom padding |
| padding-left | Property to change an object's left padding |
| padding-right | Property to change an object's right padding |
| padding-top | Property to change an object's top padding |
| padding-bottom | Property to change an object's bottom padding |

## About the Classes

With these classes, you can change the padding of an object by amounts between 0 and 100 pixels, in steps of 10, and also by 5 pixels. The _h suffix for the classes is supported to change a property only when it is being hovered over. The other standard suffixes are not available since they are highly unlikely to be used.

Here are some examples of the CSS rules used by these classes:

```
padding-left:5px;
padding-right:20px;
padding-top:0px;
padding-bottom:-10px;
```

## How to Use Them

These classes provide similar results to the margin classes in the previous plug-in group, except that the padding of an object is internal to it and so the padded area assumes the properties of the rest of the object. This can be seen in Figure 3-15, in which the 90-pixels wide padding that has been applied to the left side of the indented span has assumed the lime green background color of the object. Here is the code used to create the screen grab:

```
<span class='leftpadding5_h   lime_b'>Using leftpadding5_h  </span><br />
<span class='leftpadding10_h  lime_b'>Using leftpadding10_h </span><br />
<span class='leftpadding20_h  lime_b'>Using leftpadding20_h </span><br />
<span class='leftpadding30_h  lime_b'>Using leftpadding30_h </span><br />
<span class='leftpadding40_h  lime_b'>Using leftpadding40_h </span><br />
<span class='leftpadding50_h  lime_b'>Using leftpadding50_h </span><br />
<span class='leftpadding60_h  lime_b'>Using leftpadding60_h </span><br />
<span class='leftpadding70_h  lime_b'>Using leftpadding70_h </span><br />
<span class='leftpadding80_h  lime_b'>Using leftpadding80_h </span><br />
<span class='leftpadding90_h  lime_b'>Using leftpadding90_h </span><br />
<span class='leftpadding100_h lime_b'>Using leftpadding100_h</span>
```

Because of the padding property's ability to seem to stretch an object, you will see this feature used to good effect in Chapter 12, in conjunction with animated transitions to smoothly move menu items in and out again as the mouse hovers over them.

## The Classes

```
.leftpadding0,    .leftpadding0_h:hover    { padding-left:0px;    }
.leftpadding5,    .leftpadding5_h:hover    { padding-left:5px;    }
.leftpadding10,   .leftpadding10_h:hover   { padding-left:10px;   }
.leftpadding20,   .leftpadding20_h:hover   { padding-left:20px;   }
.leftpadding30,   .leftpadding30_h:hover   { padding-left:30px;   }
.leftpadding40,   .leftpadding40_h:hover   { padding-left:40px;   }
.leftpadding50,   .leftpadding50_h:hover   { padding-left:50px;   }
.leftpadding60,   .leftpadding60_h:hover   { padding-left:60px;   }
.leftpadding70,   .leftpadding70_h:hover   { padding-left:70px;   }
.leftpadding80,   .leftpadding80_h:hover   { padding-left:80px;   }
.leftpadding90,   .leftpadding90_h:hover   { padding-left:90px;   }
.leftpadding100,  .leftpadding100_h:hover  { padding-left:100px;  }

.rightpadding0,   .rightpadding0_h:hover   { padding-right:0px;   }
.rightpadding5,   .rightpadding5_h:hover   { padding-right:5px;   }
.rightpadding10,  .rightpadding10_h:hover  { padding-right:10px;  }
.rightpadding20,  .rightpadding20_h:hover  { padding-right:20px;  }
.rightpadding30,  .rightpadding30_h:hover  { padding-right:30px;  }
.rightpadding40,  .rightpadding40_h:hover  { padding-right:40px;  }
.rightpadding50,  .rightpadding50_h:hover  { padding-right:50px;  }
.rightpadding60,  .rightpadding60_h:hover  { padding-right:60px;  }
```

```
.rightpadding70,    .rightpadding70_h:hover   { padding-right:70px;  }
.rightpadding80,    .rightpadding80_h:hover   { padding-right:80px;  }
.rightpadding90,    .rightpadding90_h:hover   { padding-right:90px;  }
.rightpadding100,   .rightpadding100_h:hover  { padding-right:100px; }

.toppadding0,       .toppadding0_h:hover      { padding-top:0px;     }
.toppadding5,       .toppadding5_h:hover      { padding-top:5px;     }
.toppadding10,      .toppadding10_h:hover     { padding-top:10px;    }
.toppadding20,      .toppadding20_h:hover     { padding-top:20px;    }
.toppadding30,      .toppadding30_h:hover     { padding-top:30px;    }
.toppadding40,      .toppadding40_h:hover     { padding-top:40px;    }
.toppadding50,      .toppadding50_h:hover     { padding-top:50px;    }
.toppadding60,      .toppadding60_h:hover     { padding-top:60px;    }
.toppadding70,      .toppadding70_h:hover     { padding-top:70px;    }
.toppadding80,      .toppadding80_h:hover     { padding-top:80px;    }
.toppadding90,      .toppadding90_h:hover     { padding-top:90px;    }
.toppadding100,     .toppadding100_h:hover    { padding-top:100px;   }

.bottompadding0,    .bottompadding0_h:hover   { padding-bottom:0px;   }
.bottompadding5,    .bottompadding5_h:hover   { padding-bottom:5px;   }
.bottompadding10,   .bottompadding10_h:hover  { padding-bottom:10px;  }
.bottompadding20,   .bottompadding20_h:hover  { padding-bottom:20px;  }
.bottompadding30,   .bottompadding30_h:hover  { padding-bottom:30px;  }
.bottompadding40,   .bottompadding40_h:hover  { padding-bottom:40px;  }
.bottompadding50,   .bottompadding50_h:hover  { padding-bottom:50px;  }
.bottompadding60,   .bottompadding60_h:hover  { padding-bottom:60px;  }
.bottompadding70,   .bottompadding70_h:hover  { padding-bottom:70px;  }
.bottompadding80,   .bottompadding80_h:hover  { padding-bottom:80px;  }
.bottompadding90,   .bottompadding90_h:hover  { padding-bottom:90px;  }
.bottompadding100,  .bottompadding100_h:hover { padding-bottom:100px; }
```

## PLUG-IN 16   Border Style

Using the classes in plug-in group 16, you can choose exactly the kind of border you want for an object. For example, Figure 3-16 shows two rows of objects, the first of which has one of each different border style, while the second is the same, but the border styles are activated

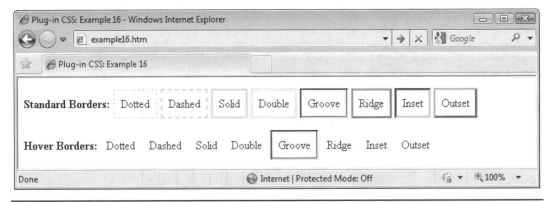

**FIGURE 3-16**   The eight different border style classes and their hover equivalents

only when the mouse passes over them. In the screen grab, the mouse is currently hovering over the object with grooved borders in the second row.

## Classes and Properties

| | |
|---|---|
| bdotted<br>bdotted_h | Classes to set an object's border style to dotted either immediately, or when hovered over |
| bdashed<br>bdashed_h | Classes to set an object's border style to dashed either immediately, or when hovered over |
| bsolid<br>bsolid_h | Classes to set an object's border style to solid either immediately, or when hovered over |
| bdouble<br>bdouble_h | Classes to set an object's border style to double either immediately, or when hovered over |
| bgroove<br>bgroove_h | Classes to set an object's border style to groove either immediately, or when hovered over—this effect depends on the border color |
| bridge<br>bridge_h | Classes to set an object's border style to ridge either immediately, or when hovered over—this effect depends on the border color |
| binset<br>binset_h | Classes to set an object's border style to inset either immediately, or when hovered over—this effect depends on the border color |
| boutset<br>boutset_h | Classes to set an object's border style to outset either immediately, or when hovered over—this effect depends on the border color |
| border-style | Property for changing an object's border style |

## About the Classes

These classes enable the selection of all eight different types of border style, which can be applied immediately, or only when hovered over. They achieve this effect using the border-style property, like this:

**border-style**:dashed;

## How to Use Them

As soon as you choose a border style for an object, the border will be displayed, but some of the classes only show these styles at their best when a mid-range color is also supplied (see the Border Color plug-in group).

To add a border to an object, refer to the border style in a class, like this:

```
<span class='bdouble'>Double</span>
```

Following is the HTML used to create the screen grab in Figure 3-16:

```
<br /><b>Standard Borders:</b>
<span class='bdotted padding blime'>Dotted</span>
<span class='bdashed padding blime'>Dashed</span>
<span class='bsolid  padding blime'>Solid </span>
<span class='bdouble padding blime'>Double</span>
<span class='bgroove padding blime'>Groove</span>
```

```
<span class='bridge  padding blime'>Ridge </span>
<span class='binset  padding blime'>Inset </span>
<span class='boutset padding blime'>Outset</span>

<br /><br /><br /><b>Hover Borders:</b>
<span class='bdotted_h padding blime'>Dotted</span>
<span class='bdashed_h padding blime'>Dashed</span>
<span class='bsolid_h  padding blime'>Solid </span>
<span class='bdouble_h padding blime'>Double</span>
<span class='bgroove_h padding blime'>Groove</span>
<span class='bridge_h  padding blime'>Ridge </span>
<span class='binset_h  padding blime'>Inset </span>
<span class='boutset_h padding blime'>Outset</span>
```

To create space around the text, the padding class has been used, as has the class blime (explained a little further on), which sets the border color to lime green in order to clearly display the different border types that rely on color.

The first set of objects displays the borders immediately, while the second does so only when hovered over.

### The Classes

```
.bdotted,  .bdotted_h:hover { border-style:dotted; }
.bdashed,  .bdashed_h:hover { border-style:dashed; }
.bsolid,   .bsolid_h:hover  { border-style:solid;  }
.bdouble,  .bdouble_h:hover { border-style:double; }
.bgroove,  .bgroove_h:hover { border-style:groove; }
.bridge,   .bridge_h:hover  { border-style:ridge;  }
.binset,   .binset_h:hover  { border-style:inset;  }
.boutset,  .boutset_h:hover { border-style:outset; }
```

## PLUG-IN 17 Border Width

With the plug-in group 17 classes, you can specify ten different border widths either immediately, or when the mouse hovers over an object. Figure 3-17 shows the same code from the previous example except that all the borders have been given widths of 10 pixels.

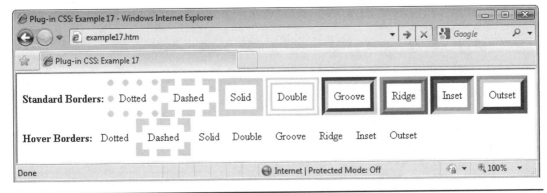

**Figure 3-17**   You can specify up to 10 different border widths with these classes.

## Classes and Properties

| | |
|---|---|
| `bwidth1`<br>`bwidth1_h` | Classes to set an object's border width to 1 pixel either immediately or when hovered over |
| `bwidth2`<br>`bwidth2_h` | Classes to set an object's border width to 2 pixels either immediately or when hovered over |
| `bwidth3`<br>`bwidth3_h` | Classes to set an object's border width to 3 pixels either immediately or when hovered over |
| `bwidth4`<br>`bwidth4_h` | Classes to set an object's border width to 4 pixels either immediately or when hovered over |
| `bwidth5`<br>`bwidth5_h` | Classes to set an object's border width to 5 pixels either immediately or when hovered over |
| `bwidth10`<br>`bwidth10_h` | Classes to set an object's border width to 10 pixels either immediately or when hovered over |
| `bwidth15`<br>`bwidth15_h` | Classes to set an object's border width to 15 pixels either immediately or when hovered over |
| `bwidth20`<br>`bwidth20_h` | Classes to set an object's border width to 20 pixels either immediately or when hovered over |
| `bwidth25`<br>`bwidth25_h` | Classes to set an object's border width to 25 pixels either immediately or when hovered over |
| `bwidth50`<br>`bwidth50_h` | Classes to set an object's border width to 50 pixels either immediately or when hovered over |
| `border-width` | Property for changing the width of a border |

## About the Classes

These classes let you change the width of a border to a value from 1 through 5 pixels, 10 through 25 pixels in steps of 5, or 50 pixels. You can also use the hover versions of the classes to apply the change only when an object is being hovered over by the mouse.

To achieve this effect, the classes use the `border-width` property, like this:

**border-width**:20px;

## How to Use Them

Simply use the name of the class you need for the width you want in your HTML, like this:

```
<span class='bsolid'>This object has a solid border</span>
```

You can also use the hover versions of these classes, as with the following HTML which was used to create Figure 3-17:

```
<br /><b>Standard Borders:</b>
<span class='bdotted bwidth10 padding blime'>Dotted</span>
<span class='bdashed bwidth10 padding blime'>Dashed</span>
<span class='bsolid  bwidth10 padding blime'>Solid </span>
<span class='bdouble bwidth10 padding blime'>Double</span>
<span class='bgroove bwidth10 padding blime'>Groove</span>
```

```
<span class='bridge  bwidth10 padding blime'>Ridge </span>
<span class='binset  bwidth10 padding blime'>Inset </span>
<span class='boutset bwidth10 padding blime'>Outset</span>

<br /><br /><br /><b>Hover Borders:</b>
<span class='bdotted_h bwidth10 padding blime'>Dotted</span>
<span class='bdashed_h bwidth10 padding blime'>Dashed</span>
<span class='bsolid_h  bwidth10 padding blime'>Solid </span>
<span class='bdouble_h bwidth10 padding blime'>Double</span>
<span class='bgroove_h bwidth10 padding blime'>Groove</span>
<span class='bridge_h  bwidth10 padding blime'>Ridge </span>
<span class='binset_h  bwidth10 padding blime'>Inset </span>
<span class='boutset_h bwidth10 padding blime'>Outset</span>
```

In each of these objects, a different border style is specified, with a width of 10 pixels and standard padding. Once again, the `blime` class (see the next section) has been used to set a border color that will show all the styles to their best effect.

### The Classes

```
.bwidth1,  .bwidth1_h:hover  { border-width:1px;  }
.bwidth2,  .bwidth2_h:hover  { border-width:2px;  }
.bwidth3,  .bwidth3_h:hover  { border-width:3px;  }
.bwidth4,  .bwidth4_h:hover  { border-width:4px;  }
.bwidth5,  .bwidth5_h:hover  { border-width:5px;  }
.bwidth10, .bwidth10_h:hover { border-width:10px; }
.bwidth15, .bwidth15_h:hover { border-width:15px; }
.bwidth20, .bwidth20_h:hover { border-width:20px; }
.bwidth25, .bwidth25_h:hover { border-width:25px; }
.bwidth50, .bwidth50_h:hover { border-width:50px; }
```

## PLUG-IN 18 Border Color

With this final group of border classes, you can choose any of 21 different colors to apply to a border either immediately, or when it is moused over. Figure 3-18 expands on the example in the previous section to present two rows of objects using a variety of different border styles, widths, and colors. The second row of classes apply only when the mouse passes over an object. In the figure, it is currently over the Inset object.

### Classes and Properties

| | |
|---|---|
| baqua baqua_h bblack bblack_h bblue bblue_h bbrown bbrown_h bfuchsia bfuchsia_h bgold bgold_h bgray bgray_h bgreen bgreen_h bkhaki bkhaki_h blime blime_h bmaroon bmaroon_h bnavy bnavy_h bolive bolive_h borange borange_h bpink bpink_h bpurple bpurple_h bred bred_h bsilver bsilver_h bteal bteal_h bwhite bwhite_h byellow byellow_h | Classes to change the border color of an object either immediately, or when it is moused over |
| Border-color | Property to change the border color of an object |

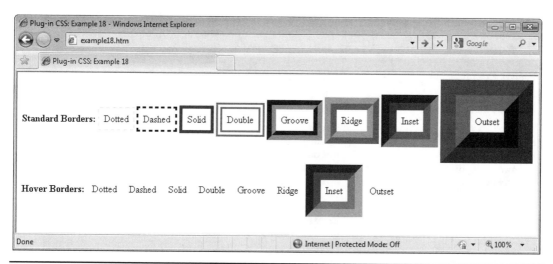

**Figure 3-18**    A selection of the different border types, widths, and colors available

## About the Classes

These classes provide a wide range of colors that you can apply to borders either immediately or when they are moused over. The property that is manipulated is border-color, like this:

```
border-color:#c44;
```

## How to Use Them

Using these color classes is as easy as putting their names within an object's class='...' argument, like this:

```
<span class='bbrown'>This object has a brown border</span>
```

In the following example HTML (which was used to create Figure 3-18), a variety of different colors has been used, along with different border styles and widths:

```
<br /><br /><br /><b>Standard Borders:</b>
<span class='bdotted bwidth1  padding baqua'>Dotted</span>
<span class='bdashed bwidth3  padding bblack'   >Dashed</span>
<span class='bsolid  bwidth5  padding bblue'    >Solid </span>
<span class='bdouble bwidth10 padding bbrown'   >Double</span>
<span class='bgroove bwidth15 padding bfuchsia' >Groove</span>
<span class='bridge  bwidth20 padding bgold'    >Ridge </span>
<span class='binset  bwidth25 padding bgray'    >Inset </span>
<span class='boutset bwidth50 padding bgreen'   >Outset</span>

<br /><br /><br /><br /><br /><br /><b>Hover Borders:</b>
<span class='bdotted_h bwidth1  padding bkhaki' >Dotted</span>
<span class='bdashed_h bwidth3  padding bmaroon'>Dashed</span>
<span class='bsolid_h  bwidth5  padding bnavy'  >Solid </span>
```

```
<span class='bdouble_h bwidth10 padding bolive' >Double</span>
<span class='bgroove_h bwidth15 padding borange'>Groove</span>
<span class='bridge_h  bwidth20 padding bpurple'>Ridge </span>
<span class='binset_h  bwidth25 padding bpink'  >Inset </span>
<span class='boutset_h bwidth50 padding bred'   >Outset</span>
```

## The Classes

```
.baqua,    .baqua_h:hover   { border-color:#0ff; }
.bblack,   .bblack_h:hover  { border-color:#000; }
.bblue,    .bblue_h:hover   { border-color:#00f; }
.bbrown,   .bbrown_h:hover  { border-color:#c44; }
.bfuchsia, .bfuchsia_h:hover { border-color:#f0f; }
.bgold,    .bgold_h:hover   { border-color:#fc0; }
.bgray,    .bgray_h:hover   { border-color:#888; }
.bgreen,   .bgreen_h:hover  { border-color:#080; }
.bkhaki,   .bkhaki_h:hover  { border-color:#cc8; }
.blime,    .blime_h:hover   { border-color:#0f0; }
.bmaroon,  .bmaroon_h:hover { border-color:#800; }
.bnavy,    .bnavy_h:hover   { border-color:#008; }
.bolive,   .bolive_h:hover  { border-color:#880; }
.borange,  .borange_h:hover { border-color:#f80; }
.bpink,    .bpink_h:hover   { border-color:#f88; }
.bpurple,  .bpurple_h:hover { border-color:#808; }
.bred,     .bred_h:hover    { border-color:#f00; }
.bsilver,  .bsilver_h:hover { border-color:#ccc; }
.bteal,    .bteal_h:hover   { border-color:#088; }
.bwhite,   .bwhite_h:hover  { border-color:#fff; }
.byellow,  .byellow_h:hover { border-color:#ff0; }
```

## PLUG-IN 19 No Outline

To enable people to tab through a document more easily, some browsers display a dotted outline around the object being focused on, as well as highlight it. This certainly helps make it clear which object has the focus, but as you can see in Figure 3-19 where Button 2 has the focus, the dotted border inset into the button destroys much of the button's 3D gradient effect.

**FIGURE 3-19**
Button 2 shows a highlight and a dotted outline.

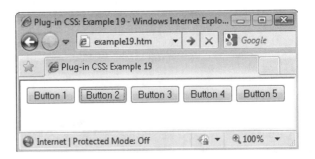

**FIGURE 3-20**
The dotted outline has been removed from Button 3, leaving only the highlight.

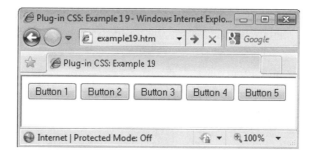

On the other hand, in Figure 3-20, Button 3 is now focused on, and because it is using the `nooutline` class, there is no dotted outline. As you can see, there is still a highlight around the button, which is sufficient to inform you that the button has the focus, and the button itself looks much cleaner as a result. And on a color monitor (rather than a grayscale printed page like this), it looks even better.

## Classes and Properties

| | |
|---|---|
| `nooutline` | Class to remove the dotted border from an object that has focus |
| `outline` | Property used by most browsers to enable or disable the outline |
| `border` | Property used by Firefox and other Mozilla-based browsers (in conjunction with the `::-moz-focus-inner` pseudo class) to enable or disable the outline |

## About the Class

When applied to an object, this class prevents it from displaying a dotted outline when it has focus. This is achieved on most browsers with the `:focus` pseudo class and the `outline` property, like this:

```
.nooutline:focus { outline:none; }
```

However, Firefox and other Mozilla-based browsers need to be handled differently, so the following alternative is used:

```
.nooutline::-moz-focus-inner { border:none; padding:1px 3px; }
```

When the outline is removed in a Firefox browser, it reduces the size of a button by the amount of the removed outline, so the padding property is updated to increase the button's size back again.

## How to Use It

To prevent an object that has focus from displaying a dotted outline, just insert the `nooutline` class into the object's `class='...'` argument, like this:

```
<button class='nooutline'>Click me</button>
```

Here is the HTML used to create Figures 3-19 and 3-20. If you press the TAB key several times or click the buttons, you'll see that Button 3 does not show the dotted outline that the others display:

```
<button>Button 1</button>
<button>Button 2</button>
<button class='nooutline'>Button 3</button>
<button>Button 4</button>
<button>Button 5</button>
```

## The Class

```
.nooutline:focus               { outline:none;  }
.nooutline::-moz-focus-inner  { border :none; padding:1px 3px; }
```

# CHAPTER 4

## Text and Typography

This chapter features a wide range of powerful plug-ins for managing most aspects of using and presenting fonts. These include quick access to font families, embedding any of an additional 19 fonts courtesy of Google, changing text size alignment and styles, and adding colors and drop shadows.

There are also handy classes to transform your text, automatically add icons and other characters such as quotation marks, create professional drop cap effects, and more. Between them, there are over 720 classes for doing almost everything you could want to do with text, without having to write your own CSS rules.

## 20 Fonts

Choosing a font for displaying text is very easy using the classes in this plug-in group, as you only need to enter a short name into the `class` argument of an object. Plus, each font offers fallback fonts so that systems without the exact font you choose will display the closest match that they have. You can also decide when to enable the fonts since there are six versions of each class.

In Figure 4-1, all the available font classes have been used twice: once to display the associated fonts immediately, and again for mouse hover versions. In the second group of fonts, "Lucida Grande" is currently being hovered over.

### Classes and Properties

| | |
|---|---|
| arial<br>arial_a<br>arial_h<br>arial_l<br>arial_la<br>arial_lh | Classes to assign a font to an object (`arial`), to do so only when it is actively being clicked (`arial_a`), or when it is being hovered over (`arial_h`), also three classes to enable a font only for a link within the object (`arial_l`), a link within the object that is being clicked (`arial_la`), or a link within the object that is being hovered over (`arial_lh`) |
| arialb (etc...) | Class – the same as Arial, but for Arial Bold |
| arialn (etc...) | Class – the same as Arial, but for Arial Narrow |
| avant (etc...) | Class – the same as Arial, but for Avant Garde |
| bookman (etc...) | Class – the same as Arial, but for Bookman |
| century (etc...) | Class – the same as Arial, but for Century Gothic |
| copper (etc...) | Class – the same as Arial, but for Copperplate |
| comic (etc...) | Class – the same as Arial, but for Comic Sans MS |
| courier (etc...) | Class – the same as Arial, but for Courier |
| couriern (etc...) | Class – the same as Arial, but for Courier New |
| garamond (etc...) | Class – the same as Arial, but for Garamond |
| gill (etc...) | Class – the same as Arial, but for Gill Sans MT |
| georgia (etc...) | Class – the same as Arial, but for Georgia |
| helvetica (etc...) | Class – the same as Arial, but for Helvetica |
| impact (etc...) | Class – the same as Arial, but for Impact |

| | |
|---|---|
| lucida (etc...) | Class – the same as Arial, but for Lucida |
| lucidac (etc...) | Class – the same as Arial, but for Lucida Console |
| palatino (etc...) | Class – the same as Arial, but for Palatino |
| tahoma (etc...) | Class – the same as Arial, but for Tahoma |
| times (etc...) | Class – the same as Arial, but for Times |
| timesnr (etc...) | Class – the same as Arial, but for Times New Roman |
| trebuchet (etc...) | Class – the same as Arial, but for Trebuchet |
| verdana (etc...) | Class – the same as Arial, but for Verdana |
| font-family | Property used for changing font |

## About the Classes

These classes use the CSS font-family property to assign the font you choose. Fallback fonts are provided for each to ensure that if a computer doesn't have a particular font, it can at least display the closest one it does have.

For example, the copper class uses the following rule:

```
font-family:"Copperplate", "Copperplate Gothic Light", serif;
```

## How to Use Them

To use a font class, enter its name in the class argument of an object. For example, to change to the Impact font, you could use HTML such as this:

```
<span class='impact'>Impact</span>
```

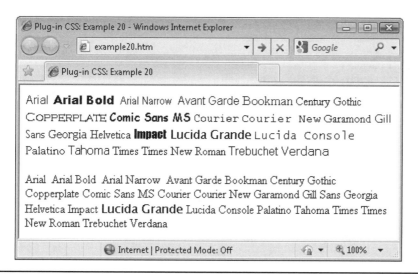

FIGURE 4-1   A typical collection of fonts on a Windows computer

Or, to change a font only when the mouse hovers over the object, you might use this:

```
<span class='impact_h'>Impact</span>
```

Or you can combine classes so that, for example, to change the font of an object to Verdana, and then to Georgia when it is hovered over, you might use this:

```
<span class='verdana Georgia_h'>Impact</span>
```

You can also use the other class suffixes to enable a font only when it is actively clicked (*classname*_a), or when it is a link that is part of the object (*classname*_l), when it is a clicked link that is part of the object (*classname*_la), or when it is a hovered link that is part of the object (*classname*_lh).

Here is the code used to create Figure 4-1:

```
<span class='arial'    >Arial</span>,
<span class='arialb'   >Arial Bold</span>,
<span class='arialn'   >Arial Narrow</span>,
<span class='avant'    >Avant Garde</span>
<span class='bookman'  >Bookman</span>
<span class='century'  >Century Gothic</span>
<span class='copper'   >Copperplate</span>
<span class='comic'    >Comic Sans MS</span>
<span class='courier'  >Courier</span>
<span class='couriern' >Courier New</span>
<span class='garamond' >Garamond</span>
<span class='gill'     >Gill Sans</span>
<span class='georgia'  >Georgia</span>
<span class='helvetica'>Helvetica</span>
<span class='impact'   >Impact</span>
<span class='lucida'   >Lucida Grande</span>
<span class='lucidacon'>Lucida Console</span>
<span class='palatino' >Palatino</span>
<span class='tahoma'   >Tahoma</span>
<span class='times'    >Times</span>
<span class='timesnr'  >Times New Roman</span>
<span class='trebuchet'>Trebuchet</span>
<span class='verdana'  >Verdana</span><br /><br />

<span class='arial_h'    >Arial</span>,
<span class='arialb_h'   >Arial Bold</span>,
<span class='arialn_h'   >Arial Narrow</span>,
<span class='avant_h'    >Avant Garde</span>
<span class='bookman_h'  >Bookman</span>
<span class='century_h'  >Century Gothic</span>
<span class='copper_h'   >Copperplate</span>
<span class='comic_h'    >Comic Sans MS</span>
<span class='courie_hr'  >Courier</span>
<span class='couriern_h' >Courier New</span>
<span class='garamond_h' >Garamond</span>
<span class='gill_h'     >Gill Sans</span>
<span class='georgia_h'  >Georgia</span>
```

```
<span class='helvetica_h'>Helvetica</span>
<span class='impact_h'   >Impact</span>
<span class='lucida_h   '>Lucida Grande</span>
<span class='lucidacon_h'>Lucida Console</span>
<span class='palatino_h' >Palatino</span>
<span class='tahoma_h'   >Tahoma</span>
<span class='times_h'    >Times</span>
<span class='timesnr_h'  >Times New Roman</span>
<span class='trebuchet_h'>Trebuchet</span>
<span class='verdana_h'  >Verdana</span>
```

## The Classes

```
.arial,          .arial_a:active,      .arial_h:hover,
.arial_l a,      .arial_la a:active,   .arial_lh a:hover
   { font-family:"Arial", sans-serif; }
.arialb,         .arialb_a:active,     .arialb_h:hover,
.arialb_l a,     .arialb_la a:active,  .arialb_lh a:hover
   { font-family:"Arial Black", sans-serif; }
.arialn,         .arialn_a:active,     .arialn_h:hover,
.arialn_l a,     .arialn_la a:active,  .arialbn_lh a:hover
   { font-family:"Arial Narrow", sans-serif; }
.avant,          .avant_a:active,      .avant_h:hover,
.avant_l a,      .avant_la a:active,   .avant_lh a:hover
   { font-family:"Avant Garde", sans-serif; }
.bookman,        .bookman_a:active,    .bookman_h:hover,
.bookman_l a,    .bookman_la a:active, .bookman_lh a:hover
   { font-family:"Bookman", "Bookman Old Style", serif; }
.century,        .century_a:active,    .century_h:hover,
.century_l a,    .century_la a:active, .century_lh a:hover
   { font-family:"Century Gothic", sans-serif; }
.copper,         .copper_a:active,     .copper_h:hover,
.copper_l a,     .copper_la a:active,  .copper_lh a:hover
   { font-family:"Copperplate", "Copperplate Gothic Light", serif; }
.comic,          .comic_a:active,      .comic_h:hover,
.comic_l a,      .comic_la a:active,   .comic_lh a:hover
   { font-family:"Comic Sans MS", cursive; }
.courier,        .courier_a:active,    .courier_h:hover,
.courier_l a,    .courier_la a:active, .courier_lh a:hover
   { font-family:"Courier", monospace; }
.couriern,       .couriern_a:active,   .couriern_h:hover,
.couriern_l a,   .couriern_la a:active, .couriern_lh a:hover
   { font-family:"Courier New", monospace; }
.garamond,       .garamond_a:active,   .garamond_h:hover,
.garamond_l a,   .garamond_la a:active, .garamond_lh a:hover
   { font-family:"Garamond", serif; }
.gill,           .gill_a:active,       .gill_h:hover,
.gill_l a,       .gill_la a:active,    .gill_lh a:hover
   { font-family:"Gill Sans", "Gill Sans MT", sans-serif; }
.georgia,        .georgia_a:active,    .georgia_h:hover,
.georgia_l a,    .georgia_la a:active, .georgia_lh a:hover
   { font-family:"Georgia", serif; }
```

```
.helvetica,      .helvetica_a:active,    .helvetica_h:hover,
.helvetica_l a, .helvetica_la a:active, .helvetica_lh a:hover
    { font-family:"Helvetica, sans-serif"; }
.impact,         .impact_a:active,       .impact_h:hover,
.impact_l a,     .impact_la a:active,    .impact_lh a:hover
    { font-family:"Impact", fantasy; }
.lucida,         .lucida_a:active,       .lucida_h:hover,
.lucida_l a,     .lucida_la a:active,    .lucida_lh a:hover
    { font-family:"Lucida Grande", "Lucida Sans Unicode", sans-serif; }
.lucidac,        .lucidac_a:active,      .lucidac_h:hover,
.lucidac_l a,    .lucidac_la a:active,   .lucidac_lh a:hover
    { font-family:"Lucida Console", monospace; }
.palatino,       .palatino_a:active,     .palatino_h:hover,
.palatino_l a,   .palatino_la a:active,  .palatino_lh a:hover
    { font-family:"Palatino", "Palatino Linotype", serif; }
.tahoma,         .tahoma_a:active,       .tahoma_h:hover,
.tahoma_l a,     .tahoma_la a:active,    .tahoma_lh a:hover
    { font-family:"Tahoma", sans-serif; }
.times,          .times_a:active,        .times_h:hover,
.times_l a,      .times_la a:active,     .times_lh a:hover
    { font-family:"Times", serif; }
.timesnr,        .timesnr_a:active,      .timesnr_h:hover,
.timesnr_l a,    .timesnr_la a:active,   .timesnr_lh a:hover
    { font-family:"Times New Roman", serif; }
.trebuchet,      .trebuchet_a:active,    .trebuchet_h:hover,
.trebuchet_l a, .trebuchet_la a:active, .trebuchet_lh a:hover
    { font-family:"Trebuchet", sans-serif; }
.verdana,        .verdana_a:active,      .verdana_h:hover,
.verdana_l a,    .verdana_la a:active,   .verdana_lh a:hover
    { font-family:"Verdana", sans-serif; }
```

## PLUG-IN 21   Font Styles

Choosing font styles with CSS can involve up to three different properties. But when you want to choose font styles such as bold, italic, or underline, these classes are much simpler. Figure 4-2 shows the various styles being applied one at a time until all are employed

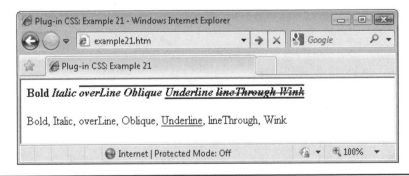

**FIGURE 4-2**   The various font styles supported by these classes

(Internet Explorer doesn't support the `blink` property, so on that browser, any blinking text is shown in bold).

In the second row, the text is set to change font only when hovered over, as is the case with the word Underline.

## Classes and Properties

| | |
|---|---|
| b<br>b_a<br>b_h<br>b_l<br>b_la<br>b_lh | Classes to assign a font to bold (b), to do so only when it is actively being clicked (b_a), or when it is being hovered over (b_h), also three classes to enable bold for a link within the object (b_l), a link within the object that is being clicked (b_la), or a link within the object that is being hovered over (b_lh) |
| i (etc...) | Class – as b but to enable italic text |
| l (etc...) | Class – as b but to enable overline text |
| n (etc...) | Class – as b but to restore normal styles |
| o (etc...) | Class – as b but to enable oblique text |
| u (etc...) | Class – as b but to enable underlined text |
| t (etc...) | Class – as b but to enable linethrough text |
| w (etc...) | Class – as b but to enable winking (or blinking) text, or bold in Internet Explorer |
| font-weight | Property for changing the weight of a font |
| font-style | Property for changing the style of a font |
| text-decoration | Property for adding a decoration to a font |

## About the Classes

These classes use three different CSS rules to create different font styles. They also support the suffixes such as _h to apply the new style only when an object is hovered over, and so on. For example, here are the CSS rules used to restore a font's styling to normal:

```
font-style:normal;
font-weight:normal;
text-decoration:none;
```

Out of all modern browsers, only Internet Explorer will not display blinking text, so the bold attribute is selected instead. This is achieved using a CSS "hack" that only Internet Explorer can see, like this:

```
font-weight:bold\0;
```

By adding the \0 to the end of the rule, all browsers except Internet Explorer will ignore the rule, while IE will accept the rule and ignore the \0. This is also the case with the current preview version of IE 9.

## How to Use Them

These font class names have been kept to single letters because they are frequently used, so it saves on typing and keeps class arguments short. To use them, just add the class letter (or letter plus suffix) to a `class` argument, like the following, which sets both an Arial font and italic styling:

```
<span class='arial i'>This text is in an italic Arial font</span>
```

This is the HTML used to create the screen grab in Figure 4-2:

```
<span class='b'>Bold
<span class='i'>Italic
<span class='l'>overLine
<span class='o'>Oblique
<span class='u'>Underline
<span class='t'>lineThrough
<span class='w'>Wink
</span></span></span></span></span></span></span><br /><br />

<span class='b_h'>Bold</span>,
<span class='i_h'>Italic</span>,
<span class='l_h'>overLine</span>,
<span class='o_h'>Oblique</span>,
<span class='u_h'>Underline</span>,
<span class='t_h'>lineThrough</span>,
<span class='w_h'>Wink</span>
```

## The Classes

```
.b,      .b_a:active,    .b_h:hover,
.b_l a,  .b_la a:active, .b_lh a:hover { font-weight:bold; }
.i,      .i_a:active,    .i_h:hover,
.i_l a,  .i_la a:active, .i_lh a:hover { font-style:italic; }
.l,      .l_a:active,    .l_h:hover,
.l_l a,  .l_la a:active, .l_lh a:hover { text-decoration:overline; }
.n,      .n_a:active,    .n_h:hover,
.n_l a,  .n_la a:active, .n_lh a:hover { font-style:normal;
                                         font-weight:normal;
                                         text-decoration:none; }

.o,      .o_a:active,    .o_h:hover,
.o_l a,  .o_la a:active, .o_lh a:hover { font-style:oblique; }
.u,      .u_a:active,    .u_h:hover,
.u_l a,  .u_la a:active, .u_lh a:hover { text-decoration:underline; }
.t,      .t_a:active,    .t_h:hover,
.t_l a,  .t_la a:active, .t_lh a:hover { text-decoration:line-through; }
.w,      .w_a:active,    .w_h:hover,
.w_l a,  .w_la a:active, .w_lh a:hover { text-decoration:blink;
                                         font-weight:bold\0;   /* IE */ }
```

## Text Alignment

With these classes, you can choose between applying left, center, right, or full justification, as shown in Figure 4-3, which includes one example of each type of justification (taken from Charles Dickens' novel, *A Tale of Two Cities*):

### Classes and Properties

| | |
|---|---|
| `leftjustify`<br>`leftjustify_a`<br>`leftjustify_h`<br>`leftjustify_l`<br>`leftjustify_la`<br>`leftjustify_lh`<br>`lj lj_a lj_h lj_l`<br>`lj_la lj_lh` | Classes to left-align text—the default—(`leftjustify`), to do so only when it is actively being clicked (`leftjustify_a`), or when it is being hovered over (`leftjustify_h`), also three classes to enable bold for a link within the object (`leftjustify_l`), a link within the object that is being clicked (`leftjustify_la`), or a link within the object that is being hovered over (`leftjustify_lh`), plus six shorthand versions (`lj...`) |
| `center` (etc...)<br>`c` (etc...) | Class – as `leftjustify` but for centered text |
| `rightjustify` (etc...)<br>`rj` (etc...) | Class – as `leftjustify` but for right-justified text |
| `justify` (etc...)<br>`j` (etc...) | Class – as `leftjustify` but for fully justified text |
| `text-align` | Property used for aligning text |

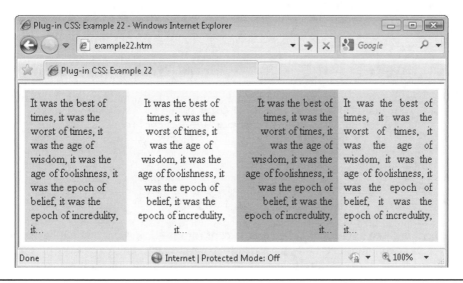

**FIGURE 4-3**  The four different types of text justification: left, center, right, and full

## About the Classes

These classes use the `text-align` property to set the alignment of some text, like this:

**`text-align`**`:right;`

## How to Use Them

You can use these classes to change the justification of text by entering their names into the `class` argument of an object, like this:

```
<span class='justify'>This text is fully justified</span>
```

Or you may prefer the shorthand class names, like this:

```
<span class='j'>This text is fully justified</span>
```

You can also use the standard suffixes to change the justification only when the text is hovered over, like this:

```
<span class=c_h'>This text is centered when hovered over</span>
```

Here is the HTML used for the screen grab in Figure 4-3:

```
<div style='width:125px' class='leftfloat padding lime_b'>
<div class='leftjustify'>It was the best of times, it was the worst of
times, it was the age of wisdom, it was the age of foolishness, it was
the epoch of belief, it was the epoch of incredulity, it...</div></div>

<div style='width:138px' class='leftfloat padding yellow_b'>
<div class='center'>It was the best of times, it was the worst of
times, it was the age of wisdom, it was the age of foolishness, it was
the epoch of belief, it was the epoch of incredulity, it...</div></div>

<div style='width:125px' class='leftfloat padding pink_b'>
<div class='rightjustify'>It was the best of times, it was the worst of
times, it was the age of wisdom, it was the age of foolishness, it was
the epoch of belief, it was the epoch of incredulity, it...</div></div>

<div style='width:125px' class='leftfloat padding aqua_b'>
<div class='justify'>It was the best of times, it was the worst of
times, it was the age of wisdom, it was the age of foolishness, it was
the epoch of belief, it was the epoch of incredulity, it...</div></div>
```

Each `<div>` is set to a width of 125 pixels, except for the second one, which has to be a little wider since centered text takes up more space. Also each one is given a different background color for clarity, and they are floated to the left so they line up in a row.

## The Classes

```
.leftjustify,       .leftjustify_a:active,    .leftjustify_h:hover,
.leftjustify_l a,   .leftjustify_la a:active, .leftjustify_lh a:hover,
.lj,                .lj_a:active,             .lj_h:hover,
.lj_l a,            .lj_la a:active,          .lj_lh a:hover
   { text-align:left;     }
.center,            .center_a:active,         .center_h:hover,
.center_l a,        .center_la a:active,      .center_lh a:hover,
.c,                 .c_a:active,              .c_h:hover,
.c_l a,             .c_la a:active,           .c_lh a:hover
   { text-align:center;   }
.rightjustify,      .rightjustify_a:active,   .rightjustify_h:hover,
.rightjustify_l a,  .rightjustify_la a:active, .rightjustify_lh a:hover,
.rj,                .rj_a:active,             .rj_h:hover,
.rj_l a,            .rj_la a:active,          .rj_lh a:hover
   { text-align:right;    }
.justify,           .justify_a:active,        .justify_h:hover,
.justify_l a,       .justify_la a:active,     .justify_lh a:hover,
.j,                 .j_a:active,              .j_h:hover,
.j_l a,             .j_la a:active,           .j_lh a:hover
   { text-align:justify; }
```

## PLUG-IN 23  Text Point Size

The classes in this group let you specify the point size for text from 1 to 100 points with varying intervals: 1–20 in steps of 1 point, 25–50 in steps of 5 points, and 60–100 in steps of 10 points.

In Figure 4-4, there are two rows of text. The first contains three immediately set font sizes, and the second uses the classes to set the font size only when an object is hovered over, as is the case with the text 25pt.

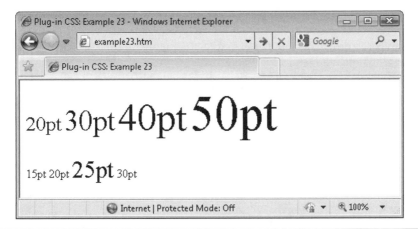

**Figure 4-4**   A variety of font sizes applied using these classes

## Classes and Properties

| | |
|---|---|
| `pt1`<br>`pt1_a`<br>`pt1_h`<br>`pt1_l`<br>`pt1_la`<br>`pt1_lh` | Class to change the text size to 1 point (`pt1`), plus classes to do so only if the object is actively being clicked (`pt1_a`) or hovered over (`pt1_h`), and another three classes to change the point size of any links within the object (`pt1_l`), any links within the object that are actively being clicked (`pt1_la`), and any links within the object that are being hovered over (`pt1_lh`) |
| `pt2 – pt20` (etc...) | Classes – in steps of 1 point, as `pt1` |
| `pt25 – pt50` (etc...) | Classes – in steps of 5 points, as `pt1` |
| `pt60 – pt100` (etc...) | Classes – in steps of 10 points, as `pt1` |
| `font-size` | Property containing the text font size |

## About the Classes

You can change the size of a font in many ways, such as by using ems or pixels and so on, but one of the most common is to use point size, and so the most useful sizes have been given class names of `pt1` through `pt20`, `pt25` through `pt50` in steps of 5 points, and `pt60` through `pt100` in steps of 10 points. These are applied using the `font-size` class, like this:

```
font-size:45pt;
```

## How to Use Them

To set the point size of some text, place the matching class name in the `class` argument of the object containing the text, like this:

```
<span class='pt14'>This is 14pt text</span>
```

You can also use the standard class suffixes to specify when the font size is applied, such as the font size hover class, like this:

```
<span class='pt20_h'>This is 20pt text when hovered over</span>
```

And you can combine classes too. For example, the following code sets the enclosed text to 10pt, or 14pt when hovered, and 12pt when clicked:

```
<span class='pt10 pt14_h pt12_a'>Hover over and click me</span>
```

Here is the code used to create the screen grab in Figure 4-4:

```
<span class='pt20'>20pt</span>
<span class='pt30'>30pt</span>
<span class='pt40'>40pt</span>
<span class='pt50'>50pt</span><br /><br />

<span class='pt15_h'>15pt</span>
<span class='pt20_h'>20pt</span>
<span class='pt25_h'>25pt</span>
<span class='pt30_h'>30pt</span>
```

## The Classes

```
.pt1,        .pt1_a:active,     .pt1_h:hover,
.pt1_l a,    .pt1_la a:active,  .pt1_lh a:hover    { font-size:1pt;  }
.pt2,        .pt2_a:active,     .pt2_h:hover,
.pt2_l a,    .pt2_la a:active,  .pt2_lh a:hover    { font-size:2pt;  }
.pt3,        .pt3_a:active,     .pt3_h:hover,
.pt3_l a,    .pt3_la a:active,  .pt3_lh a:hover    { font-size:3pt;  }
.pt4,        .pt4_a:active,     .pt4_h:hover,
.pt4_l a,    .pt4_la a:active,  .pt4_lh a:hover    { font-size:4pt;  }
.pt5,        .pt5_a:active,     .pt5_h:hover,
.pt5_l a,    .pt5_la a:active,  .pt5_lh a:hover    { font-size:5pt;  }
.pt6,        .pt6_a:active,     .pt6_h:hover,
.pt6_l a,    .pt6_la a:active,  .pt6_lh a:hover    { font-size:6pt;  }
.pt7,        .pt7_a:active,     .pt7_h:hover,
.pt7_l a,    .pt7_la a:active,  .pt7_lh a:hover    { font-size:7pt;  }
.pt8,        .pt8_a:active,     .pt8_h:hover,
.pt8_l a,    .pt8_la a:active,  .pt8_lh a:hover    { font-size:8pt;  }
.pt9,        .pt9_a:active,     .pt9_h:hover,
.pt9_l a,    .pt9_la a:active,  .pt9_lh a:hover    { font-size:9pt;  }
.pt10,       .pt10_a:active,    .pt10_h:hover,
.pt10_l a,   .pt10_l a:active,  .pt10_lh a:hover   { font-size:10pt; }
.pt11,       .pt11_a:active,    .pt11_h:hover,
.pt11_l a,   .pt11_la a:active, .pt11_lh a:hover   { font-size:11pt; }
.pt12,       .pt12_a:active,    .pt12_h:hover,
.pt12_l a,   .pt12_la a:active, .pt12_lh a:hover   { font-size:12pt; }
.pt13,       .pt13_a:active,    .pt13_h:hover,
.pt13_l a,   .pt13_la a:active, .pt13_lh a:hover   { font-size:13pt; }
.pt14,       .pt14_a:active,    .pt14_h:hover,
.pt14_l a,   .pt14_la a:active, .pt14_lh a:hover   { font-size:14pt; }
.pt15,       .pt15_a:active,    .pt15_h:hover,
.pt15_l a,   .pt15_la a:active, .pt15_lh a:hover   { font-size:15pt; }
.pt16,       .pt16_a:active,    .pt16_h:hover,
.pt16_l a,   .pt16_la a:active, .pt16_lh a:hover   { font-size:16pt; }
.pt17,       .pt17_a:active,    .pt17_h:hover,
.pt17_l a,   .pt17_la a:active, .pt17_lh a:hover   { font-size:17pt; }
.pt18,       .pt18_a:active,    .pt18_h:hover,
.pt18_l a,   .pt18_la a:active, .pt18_lh a:hover   { font-size:18pt; }
.pt19,       .pt19_a:active,    .pt19_h:hover,
.pt19_l a,   .pt19_la a:active, .pt19_lh a:hover   { font-size:19pt; }
.pt20,       .pt20_a:active,    .pt20_h:hover,
.pt20_l a,   .pt20_la a:active, .pt20_lh a:hover   { font-size:20pt; }
.pt25,       .pt25_a:active,    .pt25_h:hover,
.pt25_l a,   .pt25_la a:active, .pt25_lh a:hover   { font-size:25pt; }
.pt30,       .pt30_a:active,    .pt30_h:hover,
.pt30_l a,   .pt30_la a:active, .pt30_lh a:hover   { font-size:30pt; }
.pt35,       .pt35_a:active,    .pt35_h:hover,
.pt35_l a,   .pt35_la a:active, .pt35_lh a:hover   { font-size:35pt; }
.pt40,       .pt40_a:active,    .pt40_h:hover,
.pt40_l a,   .pt40_la a:active, .pt40_lh a:hover   { font-size:40pt; }
```

```
.pt45,        .pt45_a:active,    .pt45_h:hover,
.pt45_l a,  .pt45_la a:active,  .pt45_lh a:hover  { font-size:45pt; }
.pt50,        .pt50_a:active,    .pt50_h:hover,
.pt50_l a,  .pt50_la a:active,  .pt50_lh a:hover  { font-size:50pt; }
.pt60,        .pt60_a:active,    .pt60_h:hover,
.pt60_l a,  .pt60_la a:active,  .pt60_lh a:hover  { font-size:60pt; }
.pt70,        .pt70_a:active,    .pt70_h:hover,
.pt70_l a,  .pt70_la a:active,  .pt70_lh a:hover  { font-size:70pt; }
.pt80,        .pt80_a:active,    .pt80_h:hover,
.pt80_l a,  .pt80_la a:active,  .pt80_lh a:hover  { font-size:80pt; }
.pt90,        .pt90_a:active,    .pt90_h:hover,
.pt90_l a,  .pt90_la a:active,  .pt90_lh a:hover  { font-size:90pt; }
.pt100,       .pt100_a:active,   .pt100_h:hover,
.pt100_l a,.pt100_la a:active,  .pt100_lh a:hover { font-size:100pt;}
```

## PLUG-IN 24  Text Colors

In Chapter 3, a number of classes were provided that let you change the background color of an object. These classes partner them by letting you change the text color. The same set of 21 colors is supported, along with all the usual suffixes to control how they are applied.

In Figure 4-5, all the colors are shown twice: the first set uses the main text color class names to immediately apply the color, while the second set uses the _h suffix so the color is only applied when the mouse passes over an object.

**FIGURE 4-5**   The 21 different colors supported by these classes, followed by the same colors as hover-over classes

## Classes and Properties

| | |
|---|---|
| aqua<br>aqua_a<br>aqua_h<br>aqua_l<br>aqua_la<br>aqua_lh | Class to change the background color of an object to aqua (aqua), plus classes to do so only if the object is actively being clicked (aqua_a) or hovered over (aqua_h), and another three classes to change the background of any links within the object (aqua_l), any links within the object that are actively being clicked (aqua_la), and any links within the object that are being hovered over (aqua_lh) |
| black (etc...) | Classes – as aqua but for black |
| blue (etc...) | Classes – as aqua but for blue |
| brown (etc...) | Classes – as aqua but for brown |
| fuchsia (etc...) | Classes – as aqua but for fuchsia |
| gold (etc...) | Classes – as aqua but for gold |
| gray (etc...) | Classes – as aqua but for gray |
| green (etc...) | Classes – as aqua but for green |
| khaki (etc...) | Classes – as aqua but for khaki |
| lime (etc...) | Classes – as aqua but for lime |
| maroon (etc...) | Classes – as aqua but for maroon |
| navy (etc...) | Classes – as aqua but for navy |
| olive (etc...) | Classes – as aqua but for olive |
| orange (etc...) | Classes – as aqua but for orange |
| pink (etc...) | Classes – as aqua but for pink |
| purple (etc...) | Classes – as aqua but for purple |
| red (etc...) | Classes – as aqua but for red |
| silver (etc...) | Classes – as aqua but for silver |
| teal (etc...) | Classes – as aqua but for teal |
| white (etc...) | Classes – as aqua but for white |
| yellow (etc...) | Classes – as aqua but for yellow |
| color | Property containing text color settings |

## About the Classes

The reason for using the _b suffix for the background colors in Chapter 3 is now clear: It's because the text colors in this plug-in group have the non-_b names. As with the background classes, there are 21 color choices, and six different ways of applying them using the standard class suffixes such as _h to apply a color to an object only when it is being hovered over by the mouse.

The property being manipulated is color, like this:

```
color:#580;
```

PART II

## How to Use Them

To change the color of a section of text, enter the matching class name (and any optional suffix) in the `class` argument of the object's HTML tag, like this:

```
<span class='gold'>This text is gold</span>
```

You can also use the standard dynamic suffixes so that, for example, a section of text can be changed to navy when it is hovered over like this:

```
<span class='navy_h'>This text is navy when hovered over</span>
```

Here is the code used to create the image in Figure 4-5:

```
<div class='b pt20'>
    <span class='aqua'    >aqua   </span>
    <span class='black'   >black  </span>
    <span class='blue'    >blue   </span>
    <span class='brown'   >brown  </span>
    <span class='fuchsia' >fuchsia</span>
    <span class='gold'    >gold   </span>
    <span class='gray'    >gray   </span>
    <span class='green'   >green  </span>
    <span class='khaki'   >khaki  </span>
    <span class='lime'    >lime   </span>
    <span class='maroon'  >maroon </span>
    <span class='navy'    >navy   </span>
    <span class='olive'   >olive  </span>
    <span class='orange'  >orange </span>
    <span class='pink'    >pink   </span>
    <span class='purple'  >purple </span>
    <span class='red'     >red    </span>
    <span class='silver'  >silver </span>
    <span class='teal'    >teal   </span>
    <span class='white'   >white  </span>
    <span class='yellow'  >yellow </span><br /><br />

    <span class='aqua_h'    >aqua   </span>
    <span class='black_h'   >black  </span>
    <span class='blue_h'    >blue   </span>
    <span class='brown_h'   >brown  </span>
    <span class='fuchsia_h' >fuchsia</span>
    <span class='gold_h'    >gold   </span>
    <span class='gray_h'    >gray   </span>
    <span class='green_h'   >green  </span>
    <span class='khaki_h'   >khaki  </span>
    <span class='lime_h'    >lime   </span>
    <span class='maroon_h'  >maroon </span>
    <span class='navy_h'    >navy   </span>
    <span class='olive_h'   >olive  </span>
    <span class='orange_h'  >orange </span>
    <span class='pink_h'    >pink   </span>
    <span class='purple_h'  >purple </span>
```

```
    <span class='red_h'    >red    </span>
    <span class='silver_h' >silver </span>
    <span class='teal_h'   >teal   </span>
    <span class='white_h'  >white  </span>
    <span class='yellow_h' >yellow </span>
</div>
```

For clarity, the pair of color sets is enclosed in a `<div>` that sets the text to bold 20 point.

## The Classes

```
.aqua,         .aqua_a:active,      .aqua_h:hover,
.aqua_l a,     .aqua_la a:active,   .aqua_lh a:hover    { color:#0ff; }
.black,        .black_a:active,     .black_h:hover,
.black_l a,    .black_la a:active,  .black_lh a:hover   { color:#000; }
.blue,         .blue_a:active,      .blue_h:hover,
.blue_l a,     .blue_la a:active,   .blue_lh a:hover    { color:#00f; }
.brown,        .brown_a:active,     .brown_h:hover,
.brown_l a,    .brown_la a:active,  .brown_lh a:hover   { color:#c44; }
.fuchsia,      .fuchsia_a:active,   .fuchsia_h:hover,
.fuchsia_l a,  .fuchsia_la a:active, .fuchsia_lh a:hover { color:#f0f; }
.gold,         .gold_a:active,      .gold_h:hover,
.gold_l a,     .gold_la a:active,   .gold_lh a:hover    { color:#fc0; }
.gray,         .gray_a:active,      .gray_h:hover,
.gray_l a,     .gray_la a:active,   .gray_lh a:hover    { color:#888; }
.green,        .green_a:active,     .green_h:hover,
.green_l a,    .green_la a:active,  .green_lh a:hover   { color:#080; }
.khaki,        .khaki_a:active,     .khaki_h:hover,
.khaki_l a,    .khaki_la a:active,  .khaki_lh a:hover   { color:#cc8; }
.lime,         .lime_a:active,      .lime_h:hover,
.lime_l a,     .lime_la a:active,   .lime_lh a:hover    { color:#0f0; }
.maroon,       .maroon_a:active,    .maroon_h:hover,
.maroon_l a,   .maroon_la a:active, .maroon_lh a:hover  { color:#800; }
.navy,         .navy_a:active,      .navy_h:hover,
.navy_l a,     .navy_la a:active,   .navy_lh a:hover    { color:#008; }
.olive,        .olive_a:active,     .olive_h:hover,
.olive_l a,    .olive_la a:active,  .olive_lh a:hover   { color:#880; }
.orange,       .orange_a:active,    .orange_h:hover,
.orange_l a,   .orange_la a:active, .orange_lh a:hover  { color:#f80; }
.pink,         .pink_a:active,      .pink_h:hover,
.pink_l a,     .pink_la a:active,   .pink_lh a:hover    { color:#f88; }
.purple,       .purple_a:active,    .purple_h:hover,
.purple_l a,   .purple_la a:active, .purple_lh a:hover  { color:#808; }
.red,          .red_a:active,       .red_h:hover,
.red_l a,      .red_la a:active,    .red_lh a:hover     { color:#f00; }
.silver,       .silver_a:active,    .silver_h:hover,
.silver_l a,   .silver_la a:active, .silver_lh a:hover  { color:#ccc; }
.teal,         .teal_a:active,      .teal_h:hover,
.teal_l a,     .teal_la a:active,   .teal_lh a:hover    { color:#088; }
.white,        .white_a:active,     .white_h:hover,
.white_l a,    .white_la a:active,  .white_lh a:hover   { color:#fff; }
.yellow,       .yellow_a:active,    .yellow_h:hover,
.yellow_l a,   .yellow_la a:active, .yellow_lh a:hover  { color:#ff0; }
```

## PLUG-IN 25   Text Shadows

Using these classes, you can apply shadows of varying strengths underneath sections of text. Figure 4-6 shows two sets of shadowed text. The first has used the main class names to immediately apply the shadows, while the second has used the hover versions of the classes to apply the shadows only when the objects are hovered over, as is currently the case with the second instance of the phrase "Medium Shadow."

This grab was taken using Internet Explorer, and the `filter` property used for creating these shadows is much harsher than those created in most other modern browsers, which also blur and round the shadows for a softer effect.

### Classes and Properties

| | |
|---|---|
| `shadow`<br>`shadow_a`<br>`shadow_h`<br>`shadow_l`<br>`shadow_la`<br>`shadow_lh` | Class to place a shadow underneath some text (`shadow`), plus classes to do so only if the object is actively being clicked (`shadow_a`) or hovered over (`shadow_h`), and another three classes to place the shadow under any links within the object (`shadow_l`), any links within the object that are actively being clicked (`shadow_la`), and any links within the object that are being hovered over (`shadow_lh`) |
| `lightestshadow`<br>(etc...) | Class – as `shadow` but creates the lightest shadow |
| `lightshadow`<br>(etc...) | Class – as `shadow` but creates a light shadow |
| `darkshadow` (etc...) | Class – as `shadow` but creates a dark shadow |
| `darkestshadow`<br>(etc...) | Class – as `shadow` but creates the darkest shadow |
| `text-shadow` | Property to apply a shadow to text |
| `filter` | Property used by Internet Explorer to apply shadows and many other features to objects |

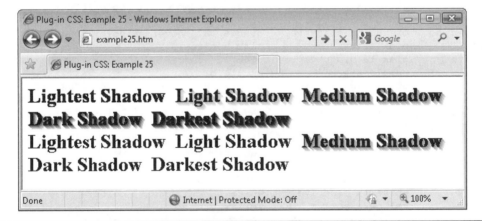

**FIGURE 4-6**   Applying shadows to text using the standard and hover versions of the classes

## About the Classes

These classes apply shadows to text using the CSS text-shadow property or the Microsoft proprietary filter property in Internet Explorer, like this:

```
text-shadow:#888888 3px 3px 4px;
filter     :progid:DXImageTransform.Microsoft.Shadow(
            color='#888888', Direction=135, Strength=5);
```

## How to Use Them

To use these classes, enter their names into the class argument of the containing object for some text. I recommend you use only the <div> tag when you want shadowed text (since Internet Explorer—even the version 9 preview—refuses to add shadows to text within a <span> or any other inline object), like this:

```
<div class='shadow'>This text is shadowed</div>
```

Alternatively, Internet Explorer *will* add shadows if a <span> is floated, as in the following, which uses the lf class (short for leftfloat):

```
<span class='shadow lf'>Shadowed text, floated left</span>
```

You can also use the hover and other forms of classes as in the following, which adds the shadow only when hovered over:

```
<div class='shadow_h'>This text is shadowed when hovered</div>
```

Following is the HML used to create Figure 4-6. In it, the <span> tags all use the lf class to float them so that Internet Explorer will be able to create shadows.

```
<div class='b pt20'>
   <span class='lightestshadow lf gray_bh'>Lightest Shadow  </span>
   <span class='lightshadow lf gray_bh'>Light Shadow  </span>
   <span class='shadow lf gray_bh'>Medium Shadow  </span>
   <span class='darkshadow lf gray_bh'>Dark Shadow  </span>
   <span class='darkestshadow lf gray_bh'>Darkest Shadow  </span>
</div><br clear='left'>

<div class='b pt20'>
   <span class='lightestshadow_h lf'>Lightest Shadow  </span>
   <span class='lightshadow_h lf'>Light Shadow  </span>
   <span class='shadow_h lf'>Medium Shadow  </span>
   <span class='darkshadow_h lf'>Dark Shadow  </span>
   <span class='darkestshadow_h lf'>Darkest Shadow  </span>
</div>
```

When you hover over the first five elements, the background changes to gray (using the gray_bh class) so you can see the effect of the different lightnesses of shadow on different backgrounds. If you hover over the second set of five elements, the shadow will be applied only as the mouse passes over them.

## The Classes

```
.shadow,                       .shadow_a:active,
.shadow_h:hover,               .shadow_l a,
.shadow_la a:active,           .shadow_lh a:hover {
   text-shadow:#888888 3px 3px 4px;
   filter      :progid:DXImageTransform.Microsoft.Shadow(
                 color='#888888', Direction=135, Strength=5);
}
.lightestshadow,               .lightestshadow_a:active,
.lightestshadow_h:hover,       .lightestshadow_l a,
.lightestshadow_la a:active,  .lightestshadow_lh a:hover {
   text-shadow:#ffffff 3px 3px 4px;
   filter      :progid:DXImageTransform.Microsoft.Shadow(
                 color='#ffffff', Direction=135, Strength=5);
}
.lightshadow,                  .lightshadow_a:active,
.lightshadow_h:hover,          .lightshadow_l a,
.lightshadow_la a:active,      .lightshadow_lh a:hover {
   text-shadow:#cccccc 3px 3px 4px;
   filter      :progid:DXImageTransform.Microsoft.Shadow(
                 color='#cccccc', Direction=135, Strength=5);
}
.darkshadow,                   .darkshadow_a:active,
.darkshadow_h:hover,           .darkshadow_l a,
.darkshadow_la a:active,       .darkshadow_lh a:hover {
   text-shadow:#444444 3px 3px 4px;
   filter      :progid:DXImageTransform.Microsoft.Shadow(
                 color='#444444', Direction=135, Strength=5);
}
.darkestshadow,                .darkestshadow_a:active,
.darkestshadow_h:hover,        .darkestshadow_l a,
.darkestshadow_la a:active,   .darkestshadow_lh a:hover {
   text-shadow:#000000 3px 3px 4px;
   filter      :progid:DXImageTransform.Microsoft.Shadow(
                 color='#000000', Direction=135, Strength=5);
}
```

## PLUG-IN 26 Text Transformations

When you need to quickly change the case of a section of text, you can simply apply one of the classes in this plug-in group. Figure 4-7 shows the four different transformations being used on a famous Albert Einstein quotation.

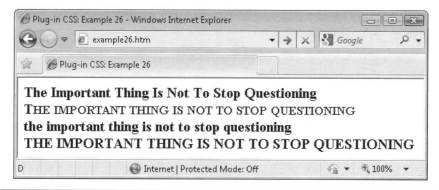

**Figure 4-7**   These classes provide a quick means of transforming sections of text.

## Classes and Properties

| | |
|---|---|
| `caps`<br>`caps_a`<br>`caps_h`<br>`caps_l`<br>`caps_la`<br>`caps_lh` | Class to change the first letter of each word in a section of text to a capital letter (`caps`), plus classes to do so only if the object is actively being clicked (`caps_a`) or hovered over (`caps_h`), and another three classes to change the case of any links within the object (`caps_l`), any links within the object that are actively being clicked (`caps_la`), and any links within the object that are being hovered over (`caps_lh`) |
| `scaps (etc...)` | Class – as `caps` but changes the entire text to small capital letters |
| `lower (etc...)` | Class – as `caps` but changes the entire text to all lowercase |
| `upper (etc...)` | Class – as `caps` but changes the text to all uppercase |
| `text-transform` | Property to capitalize text or change it to lower- or uppercase |
| `font-variant` | Property to implement a font variant such as small capital letters |

## About the Classes

These classes make use of the `text-transform` and `font-variant` properties to change a selection of text, like this:

```
text-transform:capitalize;
font-variant:small-caps;
```

## How to Use Them

You can transform a section of text by using one of these classes in the `class` argument of the containing object, like this:

```
<span class='scaps'>This text displays in small capital letters</span>
```

The standard suffixes are also available for transforming the text only under certain conditions, such as when the mouse hovers over it, like this:

```
<span class='scaps_h'>Small caps when hovered over</span>
```

Here is the HTML used for the screen grab in Figure 4-7:

```
<div class='b pt15'>
    <div class='caps' >The important thing is not to stop questioning</div>
    <div class='scaps'>The important thing is not to stop questioning</div>
    <div class='lower'>The important thing is not to stop questioning</div>
    <div class='upper'>The important thing is not to stop questioning</div>
</div>
```

## The Classes

```
.caps,          .caps_a:active,      .caps_h:hover,
.caps_l a,    .caps_la a:active,   .caps_lh a:hover
    { text-transform:capitalize; }
.scaps,         .scaps_a:active,     .scaps_h:hover,
.scaps_l a,  .scaps_la a:active,  .scaps_lh a:hover
    { font-variant   :small-caps; }
.lower,         .lower_a:active,     .lower_h:hover,
.lower_l a,  .lower_la a:active,  .lower_lh a:hover
    { text-transform:lowercase;  }
.upper,         .upper_a:active,     .upper_h:hover,
.upper_l a,  .upper_la a:active,  .upper_lh a:hover
    { text-transform:uppercase;  }
```

## PLUG-IN 27 Encapsulation

Encapsulation is a neat trick you can use to enclose a section of text within other text or objects. In this case, it is used to automatically add quotation marks and other symbols before and after a section of text, as shown in Figure 4-8, in which a phrase is repeated five times, each using a different encapsulation class.

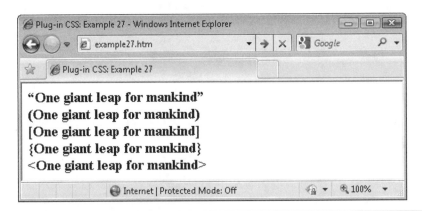

**FIGURE 4-8**   Enclosing a section of text with symbols using the encapsulation classes

## Classes and Properties

| quotes<br>quotes_h | Classes to place curly quotation marks before and after a section of text (quotes), or only when the text is hovered over (quotes_h) |
|---|---|
| parens (etc...) | Class – as quotes but for parentheses |
| brackets (etc...) | Class – as quotes but for brackets |
| braces (etc...) | Class – as quotes but for braces |
| chevrons (etc...) | Class – as quotes but for chevrons |
| content | Property used to insert content before and after some text |

## About the Classes

These classes use the pseudo classes :before and :after to insert characters before and after a section of text using the content property, as in the following, which places curly quotation marks before and after the text:

```
.quotes:before { content:'\201c'; }
.quotes:after  { content:'\201d'; }
```

## How to Use Them

When you want to encapsulate some text, enter the class needed into the class argument of the text's container, like this:

```
<div class='quotes'>This will have quotes added to it</div>
```

Or, you could add the quotes, only when the mouse hovers over the text, for example, like this:

```
<div class='quotes_h'>This has quotes added when hovered over</div>
```

The other dynamic suffixes (such as _a, and so on) are not supported by these classes since they would almost certainly never be used.

## The Classes

```
.quotes:before,    .quotes_h:hover:before   { content:'\201c'; }
.quotes:after,     .quotes_h:hover:after    { content:'\201d'; }
.parens:before,    .parens_h:hover:before   { content:'('; }
.parens:after,     .parens_h:hover:after    { content:')'; }
.brackets:before,  .brackets_h:hover:before { content:'['; }
.brackets:after,   .brackets_h:hover:after  { content:']'; }
.braces:before,    .braces_h:hover:before   { content:'{'; }
.braces:after,     .braces_h:hover:after    { content:'}'; }
.chevrons:before,  .chevrons_h:hover:before { content:'<'; }
.chevrons:after,   .chevrons_h:hover:after  { content:'>'; }
```

# Google Fonts

Google has kindly placed a number of fonts on their servers that can be easily included in your web pages by referencing them in the class arguments of this plug-in group.

Figure 4-9 shows all the Google fonts being used at the same time. This is something you may not want to do normally, since each font takes a second or two to download and install. Generally, you will only want two or three fonts on a page anyway, or it will begin to look too cluttered.

## Classes and Properties

| | |
|---|---|
| cantarell<br>cantarell_a<br>cantarell_h<br>cantarell_l<br>cantarell_la<br>cantarell_lh | Class to select a Google font (cantarell), plus classes to do so only if the object is actively being clicked (cantarell_a) or hovered over (cantarell_h), and another three classes to change the font of any links within the object (cantarell_l), any links within the object that are actively being clicked (cantarell_la), and any links within the object that are being hovered over (cantarell_lh) |
| cardo crimson droidsans<br>droidsansm droidserif<br>imfell inconsolata<br>josefin lobster molengo<br>neuton nobile oflsorts<br>oldstandard reenie<br>tangerine vollkorn yanone | Classes – as cantarell but for different font faces |
| font-family | Property for specifying a font to apply |

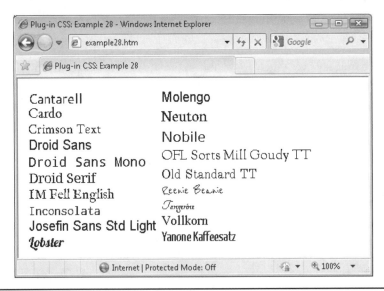

FIGURE 4-9   The 19 Google fonts supported by these classes

## About the Classes

These classes provide a shorthand way of using the Google fonts. They access the `font-family` CSS property to do so, like this:

```
font-family:"Droid Serif", serif;
```

## How to Use Them

To use the Google fonts, you will need to include a line such as the following for every Google font you plan to use:

```
<link rel='stylesheet' type='text/css'
 href='http://fonts.googleapis.com/css?family=fontfamily'>
```

The class names and their respective font family names to use in place of *fontfamily* are listed in Table 4-1. Note that the + symbol is used instead of spaces.

| Class Name | Font Name for the `<link rel...>` |
|---|---|
| cantarell | Cantarell |
| cardo | Cardo |
| crimson | Crimson+Text |
| droidsans | Droid+Sans |
| droidsansm | Droid+San+Mono |
| droidserif | Droid+Serif |
| imfell | IM+Fell+English |
| inconsolata | Inconsolata |
| josefin | Josefin+Sans+Std+Light |
| lobster | Lobster |
| molengo | Molengo |
| neuton | Neuton |
| nobile | Nobile |
| oflsorts | OFL+Sorts+Mill+Goudy+TT |
| oldstandard | Old+Standard+TT |
| reenie | Reenie+Beanie |
| tangerine | Tangerine |
| vollkorn | Vollkorn |
| yanone | Yanone+Kaffeesatz |

**TABLE 4-1**   The Google font families and plug-in class names

To load in the Crimson Text font, for example, you would, therefore, use the following code in the <head> section of a web page:

```
<link rel='stylesheet' type='text/css'
 href='http://fonts.googleapis.com/css?family=Crimson+Text'>
```

Then in the page's body you can use the font like this:

```
<span class='crimson'>This text uses the Crimson Text Font</span>
```

The following is the <head> code used to create Figure 4-9. It's a little long-winded because it loads in every single font (you will probably only want a few of them):

```
<link rel='stylesheet' type='text/css'
   href='http://fonts.googleapis.com/css?family=Cantarell'>
<link rel='stylesheet' type='text/css'
   href='http://fonts.googleapis.com/css?family=Cardo'>
<link rel='stylesheet' type='text/css'
   href='http://fonts.googleapis.com/css?family=Crimson+Text'>
<link rel='stylesheet' type='text/css'
   href='http://fonts.googleapis.com/css?family=Droid+Sans'>
<link rel='stylesheet' type='text/css'
   href='http://fonts.googleapis.com/css?family=Droid+Sans+Mono'>
<link rel='stylesheet' type='text/css'
   href='http://fonts.googleapis.com/css?family=Droid+Serif'>
<link rel='stylesheet' type='text/css'
   href='http://fonts.googleapis.com/css?family=IM+Fell+English'>
<link rel='stylesheet' type='text/css'
   href='http://fonts.googleapis.com/css?family=Inconsolata'>
<link rel='stylesheet' type='text/css'
   href='http://fonts.googleapis.com/css?family=Josefin+Sans+Std+Light'>
<link rel='stylesheet' type='text/css'
   href='http://fonts.googleapis.com/css?family=Lobster'>
<link rel='stylesheet' type='text/css'
   href='http://fonts.googleapis.com/css?family=Molengo'>
<link rel='stylesheet' type='text/css'
   href='http://fonts.googleapis.com/css?family=Neuton'>
<link rel='stylesheet' type='text/css'
   href='http://fonts.googleapis.com/css?family=Nobile'>
<link rel='stylesheet' type='text/css'
   href='http://fonts.googleapis.com/css?family=OFL+Sorts+Mill+Goudy+TT'>
<link rel='stylesheet' type='text/css'
   href='http://fonts.googleapis.com/css?family=Old+Standard+TT'>
<link rel='stylesheet' type='text/css'
   href='http://fonts.googleapis.com/css?family=Reenie+Beanie'>
<link rel='stylesheet' type='text/css'
   href='http://fonts.googleapis.com/css?family=Tangerine'>
<link rel='stylesheet' type='text/css'
   href='http://fonts.googleapis.com/css?family=Vollkorn'>
<link rel='stylesheet' type='text/css'
   href='http://fonts.googleapis.com/css?family=Yanone+Kaffeesatz'>
```

And here is the code from the body of the example:

```
<div class='pt15 lf padding'>
    <div class='cantarell'  >Cantarell             </div>
    <div class='cardo'      >Cardo                 </div>
    <div class='crimson'    >Crimson Text          </div>
    <div class='droidsans'  >Droid Sans            </div>
    <div class='droidsansm' >Droid Sans Mono       </div>
    <div class='droidserif' >Droid Serif           </div>
    <div class='imfell'     >IM Fell English       </div>
    <div class='inconsolata'>Inconsolata           </div>
    <div class='josefin'    >Josefin Sans Std Light </div>
    <div class='lobster'    >Lobster         </div></div>
<div class='pt15 padding'>
    <div class='molengo'    >Molengo               </div>
    <div class='neuton'     >Neuton                </div>
    <div class='nobile'     >Nobile                </div>
    <div class='oflsorts'   >OFL Sorts Mill Goudy TT</div>
    <div class='oldstandard'>Old Standard TT       </div>
    <div class='reenie'     >Reenie Beanie         </div>
    <div class='tangerine'  >Tangerine             </div>
    <div class='vollkorn'   >Vollkorn              </div>
    <div class='yanone'     >Yanone Kaffeesatz</div></div>
```

**NOTE** *In Chapter 9, I'll introduce a method you can use to automate all this, as long as your users have JavaScript, but the method in this plug-in will allow you to display Google fonts to all users of recent browsers, regardless of having JavaScript or not.*

## The Classes

```
.cantarell,      .cantarell_a:active,   .cantarell_h:hover,
.cantarell_l a,  .cantarell_la a:active  .cantarell_lh a:hover
   { font-family:"Cantarell", sans-serif; }
.cardo,          .cardo_a:active,       .cardo_h:hover,
.cardo_l a,      .cardo_la a:active     .cardo_lh a:hover
   { font-family:"Cardo", serif; }
.crimson,        .crimson_a:active,     .crimson_h:hover,
.crimson_l a,    .crimson_la a:active   .crimson_lh a:hover
   { font-family:"Crimson Text", serif; }
.droidsans,      .droidsans_a:active,   .droidsans_h:hover,
.droidsans_l a,  .droidsans_la a:active  .droidsans_lh a:hover
   { font-family:"Droid Sans", sans-serif; }
.droidsansm,     .droidsansm_a:active,  .droidsansm_h:hover,
.droidsansm_l a, .droidsansm_la a:active  .droidsansm_lh a:hover
   { font-family:"Droid Sans Mono", monospace; }
.droidserif,     .droidserif_a:active,  .droidserif_h:hover,
.droidserif_l a, .droidserif_la a:active  .droidserif_lh a:hover
   { font-family:"Droid Serif", serif; }
.imfell,         .imfell_a:active,      .imfell_h:hover,
.imfell_l a,     .imfell_la a:active    .imfell_lh a:hover
   { font-family:"IM Fell English", serif; }
.inconsolata,    .inconsolata_a:active,  .inconsolata_h:hover,
```

```
.inconsolata_l a, .inconsolata_la a:active .inconsolata_lh a:hover
   { font-family:"Inconsolata", monospace; }
.josefin,          .josefin_a:active,       .josefin_h:hover,
.josefin_l a,      .josefin_la a:active     .josefin_lh a:hover
   { font-family:"Josefin Sans Std Light", sans-serif; }
.lobster,          .lobster_a:active,       .lobster_h:hover,
.lobster_l a,      .lobster_la a:active     .lobster_lh a:hover
   { font-family:"Lobster", fantasy, serif; }
.molengo,          .molengo_a:active,       .molengo_h:hover,
.molengo_l a,      .molengo_la a:active     .molengo_lh a:hover
   { font-family:"Molengo", sans-serif; }
.neuton,           .neuton_a:active,        .neuton_h:hover,
.neuton_l a,       .neuton_la a:active      .neuton_lh a:hover
   { font-family:"Neuton", sans-serif; }
.nobile,           .nobile_a:active,        .nobile_h:hover,
.nobile_l a,       .nobile_la a:active      .nobile_lh a:hover
   { font-family:"Nobile", sans-serif; }
.oflsorts,         .oflsorts_a:active,      .oflsorts_h:hover,
.oflsorts_l a,     .oflsorts_la a:active    .oflsorts_lh a:hover
   { font-family:"OFL Sorts Mill Goudy TT", serif; }
.oldstandard,      .oldstandard_a:active,   .oldstandard_h:hover,
.oldstandard_l a,  .oldstandard_la a:active .oldstandard_lh a:hover
   { font-family:"Old Standard TT", serif; }
.reenie,           .reenie_a:active,        .reenie_h:hover,
.reenie_l a,       .reenie_la a:active      .reenie_lh a:hover
   { font-family:"Reenie Beanie", cursive, serif; }
.tangerine,        .tangerine_a:active,     .tangerine_h:hover,
.tangerine_l a,    .tangerine_la a:active   .tangerine_lh a:hover
   { font-family:"Tangerine", cursive, serif; }
.vollkorn,         .vollkorn_a:active,      .vollkorn_h:hover,
.vollkorn_l a,     .vollkorn_la a:active    .vollkorn_lh a:hover
   { font-family:"Vollkorn", serif; }
.yanone,           .yanone_a:active,        .yanone_h:hover,
.yanone_l a,       .yanone_la a:active      .yanone_lh a:hover
   { font-family:"Yanone Kaffeesatz", sans-serif; }
```

## PLUG-IN 29  Drop Cap

Placing a drop cap at the start of an article is a mainstay of print design, but it's also easy to achieve on the Web with Plug-in 29, as shown in Figure 4-10, which features a famous quotation from Shakespeare's play, *Macbeth*.

### Classes and Properties

| | |
|---|---|
| dropcap<br>dropcap_h | Classes to turn the contents of an object into a drop capital (dropcap), or do so only when the object is hovered over (dropcap_h) |
| font-size | Property to change the font size of text |
| line-height | Property to change the line height of text |
| margin-right | Property to change and object's right margin width |
| margin-bottom | Property to change and object's bottom margin width |
| float-left | Property to float and object to the left |

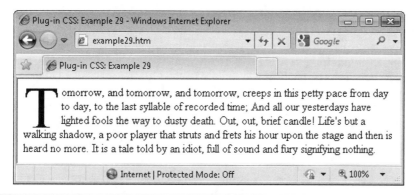

FIGURE 4-10  This plug-in makes it easy to add drop caps to your text.

## About the Class

This class enlarges the text within it by five times and lines it up with the following text to create a drop cap. This is achieved by setting the font-size property to 500 percent. Also, to neatly align the drop cap, the line-height, margin-right, and margin-bottom of the object are tweaked. Finally, the object is floated to the left using the float property to let the following text flow around it.

## How to Use It

To use this class, you should place the initial letter of some text within a <span> and use the dropcap class in the class argument, like this:

```
<span class='dropcap'>T</span>omorrow, and tomorrow, and tomorrow,
creeps in this petty pace from day to day, to the last syllable of
recorded time; And all our yesterdays have lighted fools the way to
dusty death. Out, out, brief candle! Life's but a walking shadow, a
poor player that struts and frets his hour upon the stage and then is
heard no more. It is a tale told by an idiot, full of sound and fury
signifying nothing.
```

A hover version of the class (dropcap_h) is also available, although the other dynamic versions such as _a are not, as they are most unlikely to be used.

## The Class

```
.dropcap, .dropcap_h:hover {
   font-size:500%;
   line-height:0.8em;
   margin-right:0.04em;
   margin-bottom:-0.15em;
   float:left;
}
```

## Columns

If you would like to present your text in columns to many of your users, these classes will automatically lay them out for you using between two and five columns, inclusive. I say *many* of your users because, unfortunately, no version of IE (including the preview of version 9) supports the web standard for columns, and neither does the Opera browser.

Nevertheless, on all other modern browsers columns work well, as shown by Figure 4-11, which shows these classes being used and displayed in the Google Chrome browser.

### Classes and Properties

| | |
|---|---|
| `columns2`<br>`columns2_h` | Classes to reformat text into two columns (`columns2`), or to do so only when the text is hovered over (`columns2_h`) |
| `columns3` (etc...) | Class – as `columns2` but for three columns |
| `columns4` (etc...) | Class – as `columns2` but for four columns |
| `Columns5` (etc...) | Class – as `columns2` but for five columns |
| `-moz-column-rule` | Property to specify the type of ruled line between columns on Firefox and other Mozilla browsers |
| `-webkit-column-rule` | Property to specify the type of ruled line between columns on Safari and Google Chrome |
| `-o-column-rule` | Property to specify the type of ruled line between columns on Opera (when/if it is supported) |
| `column-rule` | Property to specify the type of ruled line between columns on all other browsers (but not IE) |
| `-moz-column-gap` | Property to specify the gap between columns on Firefox and other Mozilla browsers |
| `-webkit-column-gap` | Property to specify the gap between columns on Safari and Google Chrome |
| `-o-column-gap` | Property to specify the gap between columns on Opera (when/if it is supported) |
| `column-gap` | Property to specify the gap between columns on all other browsers (but not IE) |
| `-moz-column-count` | Property to specify the number of columns on Firefox and other Mozilla browsers |
| `-webkit-column-count` | Property to specify the number of columns on Safari and Google Chrome |
| `-o-column-count` | Property to specify the number of columns on Opera (when/if it is supported) |
| `column-count` | Property to specify the number of columns on all other browsers (but not IE) |

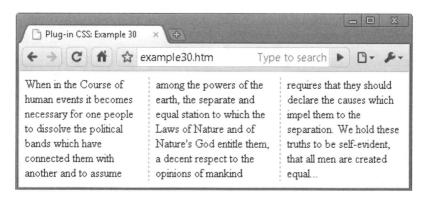

**Figure 4-11**   Create multiple columns on browsers that support the feature

## About the Classes

These classes display text in the number of columns you choose, between two and five inclusive, using the CSS `column` rules, as in the following example, which creates a two-column display:

```
column-rule:dashed 1px #888888;
column-gap:20px;
column-count:2;
```

Firefox and other Mozilla-based browsers require –moz placed before these properties, and Apple Safari and Google Chrome require –webkit. Although Opera doesn't yet support columns, it seems likely that the browser will do so soon, so to future proof the classes, versions of the properties prefaced with –o are also included.

## How to Use Them

To use these classes, decide the number of columns you want and place the relevant class in the class argument of the text's container, like the following text from the US Declaration of Independence, which was used to create the screen grab in Figure 4-11:

```
<div class='columns3'>When in the Course of human events it becomes
necessary for one people to dissolve the political bands which have
connected them with another and to assume among the powers of the earth,
the separate and equal station to which the Laws of Nature and of
Nature's God entitle them, a decent respect to the opinions of mankind
requires that they should declare the causes which impel them to the
separation. We hold these truths to be self-evident, that all men are
created equal...</div>
```

Neither Opera nor Microsoft Internet Explorer has caught up with the rest of the Web on this feature, so the text will simply display in a single column on those browsers. If you wish to have them also display columns, you will need to create an alternative section of HTML, which might look something like this:

```
<div style='width:160px' class='lf padding'>When in the Course of human
events it becomes necessary for one people to dissolve the political
bands which have connected them with another and to assume</div>

<div style='width:160px; class='lf padding'>among the powers of the
earth, the separate and equal station to which the Laws of Nature and
of Nature's God entitle them, a decent respect to the opinions of
mankind</div>

<div style='width:160px' class='lf padding'>requires that they should
declare the causes which impel them to the separation. We hold these
truths to be self-evident, that all men are created equal...</div>
```

## The Classes

```
.columns2, .columns2_h:hover {
    -moz-column-rule:     dashed 1px #888888;
    -webkit-column-rule:  dashed 1px #888888;
    -o-column-rule:       dashed 1px #888888;
    column-rule:          dashed 1px #888888;
    -moz-column-gap:      20px;
    -webkit-column-gap:   20px;
    -o-column-gap:        20px;
    column-gap:           20px;
    -moz-column-count:    2;
    -webkit-column-count: 2;
    -o-column-count:      2;
    column-count:         2;
}
.columns3, .columns3_h:hover {
    -moz-column-rule:     dashed 1px #888888;
    -webkit-column-rule:  dashed 1px #888888;
    -o-column-rule:       dashed 1px #888888;
    column-rule:          dashed 1px #888888;
    -moz-column-gap:      20px;
    -webkit-column-gap:   20px;
    -o-column-gap:        20px;
    column-gap:           20px;
    -moz-column-count:    3;
    -webkit-column-count: 3;
    -o-column-count:      3;
    column-count:         3;
}
.columns4, .columns4_h:hover {
    -moz-column-rule:     dashed 1px #888888;
    -webkit-column-rule:  dashed 1px #888888;
    -o-column-rule:       dashed 1px #888888;
    column-rule:          dashed 1px #888888;
    -moz-column-gap:      20px;
}
```

```
    -webkit-column-gap:    20px;
    -o-column-gap:         20px;
    column-gap:            20px;
    -moz-column-count:     4;
    -webkit-column-count:4;
    -o-column-count:       4;
    column-count:          4;
}
.columns5, .columns5_h:hover {
    -moz-column-rule:      dashed 1px #888888;
    -webkit-column-rule: dashed 1px #888888;
    -o-column-rule:        dashed 1px #888888;
    column-rule:           dashed 1px #888888;
    -moz-column-gap:       20px;
    -webkit-column-gap:    20px;
    -o-column-gap:         20px;
    column-gap:            20px;
    -moz-column-count:     5;
    -webkit-column-count:5;
    -o-column-count:       5;
    column-count:          5;
}
```

## PLUG-IN 31  Text Indent

Indenting the first line of a paragraph is an alternative to separating paragraphs with extra line breaks. It is commonly used in print typography. You can easily implement this feature too using these classes, as shown in Figure 4-12, in which three different indent classes have been applied to the same piece of text.

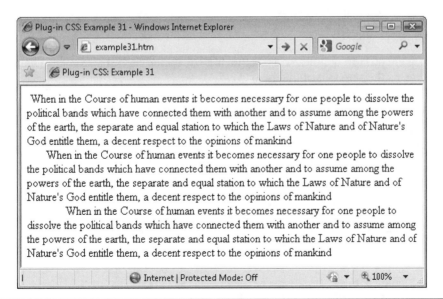

**FIGURE 4-12**   These classes enable indenting the first line of paragraphs by different amounts.

## Classes and Properties

| `indent1`<br>`indent1_h` | Classes to indent the first line of a section of text by 1 percent of the containing object's width (`indent1`), or to do so only when the text is hovered over (`indent1_h`) |
|---|---|
| `indent2` –<br>`indent10` (etc...) | Class – as `indent1` for 2 to 10 percent indent |
| `text-indent` | Property for indenting the first line of a section of text |

## About the Classes

These classes use the CSS `text-indent` property to indent the first line of a section of text by between 1 and 10 percent of the width of the containing object, like this:

**`text-indent:3%;`**

Percentage values are used to make the classes scalable for all font sizes.

## How to Use Them

When you want the first line of a section of text to be indented, use one of these classes in the `class` argument of the text's container, like the following, which indents the first line by 5 percent:

```
<div class='indent5'>When in the Course of human events it becomes
necessary for one people to dissolve the political bands which have
connected them with another and to assume among the powers of the
earth, the separate and equal station to which the Laws of Nature and
of Nature's God entitle them, a decent respect to the opinions of
mankind</div>
```

Or more likely you will use the class within a `<p>` tag, like this:

```
<p class='indent5'>When in the Course of human events (etc…) </p>
```

The hover version suffix of these classes (_h) is also supported, but the other dynamic variants are not, as they are very unlikely to ever be used.

---

*TIP*   *If you do use <p> tags with these classes, you may wish to modify the top and/or bottom margins for this tag since paragraphs will be separated and identified by indentation, rather than by spacing.*

## The Classes

```
.indent1,   .indent1_h:hover  { text-indent:1%;  }
.indent2,   .indent2_h:hover  { text-indent:2%;  }
.indent3,   .indent3_h:hover  { text-indent:3%;  }
.indent4,   .indent4_h:hover  { text-indent:4%;  }
.indent5,   .indent5_h:hover  { text-indent:5%;  }
.indent6,   .indent6_h:hover  { text-indent:6%;  }
.indent7,   .indent7_h:hover  { text-indent:7%;  }
.indent8,   .indent8_h:hover  { text-indent:8%;  }
.indent9,   .indent9_h:hover  { text-indent:9%;  }
.indent10,  .indent10_h:hover { text-indent:10%; }
```

## PLUG-IN 32

# Symbols

The final plug-ins in this chapter provide easy access to four commonly used icons: checkmark, cross, e-mail, and star. Figure 4-13 shows the icons automatically attached to a set of four buttons. A second set use the hover versions of the classes in which the icons are initially lighter, but darken when hovered over (although, unfortunately, not in Internet Explorer when used on a button).

## Classes and Properties

| | |
|---|---|
| check<br>check_h | Classes to preface text (or any object) with a checkmark icon (check), or to do so only when the text is hovered over (check_h) |
| cross | Class – as check but for a cross icon |
| email | Class – as check but for an e-mail icon |
| star | Class – as check but for a star icon |
| font-family | Property to change the font |
| font-weight | Property to change the weight of a font |
| color | Property to change the color of text |
| content | Property to add content to an object |
| opacity | Property used by non-IE browsers for opacity setting |
| filter | Property used by Internet Explorer for opacity and other features |

## About the Classes

These classes use the content property to place an icon before the text (or any object) that uses them. The text is also set to Courier with the font-family property, bold using the font-weight property, with colors set to green for check, red for cross, blue for email, and yellow for star, using the color property.

To create the hover effect, the opacity property is set to 50 percent, or 100 percent when hovered over. Microsoft browsers use the alternate filter property for this.

**FIGURE 4-13**   Use these classes to automatically add icons to text.

## How to Use Them

To use these classes, simply refer to them in the `class` argument of an object, as with the following HTML, which was used to create Figure 4-13, and also utilizes the hover versions of the classes:

```
<center>
    <button class='check'>Submit</button>
    <button class='cross'>Cancel</button>
    <button class='email'>Email Us</button>
    <button class='star'>New Stuff</button><br /><br />

    <button class='check_h'>Submit</button>
    <button class='cross_h'>Cancel</button>
    <button class='email_h'>Email Us</button>
    <button class='star_h'>New Stuff</button>
</center>
```

## The Classes

```
.check:before, .check_h:before, .check_h:hover:before {
    font-family:Courier;
    font-weight:bold;
    content:'\2713 ';
    color:#008800;
}
.cross:before, .cross_h:before, .cross_h:hover:before {
    font-family:Courier;
    font-weight:bold;
    content:'\2715 ';
    color:#ff0000;
}
.email:before, .email_h:before, .email_h:hover:before {
    font-family:Courier;
    content:'\2709 ';
    color:#0066ff;
}
.star:before, .star_h:before, .star_h:hover:before {
    font-family:Courier;
    content:'\2730 ';
    color:#888800;
}
.check_h:before, .cross_h:before, .email_h:before, .star_h:before {
    opacity:.5;
    filter :alpha(opacity = '50');
}
.check_h:hover:before, .cross_h:hover:before, .email_h:hover:before,
.star_h:hover:before {
    opacity:1;
    filter :alpha(opacity = '100');
}
```

# CHAPTER 5

## Menus and Navigation

This chapter explores a range of classes used for creating buttons and vertical and horizontal menus, and for implementing top and bottom dock bars similar to those used by Mac OS X.

There's also a handy class for creating tooltips that you can format in a variety of different ways. Between them, you can provide a professional range of menuing and navigation aids for your web visitors.

# Buttons

Plug-in group 33 makes it a simple matter to quickly create buttons when you need them. In Figure 5-1, an Internet Explorer and Safari web browser have been placed next to each other, showing the same web page. IE displays the different button sizes, but cannot manage the rounded borders, whereas Safari displays the buttons well. As you can see, even though IE is missing the rounded corners, it degrades gracefully.

## Classes and Properties

| | |
|---|---|
| `button` | Class to create a medium-sized button |
| `smallbutton` | Class to create a small button |
| `largebutton` | Class to create a large button |
| `Padding` | Property to change an object's padding |
| `border` | Property containing border details such as width and color |
| `font-size` | Property to change the size of a font |
| `text-align` | Property to align text to the left, right, center, or be fully justified |
| `width` | Property containing the width of an object |
| `overflow` | Property for setting whether and how objects overflow their boundaries |

## About the Classes

Three classes are available in this plug-in for creating medium, small, or large buttons. They also use the `:hover` pseudo class to provide professional effects when clicked or hovered over. To do this, they change the object's `border`, `font-size`, `text-align`, `width`, and `overflow` properties.

Hovered versions of the buttons change the border, while clicking them moves the button text down and to the right to emulate a 3D press.

## How to Use Them

You can use these classes with any objects, but they work best with `<input type='submit'>` and `<button>` tags. In conjunction with other classes, you can give the buttons rounded borders, different background colors, gradients that change when clicked or hovered over, add shadow effects, and more.

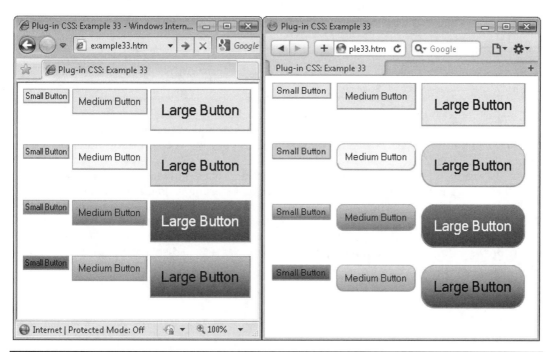

**FIGURE 5-1** These classes make it easy to create great looking buttons.

Here is the HTML used to create the screen grabs in Figure 5-1:

```
<input type='submit' class='smallbutton'
    value='Small Button' />
<input type='submit' class='button'
    value='Medium Button' />
<input type='submit' class='largebutton'
    value='Large Button' /><br /><br />

<input type='submit' class='smallbutton smallestround lime_b'
    value='Small Button' />
<input type='submit' class='button round yellow_b'
    value='Medium Button' />
<input type='submit' class='largebutton largestround aqua_b'
    value='Large Button' /><br /><br />

<input type='submit' class='smallbutton smallestround carrot1 carrot2_a'
    value='Small Button' />
<input type='submit' class='button round sky1 sky2_a'
    value='Medium Button' />
<input type='submit' class='largebutton largestround wine1 wine2_a white'
    value='Large Button' /><br /><br/>
```

PART II

```
<input type='submit' class='smallbutton smallestround rose1 rose2_a
   white_h' value='Small Button' />
<input type='submit' class='button round sunset1 sunset2_a white_h'
   value='Medium Button' />
<input type='submit' class='largebutton largestround grass1 grass2_a
   white_h' value='Large Button' /><br /><br/>
```

The first row of buttons offers plain features, while the second row adds rounded borders and background colors. In the third row, the background colors have been replaced with gradient fills that reverse when the buttons are clicked, while the fourth row adds a hover color of white to each button.

As I have already noted a few times, different browsers have different features and so they will fall back gracefully when one isn't supported. For example, Internet Explorer will not display rounded borders, but Firefox, Opera, Safari, and Chrome will. There again, Opera won't display gradient background fills, and so on.

Even so, these button classes go a long way toward producing more engaging web sites and, as browsers implement the missing features, these classes will display better, without you having to change anything.

## The Classes

```
.button {
   padding:8px;
}
.button:hover {
   border:2px solid #666666;
   padding:7px 8px 8px 7px;
}
.button:active {
   border-width:2px 1px 1px 2px;
   padding:9px 7px 7px 9px;
}
.smallbutton {
   font-size:75%;
   padding:2px;
}
.smallbutton:hover {
   border:2px solid #666666;
   padding:1px 2px 2px 1px;
}
.smallbutton:active {
   border-width:2px 1px 1px 2px;
   padding:3px 1px 1px 3px;
}
.largebutton {
   font-size:125%;
   padding:15px;
}
```

```
.largebutton:hover {
   border:2px solid #666666;
   padding:14px 15px 15px 14px;
}
.largebutton:active {
   border-width:2px 1px 1px 2px;
   padding:16px 14px 14px 16px;
}
.button, .smallbutton, .largebutton {
   text-align:center;
   border-color:#999999;
   border-width:1px 2px 2px 1px;
   vertical-align:top;
   border-style:solid; /* Required by Opera */
   width:auto;          /* Required by IE to not pad the sides */
   overflow:visible;
}
```

## PLUG-IN 34  Vertical Menu

Plug-in 34 creates a dynamic vertical menu using only unordered lists. In Figure 5-2, three levels of menu have been created, with each overlaying and offset from the previous, and with each submenu set to overlay the chevron submenu indicator of its parent.

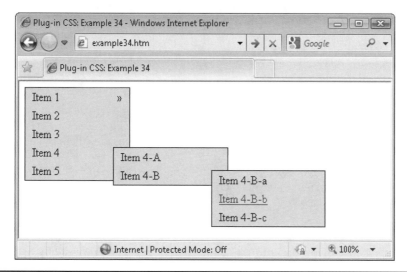

**FIGURE 5-2**   With this plug-in, you can create professional looking vertical menus.

## Classes and Properties

| vmenu | Class to create a set of vertical menus |
|---|---|
| width | Property containing the width of an object |
| height | Property containing the height of an object |
| display | Property used to set the display type of an object, such as block, inline, or none |
| text-decoration | Property containing the decoration for a section of text, such as underlines |
| border | Property containing all the border parameters of an object |
| margin | Property containing all the margin parameters of an object |
| padding | Property containing all the padding parameters of an object |
| line-height | Property containing the height of a section of text |
| list-style | Property containing the type of list |
| left | Property containing the offset of an object from the left of its containing object |
| top | Property containing the offset of an object from the top of its containing object |
| z-index | Property controlling how far behind or in front an object is compared to others |
| float | Property used to float an object to the right or left |
| position | Property used to manage the position of an object, such as relative or absolute |
| content | Property used to add content to an object from a CSS rule |

## About the Class

This class manipulates a large number of CSS properties in order to create menus and submenus that dynamically appear and disappear as required. The way it works is to make all second- and third-level menus (if any) invisible, and then it unhides them when they are due to appear.

The submenus are also given absolute positioning so they can be placed alongside the parent menu, starting at the item that calls them up, covering over the chevron symbol that indicates a submenu is available.

## How to Use It

To use this class, create a menu structure using unordered lists. The simplest of which might look like this:

```
<div class='vmenu aqua_b black_l blue_lh u_lh'>

    <ul>  <!-- Beg Level 1 -->
        <li><a href='url'>Item 1</a></li>
        <li><a href='url'>Item 2</a></li>
```

```
      <li><a href='url'>Item 3</a></li>
      <li><a href='url'>Item 4</a></li>
      <li><a href='url'>Item 5</a></li>
   </ul> <!-- End Level 1 -->

</div>
```

The entire menu is enclosed in a `<div>` with the class name of vmenu. This div has its background color set to aqua, text within links set to black (or blue when hovered over), and underlines in links are enabled when hovered over. Inside this there are five list elements within an unordered list, and each of these elements contains a link.

For clarity, I have left a line break before and after the section labeled with `<!—Beg Level 1 -->` and `<!—End Level 1 -->` comments. These breaks indicate a complete section. When you open this HTML in a web browser, it looks like Figure 5-3, in which the third menu entry is currently being hovered over.

### Creating a Two-Level Menu
Using almost the same structure it's easy to add a second level of menus, as with the following example, which has taken the preceding HTML and expanded it to add three second-level menus:

```
<div class='vmenu aqua_b black_l blue_lh u_lh'>

   <ul>  <!-- Beg Level 1 -->
      <li class='vmenu1'>
         <a href='url'>Item 1</a>

         <ul class='aqua_b'>  <!-- Beg Level 2 -->
            <li><a href='url'>Item 1-A</a></li>
            <li><a href='url'>Item 1-B</a></li>
            <li><a href='url'>Item 1-C</a></li>
         </ul>                  <!-- End Level 2 -->
```

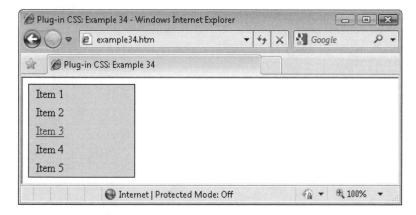

**FIGURE 5-3**    A single-level menu created with this class

```
    </li>
    <li><a href='url'>Item 2</a></li>
    <li><a href='url'>Item 3</a></li>
    <li class='vmenu1'>
       <a href='url' >Item 4</a>

       <ul class='aqua_b'>  <!-- Beg Level 2 -->
          <li><a href='url'>Item 4-A</a></li>
          <li><a href='url'>Item 4-B</a></li>
       </ul>                <!-- End Level 2 -->

    </li>
    <li class='vmenu1'>
       <a href='url'>Item 5</a>

       <ul class='aqua_b'>  <!-- Beg Level 2 -->
          <li><a href='url'>Item 5-A</a></li>
          <li><a href='url'>Item 5-B</a></li>
          <li><a href='url'>Item 5-C</a></li>
       </ul>                <!-- End Level 2 -->

    </li>
  </ul> <!-- End Level 1 -->

</div>
```

When viewed in a browser, this example looks like Figure 5-4, in which the first of the three menus has been opened by hovering over Item 1 in the main menu.

To add each second-level menu, the `<li>` and `</li>` tags surrounding the entry to which the menus are attached have been altered. The `<li>` tag has become `<li class='vmenu1'>`

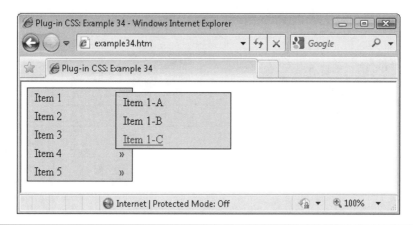

**Figure 5-4**  A two-level menu created with this class

and the `</li>` has been moved to after the position where the new menu was added. In other words, the line…

```
<li><a href='url'>Item 1</a></li>
```

…has become the following section of code (the new code being marked by the comments):

```
<li class='vmenu1'>
   <a href='url'>Item 1</a>

   <ul class='aqua_b'>  <!-- Beg Level 2 -->
      <li><a href='url'>Item 1-A</a></li>
      <li><a href='url'>Item 1-B</a></li>
      <li><a href='url'>Item 1-C</a></li>
   </ul>                    <!-- End Level 2 -->

</li>
```

## Creating a Three-Level Menu

You can take the process a step further by adding another level of menus, like the following code, which was used to create Figure 5-2:

```
<div class='vmenu aqua_b black_l blue_lh u_lh'>

   <ul>  <!-- Beg Level 1 -->
     <li class='vmenu1'>
        <a href='url'>Item 1</a>

        <ul class='aqua_b'>  <!-- Beg Level 2 -->
          <li class='vmenu1'>
             <a href='url'>Item 1-A</a>

             <ul class='aqua_b'>  <!-- Beg Level 3 -->
                <li><a href='url'>Item 1-A-a</a></li>
                <li><a href='url'>Item 1-A-b</a></li>
             </ul>                    <!-- End Level 3 -->

          </li>
          <li><a href='url'>Item 1-B</a></li>
          <li><a href='url'>Item 1-C</a></li>
        </ul>                    <!-- End Level 2 -->

     </li>
     <li><a href='url'>Item 2</a></li>
     <li><a href='url'>Item 3</a></li>
     <li class='vmenu1'>
        <a href='url'>Item 4</a>

        <ul class='aqua_b'>  <!-- Beg Level 2 -->
          <li><a href='url'>Item 4-A</a></li>
          <li class='vmenu1'>
             <a href='url'>Item 4-B</a>
```

```
                    <ul class='aqua_b'>  <!-- Beg Level 3 -->
                       <li><a href='url'>Item 4-B-a</a></li>
                       <li><a href='url'>Item 4-B-b</a></li>
                       <li><a href='url'>Item 4-B-c</a></li>
                    </ul>                <!-- End Level 3 -->

                 </li>
              </ul>                    <!-- End Level 2 -->

           </li>
           <li class='vmenu1'>
              <a href='url'>Item 5</a>

              <ul class='aqua_b'>  <!-- Beg Level 2 -->
                 <li class='vmenu1'>
                    <a href='url'>Item 5-A</a>

                    <ul class='aqua_b'>  <!-- Beg Level 3 -->
                       <li><a href='url'>Item 5-A-a</a></li>
                       <li><a href='url'>Item 5-A-b</a></li>
                    </ul>                <!-- End Level 3 -->

                 </li>
                 <li><a href='url'>Item 5-B</a></li>
                 <li><a href='url'>Item 5-C</a></li>
              </ul>                    <!-- End Level 2 -->

           </li>
        </ul>  <!-- End Level 1 -->

</div>
```

Here, one of the second-level items has been split into a menu in the same way the first-level item was split into a second-level menu.

This example is now quite long, so to make its working clearer, following is the underlying set of nested unordered list items as they would appear without the CSS styling, as you can determine for yourself by not importing the *PC.css* style sheet file:

```
Item 1
   Item 1-A
      Item 1-A-a
      Item 1-A-b
   Item 1-B
   Item 1-C
Item 2
Item 3
Item 4
   Item 4-A
   Item 4-B
      Item 4-B-a
      Item 4-B-b
      Item 4-B-c
```

```
Item 5
   Item 5-A
      Item 5-A-a
      Item 5-A-b
   Item 5-B
   Item 5-C
```

If you study the following CSS rules, you'll see references to an hmenu class. This is because the following horizontal menu plug-in (Plug-in 35) shares many of the same styles, so bringing them into the same rules is more efficient than including them twice.

By the way, a fourth (or any deeper) level of menus is not supported by this plug-in.

## The Class

```css
.vmenu, .hmenu {
   width:150px;
}
.vmenu a, .hmenu a {
   display:table-cell;
   width:150px;
   text-decoration:none;
}
.vmenu ul, .hmenu ul {
   border:1px solid #000;
   margin:0px;
   padding:0px;
}
.vmenu ul li, .hmenu ul li {
   height:25px;
   line-height:25px;
   list-style:none;
   padding-left:10px;
}
.vmenu ul li:hover, .hmenu ul li:hover {
   position:relative;
}
.vmenu ul ul, .hmenu ul ul {
   display:none;
   position:absolute;
}
.vmenu ul ul {
   left:125px;
   top:5px;
}
.vmenu ul li:hover ul, .hmenu ul li:hover ul {
   z-index:1;
}
.vmenu ul li:hover ul {
   display:block;
}
```

```
.vmenu ul ul li, .hmenu ul ul li {
   width:150px;
   float:left;
}
.vmenu ul ul li {
   display:block;
}
.vmenu li:hover ul li ul, .hmenu li:hover ul li ul {
   display:none;
}
.vmenu ul ul li ul, .hmenu ul ul li ul {
   left:137px;
}
.vmenu ul ul li:hover ul, .hmenu ul ul li:hover ul {
   z-index:1;
}
.vmenu ul ul li:hover ul {
   display:block;
}
.vmenu1:after, .hmenu1:after {
   position:relative;
   top:-25px;
   float:right;
   z-index:0;
   margin-right:10px;
   content:'\0bb';
}
```

## PLUG-IN 35 Horizontal Menu

Using this class, it is equally easy to create a horizontal menu. In fact, by swapping the class names vmenu and vmenu1 in the previous plug-in, for hmenu and hmenu1 in this one, the menu completely reorientates itself, as shown by Figure 5-5, which uses exactly the same unordered list structure.

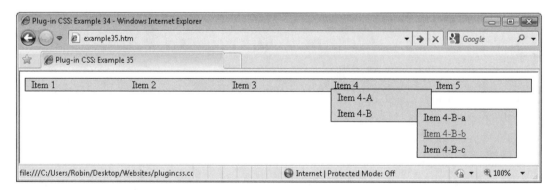

FIGURE 5-5    You can get a horizontal menu by using the hmenu classes instead of vmenu.

## Classes and Properties

| vmenu | Class to create a set of horizontal menus |
|---|---|
| width | Property containing the width of an object |
| height | Property containing the height of an object |
| display | Property used to set the display type of an object, such as block, inline, or none |
| text-decoration | Property containing the decoration for a section of text, such as underlines |
| border | Property containing all the border parameters of an object |
| margin | Property containing all the margin parameters of an object |
| padding | Property containing all the padding parameters of an object |
| line-height | Property containing the height of a section of text |
| list-style | Property containing the type of list |
| left | Property containing the offset of an object from the left of its containing object |
| top | Property containing the offset of an object from the top of its containing object |
| z-index | Property controlling how far behind or in front an object is compared to others |
| float | Property used to float an object to the right or left |
| position | Property used to manage the position of an object, such as relative or absolute |
| content | Property used to add content to an object from a CSS rule |

## About the Class

This class is almost the same as for the vertical menu, except that a few CSS rules have been modified to display the menus inline so they line up horizontally. It also moves the submenus to slightly different relative locations.

## How to Use It

You use this class in exactly the same way as the vertical menu class, just change the class names used from vmenu and vmenu1 to hmenu and hmenu1. Please refer to the Vertical Menu plug-in (Plug-in 34) for full details.

Following are the additional tweaks made to the class in the previous section to provide horizontal menus.

## The Class

```
.hmenu, .hmenu ul, .hmenu ul li, .hmenu ul li:hover ul, .hmenu ul ul li,
.hmenu ul ul li:hover ul {
   display:inline;
}
```

```
.hmenu ul ul {
   left:5px;
   top:15px;
}
.hmenu ul ul li ul {
   top:5px;
}
```

## PLUG-IN 36

## Top Dock Bar

Plug-in 36 provides a static dock bar that can be placed at the top of a web page for use as a menu or navigation aid. Figure 5-6 shows such a dock bar created from six icons, the fourth of which is currently being hovered over and has expanded under the mouse pointer.

### Classes and Properties

| | |
|---|---|
| `topdockbar` | Class for creating a dock bar container |
| `topdockitem` | Class for assigning an icon to a top dock bar |
| `position` | Property specifying whether an object has absolute or relative positioning, and so on |
| `left` | Property containing an object's left offset |
| `margin-left` | Property containing an object's left margin |
| `vertical-align` | Property containing an object's vertical alignment |
| `width` | Property containing an object's width |
| `height` | Property containing an object's height |
| `-moz-transition` | Property used by Mozilla and other Mozilla browsers to transition between two sets of property values |
| `-webkit-transition` | Property used by Safari and Chrome to transition between two sets of property values |
| `-o-transition` | Property used by Opera to transition between two sets of property values |
| `transition` | Property used by all other browsers except for Internet Explorer |

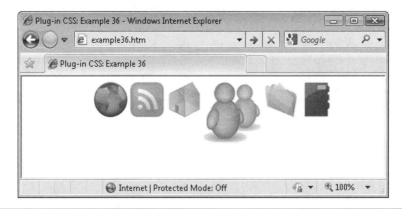

**FIGURE 5-6**   Using this class, you can create a top dock bar.

## About the Classes

This plug-in has two classes: the first (`topdockbar`) is used to create a container for the dock bar items, and the second is for attaching to icons used in the dock bar (`topdockitem`).

The `topdockbar` class moves the object that uses it to the top of the browser and centers it. The object's position is also fixed so it will not move when the browser scrolls.

The `topdockitem` class attaches a transition to the object so that any changes made to it will transition over the time period specified (on browsers that support transitions). It also aligns each item to the top of the dock bar so that passing the mouse over it will enlarge the image but keep it top-aligned.

A `:hover` pseudo class is then used to enlarge the icons when moused over, and restore them when the mouse passes away.

## How to Use Them

To use these classes, you need to have six icons that are 86 × 86 pixels in size. If they are different sizes or a different number, you may need to modify the code in the *PC.css* file.

These images are then resized to 50 × 50 pixels for the initial display (so that they can be enlarged to their full dimensions when moused over).

Then, write some HTML to contain all the images, such as this:

```
<div class='topdockbar'>
    <img class='topdockitem' src='i1.gif'>
    <img class='topdockitem' src='i2.gif'>
    <img class='topdockitem' src='i3.gif'>
    <img class='topdockitem' src='i4.gif'>
    <img class='topdockitem' src='i5.gif'>
    <img class='topdockitem' src='i6.gif'>
</div>
```

When you use this HTML in a web page, you get the result seen in Figure 5-6. Of course, you will also attach links to the images to give each a function. When you do, a border may be displayed around the images, which you can remove by adding the argument `border='0'` to the `<img...>` tag. You may also wish to use Plug-in 19 (No Outline) to remove the dotted focus outline added to clicked elements.

---

**NOTE** *In Internet Explorer, when the icons are hovered over, they will instantly enlarge, and reduce down again in size when the mouse passes away. But on all of Opera 10, Firefox 4, Safari 5, and the Chrome 5 web browsers (or better), the enlarging and reduction are animated using CSS transitions, which automatically generate and display a sequence of frames between a start and end set of styles settings.*

### Changing the Number of Icons and/or Icon Sizes

In the following CSS rules, note the value assigned to the `margin-left` property in order to center the dock bar. If you change the icon sizes or number of icons, you should calculate a new value for this property, using this formula:

```
(Reduced image size x Number of images) / 2
   +
(Actual width - Reduced width) / 4
```

So, for example, if you intend to use five 100 × 100 pixel images with a reduced size of 80 × 80 pixels, this is the calculation:

```
(5 x 100) / 2
   +
(100 - 80) / 4
```

This would give you a new value of 5 multiplied by 100 (which is 500), divided by 2 (which is 250), plus 100 – 80 (which is 20), divided by 4 (which is 5), which equals 250 plus 5, or a final value of 255 pixels.

You will also see mention of a bottomdockbar class in these rules. This is because the following plug-in shares much of the CSS, so it also shares some of the CSS rule assignments to save repeating the code.

### The Classes

```css
.topdockbar, .bottomdockbar {
   position:fixed;
   left:50%;
   margin-left:-159px;    /* Set to (total width of reduced images) / 2 */
                          /*       + (actual width -  reduced width) / 4 */
}
.topdockitem, .bottomdockitem {
   -moz-transition:    all .2s;
   -webkit-transition:all .2s;
   -o-transition:      all .2s;
   transition:         all .2s;
   vertical-align:top;
   width: 50px;           /* Set to reduced image width  */
   height:50px;           /* Set to reduced image height */
}
.topdockitem:hover, .bottomdockitem:hover {
   width: 86px;           /* Set to actual image width  */
   height:86px;           /* Set to actual image height */
}
```

## PLUG-IN 37  Bottom Dock Bar

Plug-in 37 lets you create a bottom dock bar in the same way you can create a top dock bar in the previous plug-in. Figure 5-7 shows the classes being used in the Apple Safari browser.

**Figure 5-7**   Creating a bottom dock bar in the Apple Safari Browser

## Classes and Properties

| | |
|---|---|
| `bottomdockbar` | Class for creating a bottom dock bar container |
| `bottomdockitem` | Class for assigning an icon to a bottom dock bar |
| `position` | Property specifying whether an object has absolute or relative positioning, and so on |
| `left` | Property containing an object's left offset |
| `margin-left` | Property containing an object's left margin |
| `vertical-align` | Property containing an object's vertical alignment |
| `width` | Property containing an object's width |
| `height` | Property containing an object's height |
| `-moz-transition` | Property used by Mozilla and other Mozilla browsers to transition between two sets of property values |
| `-webkit-transition` | Property used by Safari and Chrome to transition between two sets of property values |
| `-o-transition` | Property used by Opera to transition between two sets of property values |
| `transition` | Property used by all other browsers except for Internet Explorer |

### About the Classes

These classes work in exactly the same manner as the `topdockbar` and `topdockitem` classes, only replacing those class names with `bottomdockbar` and `bottomdockitem`.

### How to Use Them

Using these items is identical to creating a top dock bar, except for swapping the class names to `bottomdockbar` and `bottomdockitem`. Therefore, please refer to the previous plug-in for details.

Following are the additional CSS rules required to create bottom dock bars. If you change the height of any images, you will also need to change the `margin-top` property to the new height plus 7 pixels, and `padding-top` to the difference in pixels between the actual height of the images and their reduced heights.

### The Classes

```
.bottomdockbar {
   top:100%;
   margin-top:-93px;      /* Set to -(actual image height + 7) */
}
.bottomdockitem {
   padding-top:36px;      /* Set to (actual height) - (reduced height) */
}
.bottomdockitem:hover {
   padding-top:0px;
}
```

# 38 Tooltip and Tooltip Fade

**PLUG-IN**

Plug-in group 38 lets you add tooltips (most of whose dimensions and HTML you can decide) to any object. In Figure 5-8, the word gravity has been assigned a short tooltip, briefly providing an explanation for the term. Tooltips can also be applied to links and any other objects.

## Classes and Properties

| | |
|---|---|
| `tooltip` | Class to display a tooltip when the mouse passes over an object |
| `tooltipfade` | Class to fade in a tooltip when the mouse passes over an object (for browsers that support transitions) |
| `text-decoration` | Property for changing text decorations such as underlines |
| `position` | Property containing an objects' position, such as absolute or relative |
| `display` | Property containing the way an object displays, such as block or inline |
| `top` | Property containing the vertical offset of an object from the top of its container |
| `left` | Property containing the horizontal offset of an object from the left of its container |
| `white-space` | Property used to disallow word wrapping at spaces |
| `background` | Property containing an object's background settings |
| `border` | Property containing an object's border settings |
| `color` | Property containing an object's text color |
| `font-family` | Property specifying the font to use |
| `font-size` | Property specifying the font size to use |
| `line-height` | Property specifying the line height of a font |
| `padding` | Property containing an object's padding settings |
| `opacity` | Property used to control an object's opacity (or transparency) |
| `-moz-transition` | Property for creating transitions on Firefox and other Mozilla browsers |
| `-webkit-transition` | Property for creating transitions on Safari and Chrome |
| `-o-transition` | Property for creating transitions on Opera |
| `transition` | Property for creating transitions on all other browsers (except IE) |
| `filter` | Property used by IE for opacity and other features |

## About the Classes

The `tooltip` class takes a `<span>` that must be provided alongside the object being given a tooltip, and then hides it away to be displayed only when the mouse passes over the object.

The `tooltipfade` class is identical except that (where supported) it uses CSS transitions to slide and fade a tooltip into place.

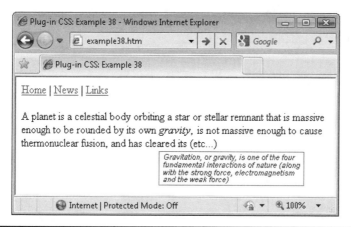

**Figure 5-8**   With this class, you can add tooltips to any object.

## How to Use Them

To use either of these classes, you must place a `<span>` directly following the object to be given the tooltip, in which you should place the tip to be displayed, like this:

```
<a class='tooltip' href='/'>Home<span>Go to the Home page</span></a>
```

The `<span>` is then lifted from the flow of the web page and made invisible, to appear only when the object is moused over.

Here is the code used to create Figure 5-8, showing the two different variants of the class in action:

```
<a href='/'>Home</a> |
<a href='/news/'>News</a> |
<a class='tooltip' href='/links/'>Links<span>Click here for a<br />
collection of great links</span></a><br /><br />

A planet is a celestial body orbiting a star or stellar remnant that is
massive enough to be rounded by its own
<span class='tooltipfade i'>gravity<span>Gravitation, or gravity, is one
of the four<br />fundamental interactions of nature (along<br />with the
strong force, electromagnetism<br />and the weak force)</span></span>,
is not massive enough to cause thermonuclear fusion, and has (etc...)
```

The first use of these classes is of the `tooltip` class in the third link from the top, and the second is of the `tooltipfade` class in the text below it. The `class` argument of `'tooltipfade i'` tells the browsers to display the text within the tooltip in italics. When displayed in either the Opera 10, Firefox 4, Safari 5, or Chrome 5 browsers (or better), the tooltip attached to the word *gravity* will slide down into place, smoothly fading in at the same time. On Internet Explorer, the tooltip will simply appear and disappear as the mouse hovers over the object and away again.

These classes disallow automatic wrapping at white space so that the width of each tooltip can be specified according to where the `<br />` tags are placed, and therefore the final width is that of the widest line.

**NOTE** *The text and background colors of the tooltips are fixed, so if you want different ones, you'll need to alter the* PC.css *file accordingly.*

## The Classes

```css
.tooltip:hover, .tooltipfade:hover {
   text-decoration:none;
   position:relative;
}
.tooltip span {
   display:none;
}
.tooltip:hover span {
   display:block;
   position:absolute;
   top:40px;
   left:0px;
   white-space:nowrap;
   background:#ffffdd;
   border:1px solid #888888;
   color:#444444;
   font-family:Arial, Helvetica, sans-serif;
   font-size:8pt;
   line-height:95%;
   padding:2px 5px;
}
.tooltipfade span {
   position:absolute;
   white-space:nowrap;
   font-family:Arial, Helvetica, sans-serif;
   font-size:8pt;
   line-height:95%;
   padding:2px 5px;
   top:0px;
   top:-10000px\0; /* IE hack to keep it out of the way */
   left:0px;
   background:#ffffdd;
   border:1px solid #888888;
   color:#444444;
   opacity:0;
   filter:alpha(opacity = '0');
}
.tooltipfade:hover span {
   -moz-transition    :all .5s linear;
   -webkit-transition:all .5s linear;
   -o-transition      :all .5s linear;
   transition         :all .5s linear;
   opacity:1;
   filter:alpha(opacity = '100');
   top:40px;
}
```

# CHAPTER 6

Page Layout

The plug-ins in this chapter provide classes for making your web pages appear as similar as possible when displayed on different web browsers; to emphasize sections of text and HTML using boxouts, sidebars, and quotes; and to format a web page so it looks its best when printed.

## PLUG-IN 39  Reset CSS

When you plan a lot of style changes, sometimes it is easier to reset all the settings so whichever browser is used the styles will be the same (or as close as possible). By resetting all the styles, when you view a web page during development it should become clear when you haven't created a style for an element, since it gives you a visual reminder.

Also, when you rely on the browser for default styles, you have no guarantee that all other browsers will use the same default setting. So by resetting all the properties, you are forced to create your own styling—which will be the same across all browsers.

For example, in Figure 6-1 I have displayed the same small segment of HTML in each of the Firefox, Internet Explorer, Chrome, Opera, and Safari web browsers.

The HTML each displays is the following, which simply creates a `<div>` with a solid one-pixel border, placing three headings within it:

```
<div class='bsolid'>
    <h1>Hello</h1>
    <h2>Hello</h2>
    <h3>Hello</h3>
</div>
```

You might think that such a tiny piece of HTML would display exactly the same way in all web browsers, but take a look at the figure and note the light line I have drawn across the top border of the `<div>` in each browser. As you can see, all the browsers have been aligned so that the top border of each `<div>` is against the line.

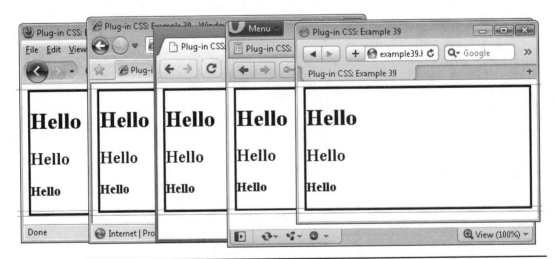

**FIGURE 6-1**  A simple section of HTML displayed in five different browsers

Now look at the bottom border of each <div>. Using a graphics program, I counted the difference in pixels and can report that the Internet Explorer <div> is three pixels shorter than the Firefox one. If you look at the two other light lines I drew—under the lowest and over the highest of the bottom borders—you can easily see this discrepancy. Also, the headings are one, one, and two pixels higher up respectively in IE.

Turning to Google Chrome, it has exactly the same appearance as IE and, therefore, is also different from Firefox in the same ways. The Opera <div>, on the other hand, is one pixel shorter than these two, and therefore four pixels shorter than the one in Firefox one. Also, its headings are zero, one, and one pixel higher than IE and Chrome, or one, two, and three pixels higher than Firefox.

Finally, Apple Safari has the same height <div> as IE and Chrome. Therefore, it is three pixels shorter than Firefox—and its headings are also slightly higher than Firefox.

Perhaps you never realized how different all the browsers are—and this example uses only a couple of elements. But by using the reset class, you can remove all these different attributes and start again with your own settings.

## Classes and Properties

| reset | Class to reset all the major properties of an object—can be applied to a document to reset all of the document's properties |
|---|---|
| (numerous properties) | Properties of an object that are too numerous to mention here |

## About the Class

This class resets all the properties of an object that sensibly can be reset, leaving them ready for you to assign your own values. These will then be the same on all browsers.

## How to Use It

You can use this class in a couple of ways. First, to reset only the properties of an object and its subobjects, you might use code such as this:

```
<div id='obj' class='reset'>Everything in this div is reset</div>
```

You would then need to write CSS rules for the ID obj to create the property values you want, such as:

```
#obj p {
   display:block;
   Margin:1.12em;
}
```

Alternatively (and probably the most useful method), you can attach the class to the <html> tag, like this:

```
<html class='reset'>
```

Once you do this, your whole web page will lose almost all its styling, ready for you to provide the styles you need.

## The Class

```css
.reset a,            .reset abbr,        .reset acronym,
.reset address,      .reset applet,      .reset big,
.reset blockquote,   .reset body,        .reset caption,
.reset cite,         .reset code,        .reset dd,
.reset del,          .reset dl,          .reset dfn,
.reset div,          .reset dt,          .reset em,
.reset fieldset,     .reset font,        .reset form,
.reset h1,           .reset h2,          .reset h3,
.reset h4,           .reset h5,          .reset h6,
.reset html,         .reset iframe,      .reset img,
.reset ins,          .reset kbd,         .reset label,
.reset legend,       .reset li,          .reset object,
.reset ol,           .reset p,           .reset pre,
.reset span,         .reset q,           .reset s,
.reset samp,         .reset small,       .reset strike,
.reset strong,       .reset sub,         .reset sup,
.reset table,        .reset tbody,       .reset td,
.reset tfoot,        .reset th,          .reset thead,
.reset tr,           .reset tt,          .reset ul,
.reset var {
    margin          :0;
    padding         :0;
    border          :0;
    outline         :0;
    font-family     :inherit;
    font-style      :inherit;
    font-weight     :inherit;
    font-size       :100%;
    vertical-align  :baseline;
}
.reset address,      .reset ar,          .reset caption,
.reset cite,         .reset code,        .reset dfn,
.reset em,           .reset strong,      .reset th,
.reset v {
    font-style      :normal;
    font-weight     :normal;
}
.reset h1,           .reset h2,          .reset h3,
.reset h4,           .reset h5,          .reset h6 {
    font-weight     :normal;
    font-size       :100%;
}
.reset blockquote:after, .reset blockquote:before,
.reset q:after,          .reset q:before {
    content         :'';
}
.reset caption,      .reset th,          .reset td {
    font-weight     :normal;
    text-align      :left;
}
```

```
.reset                  .reset fieldset, .reset img {
   border               :0;
}
.reset abbr,            .reset acronym {
   border               :0;
}
.reset ol,              .reset ul {
   list-style           :none;
}
.reset body {
   line-height          :1;
   background           :#ffffff;
   color                :#000000;
}
.reset table {
   border-collapse:separate;
   border-spacing :0;
}
.reset:focus {
   outline              :0;
}
```

## PLUG-IN 40  Default CSS

As an alternative to resetting all the CSS values, you can use this class, which creates a set of default property values, as recommended by the World Wide Web Consortium (*w3.org/TR/CSS2/sample.html*).

Figure 6-2 shows the same code as in the previous plug-in, displayed in the same browsers, with a single difference—the default class has been attached to the <html> tag. Now that all the browsers are using the same settings, their display is much more similar.

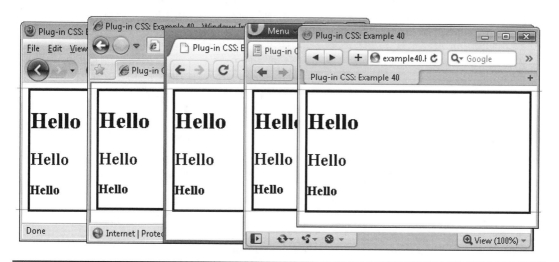

**FIGURE 6-2**  Using the default class the differences in display between browsers are reduced.

However, some slight differences still remain. This is because it is necessary to allow fonts and margins to scale up or down, so relative em measurements have been used for their values and, due to the different ways each browser calculates them, there is still a slight difference between them. Overall, however, you have a lot more control over a web page's display using this class, instead of relying on each browser's default settings.

## Classes and Properties

| default | Class to reset all the major properties of an object—can be applied to a document to reset all of the document's properties |
| --- | --- |
| (numerous properties) | Properties of an object that are too numerous to mention here |

## About the Class

This class resets all the properties of an object to sensible defaults, as recommended by *w3.org*, the web standards body, so your pages look much more alike on different browsers.

## How to Use It

You can use this class in a couple of ways. First, to set default styles only for the properties of an object and its subobjects, you might use code such as this:

```
<div id='obj' class='default'>This div has default settings</div>
```

Alternatively, you might be more likely to attach the class to the <html> tag, like this:

```
<html class='default'>
```

***

**TIP**  *In the case of both the* reset *and* default *classes, you may prefer to extract the CSS rules for these classes from the PC.css file into separate CSS style sheets that you can import before any others. In which case, use a search and replace facility to remove all instances of* .reset *for the* reset *class or* .default *for the* default *class, and then the styles will apply to the entire document, not just to classes using those names. For example, the rule* .default h1 *applies only to* <h1> *tags with an element ID of* default. *But by removing the* .default *prior to the* h1, *the rule will apply to all instances of the* <h1> *tag anywhere in a web page.*

## The Class

```
.default address,     .default blockquote,   .default body,
.default center,      .default dd,           .default dir,
.default div,         .default dl,           .default dt,
.default fieldset,    .default form,         .default frame,
.default frameset,    .default h1,           .default h2,
.default h3,          .default h4,           .default h5,
.default h6,          .default hr,           .default html,
.default menu,        .default noframes,     .default ol,
.default p,           .default pre,          .default ul
```

```
          { display:block; }
.default blockquote, .default dir,      .default dl,
.default fieldset,    .default form,     .default h4,
.default menu,        .default ol,       .default p,
.default ul
          { margin:1.12em 0; }
.default b,           .default h1,       .default h2,
.default h3,          .default h4,       .default h5,
.default h6,          .default strong
          { font-weight:bolder; }
.default address,     .default cite,     .default em,
.default i,           .default var
          { font-style:italic; }
.default code,        .default kbd,      .default pre,
.default samp,        .default tt
          { font-family:monospace; }
.default dd,          .default dir,      .default menu,
.default ol,          .default ul
          { margin-left:40px; }
.default button,      .default input,    .default select,
.default textarea
          { display:inline-block; }
.default ol ol,       .default ol ul,    .default ul ol,
.default ul ul
          { margin-top:0; margin-bottom:0; }
.default del,         .default s,        .default strike
          { text-decoration:line-through; }
.default small,       .default sub,      .default sup
          { font-size:0.83em; }
.default tbody,       .default tfoot,    .default thead
          { vertical-align :middle; }
.default td,          .default th,       .default tr
          { vertical-align :inherit; }
.default ins,         .default u
          { text-decoration:underline; }
.default td,          .default th
          { display:table-cell; padding:2px; }
.default a:active,    .default a:link
          { text-decoration:underline; color:#0000ff; }
.default big
          { font-size:1.17em; }
.default blockquote
          { margin-left:40px; margin-right:40px; }
.default body
          { margin:8px; }
.default br:before
          { content:"\A"; white-space:pre-line; }
.default caption
          { display:table-caption; text-align:center; }
.default center
          { text-align:center; }
.default col
          { display:table-column; }
```

```
.default colgroup
    { display:table-column-group; }
.default h1
    { font-size:2em; margin:0.7em 0; }
.default h2
    { font-size:1.5em; margin:0.75em 0; }
.default h3
    { font-size:1.17em; margin:0.83em 0; }
.default h5
    { font-size:0.83em; margin:1.5em 0; }
.default h6
    { font-size:0.75em; margin:1.67em 0; }
.default head
    { display:none; }
.default hr
    { border:1px inset; }
.default li
    { display:list-item; }
.default ol
    { list-style-type:decimal; }
.default table
    { display:table; }
.default tbody
    { display:table-row-group; }
.default tfoot
    { display:table-footer-group; }
.default th
    { font-weight:bolder; text-align:center; }
.default thead
    { display:table-header-group;  }
.default tr
    { display:table-row; }
.default pre
    { white-space:pre; }
.default sub
    { vertical-align:sub;  }
.default sup
    { vertical-align:super; }
.default table
    { border-spacing:2px; }
.default a:visited
    { color:#800080; }
.default :focus
    { outline:thin dotted invert; }
```

## Boxout

**PLUG-IN 41**

With the boxout class, you can easily place a section of HTML within a special boxout to make it stand out from the rest of the page. Figure 6-3 shows the class being used to emphasize some information in an article on global warming (taken from *wikipedia.org*).

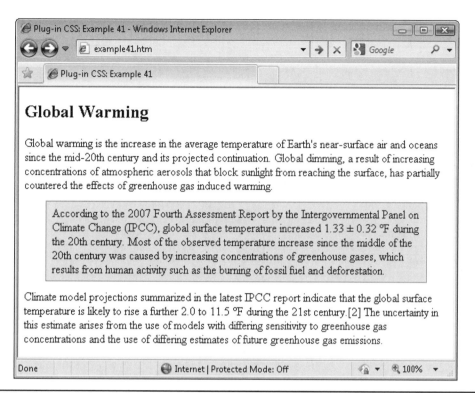

**FIGURE 6-3**     The boxout class helps add emphasis to important sections of a page.

## Classes and Properties

| | |
|---|---|
| boxout<br>boxout_h | Class to create a boxout around a section of HTML (boxout), or to do so only when the text is hovered over (boxout_h) |
| margin | Property containing the various margin settings of an object |
| padding | Property containing the various padding settings of an object |
| border | Property containing the various border settings of an object |
| background | Property containing the various background settings of an object |

## About the Classes

These classes create a professional looking boxout around any section of HTML. They do so either immediately or only when hovered over, and completely restyle the HTML by altering the margin, padding, border, and background properties of an object.

## How to Use Them

To place a section of HTML into a boxout, you would use HTML such as this:

```
<div class='boxout'>This text will appear in a boxout</div>
```

Or you can choose to make the boxout appear only when the HTML is hovered over, like this:

```
<div class='boxout_h'>This is a boxout when hovered</div>
```

***Tip***   *If you use the hover version of the class, it's a good idea to ensure the section is already separated from the text above and below, otherwise the change when hovered over may be too much on the eye.*

Following is the HTML used to create Figure 6-3. As you can see, when writing, it's easy to drop the class into a section of text without distracting you from your creative flow:

```
<h2>Global Warming</h2>
Global warming is the increase in the average temperature of Earth's
near-surface air and oceans since the mid-20th century and its projected
continuation. Global dimming, a result of increasing concentrations of
atmospheric aerosols that block sunlight from reaching the surface, has
partially countered the effects of greenhouse gas induced warming.

<div class='boxout_h'>
According to the 2007 Fourth Assessment Report by the Intergovernmental
Panel on Climate Change (IPCC), global surface temperature increased
1.33 +/- 0.32 &deg;F during the 20th century. Most of the observed
temperature increase since the middle of the 20th century was caused by
increasing concentrations of greenhouse gases, which results from human
activity such as the burning of fossil fuel and deforestation.</div>

Climate model projections summarized in the latest IPCC report indicate
that the global surface temperature is likely to rise a further 2.0 to
11.5 &deg;F during the 21st century. The uncertainty in this estimate
arises from the use of models with differing sensitivity to greenhouse
gas concentrations and the use of differing estimates of future
greenhouse gas emissions.
```

## The Classes

```
.boxout, .boxout_h:hover {
   margin:2% 5%;
   padding:1% 1.4%;
   border:1px solid #888;
   background:#eeeeee;
}
```

## PLUG-IN 42   Quote

Another great way to emphasize a section of text is to change the font style to something like italic and add a faded-out icon behind it, as with the quote class. In Figure 6-4, an article about the poet William Wordsworth (from *wikipedia.org*) has been displayed, with a few lines from one of his poems shown using this class.

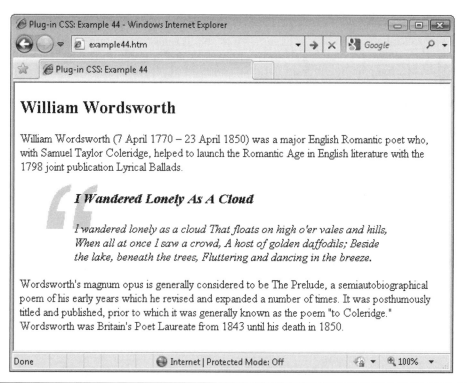

**Figure 6-4**    Using the quote class automatically sets up an appealing style.

## Classes and Properties

| Quote<br>quote_h | Class to enclose a section of HTML in a quote (quote), or to do so only when the text is hovered over (quote_h) |
| --- | --- |
| margin | Property containing the various margin settings of an object |
| padding | Property containing the various padding settings of an object |
| font-style | Property containing the style of a font |
| font-size | Property containing the size of a font |
| content | Property for adding content via CSS |
| position | Property specifying an object's position, such as absolute or relative |
| left | Property containing the offset from the left of an object |
| top | Property containing the offset from the top of an object |
| line-height | Property specifying the line height of a font |
| margin-bottom | Property specifying the bottom margin height |
| color | Property containing the text color |
| opacity | Property specifying the opacity (or transparency) of an object (except IE) |
| float | Property used to float an object to the left or right |

## About the Classes

These classes present a section of text in such a way that it is clearly obvious the text is a quotation. They do so by changing the text font to italic and resizing the margins and padding. Then, a large pale opening quotation mark symbol is placed at the top left of, and behind, the text.

Internet Explorer refuses to use the `filter` property to change the large quotation mark's opacity. For some reason, `filter` seems to not like operating within a `:before` or `:after` pseudo class. Therefore, an IE-specific hack is used to set the color of the symbol to very light gray instead.

## How to Use Them

To use these classes, simply mention one or the other in the `class` argument of an object, like this:

```
iv class='quote'>This text will appear as a quote</div>
```

Or you can choose to make the quote appear only when the HTML is hovered over, like this:

```
<div class='quote_h'>This appears as a quote when hovered over</div>
```

Here is the HTML used for the screen grab in Figure 6-4:

```
<h2>William Wordsworth</h2>
William Wordsworth (7 April 1770 - 23 April 1850) was a major English
Romantic poet who, with Samuel Taylor Coleridge, helped to launch the
Romantic Age in English literature with the 1798 joint publication
Lyrical Ballads.

<div class='quote'><h3>I Wandered Lonely As A Cloud</h3>
I wandered lonely as a cloud That floats on high o'er vales and hills,
When all at once I saw a crowd, A host of golden daffodils; Beside the
lake, beneath the trees, Fluttering and dancing in the breeze.</div>

Wordsworth's magnum opus is generally considered to be The Prelude, a
semiautobiographical poem of his early years which he revised and
expanded a number of times. It was posthumously titled and published,
prior to which it was generally known as the poem "to Coleridge."
Wordsworth was Britain's Poet Laureate from 1843 until his death in 1850.
```

You can change the quotation mark to one of many different styles by changing the font-family assignment in the following class in the *PC.css* file (available at *plugincss.com*). You may find you also need to play with the `padding` and `left` properties if you do so, since different fonts display at different sizes and in different ways.

## The Classes

```
.quote, .quote_h {
    margin:2% 10%;
    padding:1% 3%;
    font-style:italic
}
```

```
.quote:before, .quote_h:hover:before  {
   font-size:1500%;
   font-family:Arial, serif;
   content:'\201c';
   position:relative;
   left:-15%;
   top:-1%;
   line-height:0.7em;
   margin-bottom:-2em;
   color:#dddddd\0;    /* hack for IE only */
   opacity:.1;
   float:left;
}
```

## 43 Left Sidebar

Another way of emphasizing a section of HTML is to move it to one side as a boxout and let the main article flow around it. Figure 6-5 shows this class being used to do exactly that on the example from the previous plug-in.

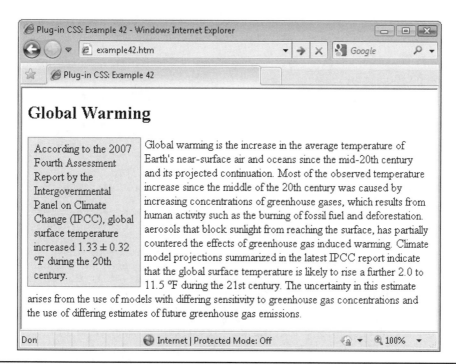

**FIGURE 6-5**    Boxouts are another great way to make your text more interesting.

## Classes and Properties

| | |
|---|---|
| leftsidebar | Class to float a section of HTML to the left of the main text |
| padding | Property containing all the padding settings of an object |
| margin-right | Property specifying the width of an object's right margin |
| border | Property containing all the border settings of an object |
| background | Property containing all the background settings of an object |
| width | Property specifying an object's width |
| float | Property for floating an object to the left or right |

## About the Class

This class floats a section of HTML to the left using the float property and then adds padding around it and a suitable margin to the right. The background is set to very light gray and the object's width is set to 25 percent of its containing object.

## How to Use It

To use this class, decide exactly where in the flow of your HTML you would like it to appear and then enclose the section for placement in the sidebar in a <div> using the class name leftsidebar, like this:

```
<div class='leftsidebar'>This text will appear in a left sidebar</div>
```

For example, here is the HTML used to create Figure 6-5, with the sidebar starting at the same vertical position as the main text:

```
<h2>Global Warming</h2>
<div class='leftsidebar'>
According to the 2007 Fourth Assessment Report by the Intergovernmental
Panel on Climate Change (IPCC), global surface temperature increased
1.33 +/- 0.32 &deg;F during the 20th century.</div>

Global warming is the increase in the average temperature of Earth's
near-surface air and oceans since the mid-20th century and its projected
continuation. Most of the observed temperature increase since the middle
of the 20th century was caused by increasing concentrations of greenhouse
gases, which result from human activity such as the burning of fossil
fuel and deforestation. Aerosols that block sunlight from reaching the
surface, have partially countered the effects of greenhouse-gas-induced
warming. Climate model projections summarized in the latest IPCC report
indicate that the global surface temperature is likely to rise a further
2.0 to 11.5 &deg;F during the 21st century. The uncertainty in this
estimate arises from the use of models with differing sensitivity to
greenhouse gas concentrations and the use of differing estimates of
future greenhouse gas emissions.
```

## The Class

```
.leftsidebar {
    padding:1% 1.4%;
    margin-right:1%;
    border:1px solid #888;
    background:#eeeeee;
    width:25%;
    float:left;
}
```

## 44  Right Sidebar

This is the partner class to Left Sidebar. It works in exactly the same way, but moves the sidebar to the right-hand side of the main text. Figure 6-6 shows the same example used in the previous plug-in, with only the class used being changed to `rightsidebar`:

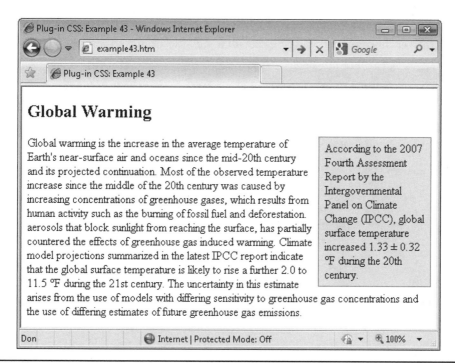

**FIGURE 6-6**   You can also create a sidebar on the right if you prefer.

## Classes and Properties

| rightsidebar | Class to float a section of HTML to the right of the main text |
|---|---|
| padding | Property containing all the padding settings of an object |
| margin-left | Property specifying the width of an object's left margin |
| border | Property containing all the border settings of an object |
| background | Property containing all the background settings of an object |
| width | Property specifying an object's width |
| float | Property for floating an object to the left or right |

## About the Class

This class floats a section of HTML to the right using the float property and then adds padding around it and a suitable margin to the left. The background is very light gray and the object's width is set to 25 percent of its containing object.

## How to Use It

To use this class, decide exactly where in the flow of your HTML you would like it to appear and then enclose the section for placement in the sidebar in a <div>, with the class name rightsidebar, like this:

```
<div class='rightsidebar'>This text will appear in a right sidebar</div>
```

For example, here is the HTML used to create Figure 6-6, with the sidebar starting at the same vertical position as the main text (since the article text is identical to that in the previous plug-in, only the first five lines are shown):

```
<h2>Global Warming</h2>
<div class='rightsidebar'>
According to the 2007 Fourth Assessment Report by the Intergovernmental
Panel on Climate Change (IPCC), global surface temperature increased
1.33 +/- 0.32 &deg;F during the 20th century.</div>
(etc…)
```

## The Class

```
.rightsidebar {
    padding:1% 1.4%;
    margin-left:1%;
    border:1px solid #888;
    background:#eeeeee;
    width:25%;
    float:right;
}
```

# Page Break

Plug-in 45 is a short and sweet class that you will find useful when visitors print out a web page, because with it you can specify where the page breaks should be located, so the printout will look much cleaner than web pages printed without using such a feature. For example, although the text is too small to read clearly, Figure 6-7 shows a copy of the Wikipedia Computer Printers page being viewed using Internet Explorer's Print Preview mode.

Immediately, you may notice that a couple of things could be improved here, such as the heading near the bottom left of the first page, which would be better moved over to the top of the following page. At the same time, there's a heading at the bottom of the second page that currently isn't too short, but if the first heading is moved to that page, it will become so. Therefore, it could also be moved to the following page.

However, in Figure 6-8, by placing a `<br />` tag containing this class just before each of the headings, you can see that the page layout is clearer—without headings commencing too near the bottom of any page.

After adding these two page breaks, it looks like a page break should also be forced at the start of the short paragraph at the bottom of the third page in Figure 6-8, which is also easily achieved.

## Classes and Properties

| | |
|---|---|
| `break` | Class to force a page break at the current location when it is printed |
| `page-break-before` | Property to set up page breaks for printing purposes |

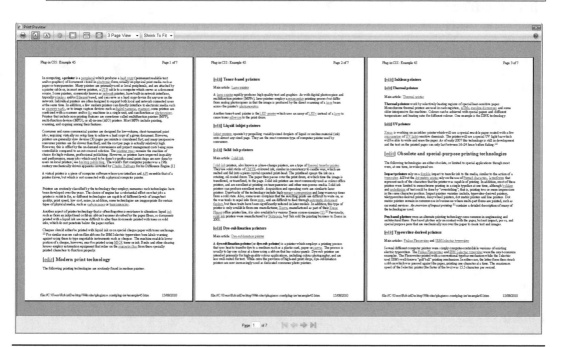

**FIGURE 6-7** A copy of Wikipedia's Computer Printers page in Print Preview mode

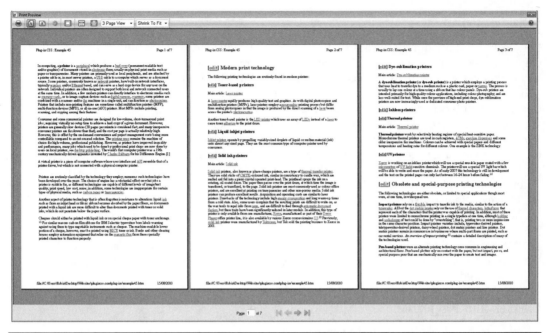

**FIGURE 6-8**   Using this class, printouts can be made much easier to read.

### About the Class

This class is acted on only when a web page is being printed (or print previewed). With it, you specify where you want printing to continue on a new page of paper. To do this, the plug-in makes use of the `page-break-before` property.

### How to Use It

The best way to use this class is to drop it in at the start of a heading you would like to ensure appears on a new sheet of paper when printed, like this:

```
<h1 class='break'>This is a heading</h1>
```

Or you may wish to attach it to a `<p>` or `<br />` tag, like this:

```
<p class='break'>The start of a paragraph...
<br class='break' />Text after a line break...
```

*CAUTION   Usually, it's best to add this class to an existing tag because if you add it to a new `<p>` or other tag, you may see unwanted extra line breaks or other styling when the web page is viewed normally.*

### The Class

```
.break { page-break-before:always; }
```

# CHAPTER 7

## Visual Effects

This chapter provides a wide range of visual effects such as star ratings (similar to those used on the Amazon website), progress bars or bar ratings, the scaling of images up or down, animating transitions at different speeds (and using different types of motion), viewing enlarged versions of thumbnail images, captioning and the rotation of images, changing the mouse pointer, and alternating the text and background colors of table rows.

Between them, you'll find you can build an amazing variety of different effects just by applying the right classes to the right elements, all without JavaScript or having to write your own CSS (unless you want to).

# Star Rating

Many sites use rating systems comprised of stars, the most notable probably being Amazon with its five-star ratings. Using this class, you can easily achieve a similar effect, as shown in Figure 7-1, in which a 65 percent popularity rating is displayed.

## Classes and Properties

| | |
|---|---|
| `starrating`<br>`starrating_h` | Classes to display a star rating of between 0 and 100 percent (`starrating`), or to do so only when hovered over (`starrating_h`) |
| `position` | Property specifying an object's position, such as absolute or relative |
| `color` | Property containing the text color of an object |
| `width` | Property containing the width of an object |
| `font-size` | Property containing the font size |
| `display` | Property specifying how to display an object, such as `block`, `inline`, or `none` |
| `overflow` | Property specifying what to do with any text that overflows the object's boundaries |
| `top` | Property containing an object's vertical offset from the top of its container |
| `left` | Property containing an object's horizontal offset from the left of its container |

**FIGURE 7-1**
Using this class makes it easy to display star ratings.

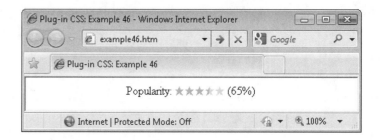

## About the Classes

These classes display a star rating using a star symbol already available as a character; therefore, they need no external image. This is achieved by overlaying two sets of stars. The first is a set of five very light stars, and the second is a set of darker stars truncated to the right at whatever percent value is to be displayed.

## How to Use Them

To use these classes, embed a <div> (whose width is set using a `style` argument to the percent value to display) within another container such as a <span>, like this:

```
<span class='starrating'>&#9733;&#9733;&#9733;&#9733;&#9733;
   <div style='width:65%'>&#9733;&#9733;&#9733;&#9733;&#9733;</div>
</span>
```

The &#9733; HTML entity represents the solid star symbol, and the `width` parameter of the `style` argument restricts the width of the inner <div> to only 65 percent of the outer <span>.

You can also choose to display the rating only when hovered over, by using the `starrating_h` class instead of `starrating`. Also, because of the simplicity of this plug-in's design, you can easily use other characters instead of stars.

## The Classes

```
.starrating, .starrating_h {
   position:relative;
   color:#ffddcc;
   width:65px;
   font-size:10pt;
}
.starrating_h div {
   display:none;
}
.starrating div, .starrating_h:hover div {
   display:block;
   position:absolute;
   overflow:hidden;
   color:#ff9900;
   top:0px;
   left:0px;
}
```

## PLUG-IN 47  Star Rating Using Images

In much the same way that you can use different characters instead of the star in the previous plug-in, with this plug-in you can use images of your choice. In Figure 7-2, this class has been used with a pair of star images for a more interesting effect, due to the range of colors an image can use.

**Figure 7-2**
Using images for
the stars provides
greater color
depth.

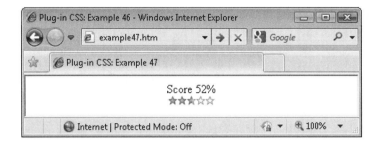

## Classes and Properties

| | |
|---|---|
| `starratingi`<br>`starratingi_h` | Classes to display a star rating of between 0 and 100 percent using gif images (`starratingi`), or to do so only when hovered over (`starratingi_h`) |
| `position` | Property specifying an object's position, such as absolute or relative |
| `width` | Property containing the width of an object |
| `height` | Property containing the height of an object |
| `background` | Property containing an object's various background settings |
| `top` | Property containing an object's vertical offset from the top of its container |
| `left` | Property containing an object's horizontal offset from the left of its container |

## About the Classes

These classes display a star rating using an image. This is achieved by using images for the backgrounds of two objects that are overlaid on each other. The first is a set of five very light stars, and the second is a set of darker stars with the right cut off at whatever percent value is to be displayed.

## How to Use Them

To use these classes, embed a `<div>` (whose width is set to the percent value to display) within another `<div>` (not a `<span>`), like this:

```
<div class='starratingi'><div style='width:52%'></div></div>
```

In this example the `width` parameter of the `style` argument restricts the width of the inner `<div>` to only 52 percent of the outer `<div>`. You can also choose to display the rating only when hovered over by using the `starratingi_h` class instead of `starratingi`.

You can change the images for any others of your choosing by altering the *PC.css* file (by either editing the `starratingi` class, or copying it and creating a new one), but if they will have dimensions other than 13 × 12 pixels, you will need to also alter the `width` and `height` properties in the class definition to the new image width (multiplied by the number of images used) and height. You will also need to change the filenames if you aren't using *star1.gif* and *star2.gif*. Don't forget that all the examples, classes, and images are available for download at *plugincss.com*.

## The Classes

```
.starratingi, .starratingi_h {
   position:relative;
   width:65px;
   height:12px;
   background:url(star1.gif) 0 0 repeat-x;
}
.starratingi div, .starratingi_h:hover div {
   position:absolute;
   height:12px;
   background:url(star2.gif) 0 0 repeat-x;
   top:0px;
   left:0px;
}
```

**PLUG-IN 48**

# Progress Bar

By relying on changing only an object's background color, the class in this plug-in lets you create a progress or rating bar you can use to indicate how far a particular action has progressed, or the rating given to something, as shown in Figure 7-3, which shows 65 percent progress of a loading action.

## Classes and Properties

| | |
|---|---|
| progress<br>progress_h | Classes to display a progress bar of between 0 and 100 percent using background colors (progress), or to do so only when hovered over (progress_h) |
| position | Property specifying an object's position, such as absolute or relative |
| width | Property containing the width of an object |
| height | Property containing the height of an object |
| top | Property containing an object's vertical offset from the top of its container |
| left | Property containing an object's horizontal offset from the left of its container |

**FIGURE 7-3**
Show how far an action has progressed with this plug-in.

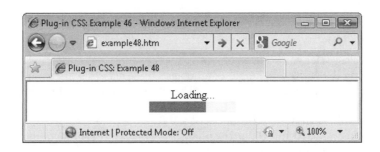

## About the Classes

These classes display a progress bar using only the background colors of two objects that are overlaid on each other.

## How to Use Them

To display a progress bar `<div>` inside another and give each a background color or perhaps a gradient fill using a suitable class (and use the `style` argument to set the width of the inner `<div>`), you would use code such as this:

```
<div class='progress yellow_b'>
   <div class='red_b' style='width:65%'></div>
</div>
```

In this example, a yellow progress bar is created with a red bar on top of it showing 65 percent progress. Or here's an example that uses gradient fills:

```
<div class='progress sunset1'>
   <div class='sky1' style='width:23%'></div>
</div>
```

You can also use the `progress_h` class to show the progress only when the object is hovered over by the mouse.

As you can see, you can specify both colors and the percentage to indicate directly from HTML. But, if you would like to have a progress bar with dimensions other than 120 × 15 pixels, you'll need to modify the class rules in the *PC.css* file.

## The Classes

```
.progress, .progress_h {
   position:relative;
   width:120px;
   height:15px;
}
.progress div, .progress_h:hover div {
   position:absolute;
   height:15px;
   top:0px;
   left:0px;
}
```

## PLUG-IN 49 Scale Up

These classes let you scale an object up by between 110 and 200 percent. Rather than simply changing the width and height of an object, these classes scale it in place, without pushing other objects around to make room. Therefore, they are great for special effects such as rollovers.

Figure 7-4 shows ten instances of a 100 × 100–pixel image displayed at dimensions between 110 × 110 and 200 × 200 pixels. As you can see, none of them has affected the location of any of the other images.

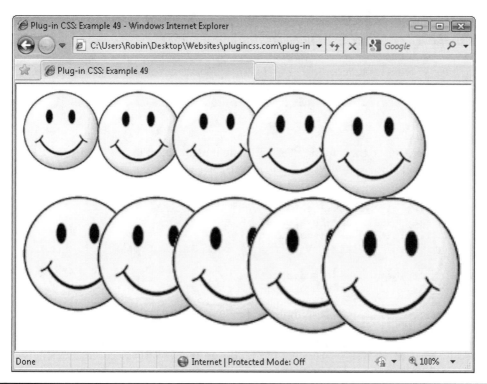

**FIGURE 7-4**    These classes let you resize an image in situ without affecting other objects.

## Classes and Properties

| | |
|---|---|
| `scaleup1`<br>`scaleup1_h` | Classes to scale up an image by 110 percent (`scaleup1`), or to do so only when hovered over (`scaleup1_h`) |
| `scaleup2 –`<br>`scaleup10` (etc...) | Class – as `scaleup1` but for scaling between 120 and 200 percent |
| `-moz-transform` | Property for transforming an object in Firefox and other Mozilla browsers |
| `-webkit-transform` | Property for transforming an object in Safari and Chrome |
| `-o-transform` | Property for transforming an object in Opera |
| `transform` | Property for transforming an object in all other browsers (except IE) |
| `filter` | Property for transforming an image in Internet Explorer |

## About the Classes

These classes are particularly useful in that they create effects you don't often see so easily implemented. What they do is use the CSS `transform` property (or browser-specific versions of it) along with the `scale()` argument, like this:

```
transform:scale(1.5);
```

---

*CAUTION  On Internet explorer, the* `filter` *property is used instead of* `transform` *to achieve a similar effect. However, this means that on IE only images can be scaled (whereas you can scale* `<div>`, `<span>`, *and other objects with other browsers). And there's another couple of provisos: While all other browsers scale using the object's center, IE scales from the top left. It also scales objects up* behind *other objects. Therefore, elements that may be scaled up should be separated from others that could obscure it, or vice versa. There is more on this topic in Plug-in 51.*

---

## How to Use Them

To use these classes, place them in the `class` argument of an object to be scaled, as in the following example, which was used to create Figure 7-4:

```
<img src='smiley.gif' class='scaleup1' />
<img src='smiley.gif' class='scaleup2' />
<img src='smiley.gif' class='scaleup3' />
<img src='smiley.gif' class='scaleup4' />
<img src='smiley.gif' class='scaleup5' /><br /><br /><br />

<img src='smiley.gif' class='scaleup6' />
<img src='smiley.gif' class='scaleup7' />
<img src='smiley.gif' class='scaleup8' />
<img src='smiley.gif' class='scaleup9' />
<img src='smiley.gif' class='scaleup10' />
```

You can also use the _h hover versions of the classes to resize an object only when it is hovered over, like this:

```
<img src='smiley.gif' class='scaleup5_h' />
```

---

*NOTE  When scaling up an object in the Opera or Firefox browsers, if the new size of the object will place its boundaries outside the browser's borders, scroll bars will be added to the browser. This behavior does not occur on other browsers.*

---

## The Classes

```
.scaleup1, .scaleup1_h:hover {
   -moz-transform    :scale(1.1);
   -webkit-transform:scale(1.1);
   -o-transform      :scale(1.1);
   transform         :scale(1.1);
   filter            :progid:DXImageTransform.Microsoft.Matrix(
                      SizingMethod='auto expand', M11='1.1', M22='1.1');
}
.scaleup2, .scaleup2_h:hover {
   -moz-transform    :scale(1.2);
   -webkit-transform:scale(1.2);
   -o-transform      :scale(1.2);
   transform         :scale(1.2);
```

```
   filter              :progid:DXImageTransform.Microsoft.Matrix(
                        SizingMethod='auto expand', M11='1.2', M22='1.2');
}
.scaleup3, . :hover {
   -moz-transform     :scale(1.3);
   -webkit-transform:scale(1.3);
   -o-transform       :scale(1.3);
   transform          :scale(1.3);
   filter              :progid:DXImageTransform.Microsoft.Matrix(
                        SizingMethod='auto expand', M11='1.3', M22='1.3');
}
.scaleup4, .scaleup4_h:hover {
   -moz-transform     :scale(1.4);
   -webkit-transform:scale(1.4);
   -o-transform       :scale(1.4);
   transform          :scale(1.4);
   filter              :progid:DXImageTransform.Microsoft.Matrix(
                        SizingMethod='auto expand', M11='1.4', M22='1.4');
}
.scaleup5, .scaleup5_h:hover {
   -moz-transform      :scale(1.5);
   -webkit-transform:scale(1.5);
   -o-transform       :scale(1.5);
   transform          :scale(1.5);
   filter              :progid:DXImageTransform.Microsoft.Matrix(
                        SizingMethod='auto expand', M11='1.5', M22='1.5');
}
.scaleup6, .scaleup6_h:hover {
   -moz-transform     :scale(1.6);
   -webkit-transform:scale(1.6);
   -o-transform       :scale(1.6);
   transform          :scale(1.6);
   filter              :progid:DXImageTransform.Microsoft.Matrix(
                        SizingMethod='auto expand', M11='1.6', M22='1.6');
}
.scaleup7, .scaleup7_h:hover {
   -moz-transform     :scale(1.7);
   -webkit-transform:scale(1.7);
   -o-transform       :scale(1.7);
   transform          :scale(1.7);
   filter              :progid:DXImageTransform.Microsoft.Matrix(
                        SizingMethod='auto expand', M11='1.7', M22='1.7');
}
.scaleup8, .scaleup8_h:hover {
   -moz-transform     :scale(1.8);
   -webkit-transform:scale(1.8);
   -o-transform       :scale(1.8);
   transform          :scale(1.8);
   filter              :progid:DXImageTransform.Microsoft.Matrix(
                        SizingMethod='auto expand', M11='1.8', M22='1.8');
}
```

```
.scaleup9, .scaleup9_h:hover {
    -moz-transform    :scale(1.9);
    -webkit-transform:scale(1.9);
    -o-transform      :scale(1.9);
    transform         :scale(1.9);
    filter            :progid:DXImageTransform.Microsoft.Matrix(
                       SizingMethod='auto expand', M11='1.9', M22='1.9');
}
.scaleup10, .scaleup10_h:hover {
    -moz-transform    :scale(2);
    -webkit-transform:scale(2);
    -o-transform      :scale(2);
    transform         :scale(2);
    filter            :progid:DXImageTransform.Microsoft.Matrix(
                       SizingMethod='auto expand', M11='2', M22='2');
}
```

## PLUG-IN 50 | Scale Down

These classes offer the inverse functionality to the previous plug-in group, in that they reduce an object down by between 10 and 100 percent, as shown in Figure 7-5, in which ten instances of an image have been reduced by these amounts.

As with the previous group of Scale Up classes, these classes do not alter the position of surrounding objects.

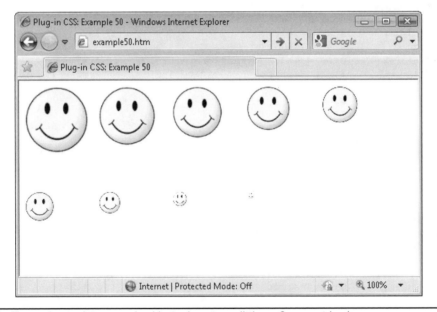

**Figure 7-5**   These classes let you scale objects down to as little as 0 percent in size.

## Classes and Properties

| | |
|---|---|
| `scaledown1`<br>`scaledown1_h` | Classes to scale down an image by 10 percent (`scaledown1`), or to do so only when hovered over (`scaledown1_h`) |
| `scaledown2 –`<br>`scaledown10 (etc...)` | Classes – as `scaledown1` but for scaling down between 20 and 100 percent |
| `-moz-transform` | Property for transforming an object in Firefox and other Mozilla browsers |
| `-webkit-transform` | Property for transforming an object in Safari and Chrome |
| `-o-transform` | Property for transforming an object in Opera |
| `transform` | Property for transforming an object in all other browsers (except IE) |
| `filter` | Property for transforming an image in Internet Explorer |

## About the Classes

These classes use the CSS `transform` property (or browser-specific versions of it) along with the `scale()` argument, like this:

```
transform:scale(0.5);
```

On Internet Explorer, the `filter` property achieves a similar effect. However, this means that on IE only images can be scaled. Also, while all other browsers scale using the object's center, IE scales from the top left.

## How to Use Them

To use these classes, place them in the `class` argument of an object to be scaled, as in the following example, which was used to create Figure 7-5:

```
<img src='smiley.gif' class='scaledown1' />
<img src='smiley.gif' class='scaledown2' />
<img src='smiley.gif' class='scaledown3' />
<img src='smiley.gif' class='scaledown4' />
<img src='smiley.gif' class='scaledown5' /><br /><br /><br />

<img src='smiley.gif' class='scaledown6' />
<img src='smiley.gif' class='scaledown7' />
<img src='smiley.gif' class='scaledown8' />
<img src='smiley.gif' class='scaledown9' />
<img src='smiley.gif' class='scaledown10' />
```

You can also use the _h hover versions of the classes to resize an object only when it is hovered over, like this:

```
<img src='smiley.gif' class='scaledown5_h' />
```

## The Classes

```css
.scaledown1, .scaledown1_h:hover {
   -moz-transform    :scale(0.9);
   -webkit-transform:scale(0.9);
   -o-transform      :scale(0.9);
   transform         :scale(0.9);
   filter            :progid:DXImageTransform.Microsoft.Matrix(
                      SizingMethod='auto expand', M11='0.9', M22='0.9');
}
.scaledown2, .scaledown2_h:hover {
   -moz-transform    :scale(0.8);
   -webkit-transform:scale(0.8);
   -o-transform      :scale(0.8);
   transform         :scale(0.8);
   filter            :progid:DXImageTransform.Microsoft.Matrix(
                      SizingMethod='auto expand', M11='0.8', M22='0.8');
}
.scaledown3, . :hover {
   -moz-transform    :scale(0.7);
   -webkit-transform:scale(0.7);
   -o-transform      :scale(0.7);
   transform         :scale(0.7);
   filter            :progid:DXImageTransform.Microsoft.Matrix(
                      SizingMethod='auto expand', M11='0.7', M22='0.7');
}
.scaledown4, .scaledown4_h:hover {
   -moz-transform    :scale(0.6);
   -webkit-transform:scale(0.6);
   -o-transform      :scale(0.6);
   transform         :scale(0.6);
   filter            :progid:DXImageTransform.Microsoft.Matrix(
                      SizingMethod='auto expand', M11='0.6', M22='0.6');
}
.scaledown5, .scaledown5_h:hover {
   -moz-transform    :scale(0.5);
   -webkit-transform:scale(0.5);
   -o-transform      :scale(0.5);
   transform         :scale(0.5);
   filter            :progid:DXImageTransform.Microsoft.Matrix(
                      SizingMethod='auto expand', M11='0.5', M22='0.5');
}
.scaledown6, .scaledown6_h:hover {
   -moz-transform    :scale(0.4);
   -webkit-transform:scale(0.4);
   -o-transform      :scale(0.4);
   transform         :scale(0.4);
   filter            :progid:DXImageTransform.Microsoft.Matrix(
                      SizingMethod='auto expand', M11='0.4', M22='0.4');
}
.scaledown7, .scaledown7_h:hover {
   -moz-transform    :scale(0.3);
   -webkit-transform:scale(0.3);
```

```
    -o-transform      :scale(0.3);
    transform         :scale(0.3);
    filter            :progid:DXImageTransform.Microsoft.Matrix(
                       SizingMethod='auto expand', M11='0.3', M22='0.3');
}
.scaledown8, .scaledown8_h:hover {
    -moz-transform    :scale(0.2);
    -webkit-transform:scale(0.2);
    -o-transform      :scale(0.2);
    transform         :scale(0.2);
    filter            :progid:DXImageTransform.Microsoft.Matrix(
                       SizingMethod='auto expand', M11='0.2', M22='0.2');
}
.scaledown9, .scaledown9_h:hover {
    -moz-transform    :scale(0.1);
    -webkit-transform:scale(0.1);
    -o-transform      :scale(0.1);
    transform         :scale(0.1);
    filter            :progid:DXImageTransform.Microsoft.Matrix(
                       SizingMethod='auto expand', M11='0.1', M22='0.1');
}
.scaledown10, .scaledown10_h:hover {
    -moz-transform    :scale(0);
    -webkit-transform:scale(0);
    -o-transform      :scale(0);
    transform         :scale(0);
    filter            :progid:DXImageTransform.Microsoft.Matrix(
                       SizingMethod='auto expand', M11='0', M22='0');
}
```

## PLUG-IN 51 | Transition All

For browsers that support the new transition property, including Opera 10, Firefox 4, Apple Safari 5, and Google Chrome 5 (but, sadly, not Internet Explorer), you can use this plug-in to make any changes made to an object transition smoothly, over a time between 0.1 and 2.0 seconds. Browsers that do not support transitions ignore these classes and will change properties immediately rather than transitioning.

In Figure 7-6 (a screen grab taken using the Apple Safari browser), the mouse is currently hovering over the middle smiley in the bottom row, which has smoothly enlarged—and it will gently shrink back down in size when the mouse moves away.

However, a word of caution when using scaling.... In Figure 7-7 (a screen grab taken using Internet Explorer), the object has correctly enlarged (but not transitioned, as IE doesn't support it), and you can see the reason for the warning I gave in Plug-in 49 about ensuring objects that may be scaled up in an IE window are separated from each other (since scaled-up objects appear *behind* others in IE). Other browsers do, however, correctly bring an object to the front when scaled, and move it back to its previous position when not scaled.

**FIGURE 7-6**   Combining the `transitionall` and `scale8_h` classes to create a rollover effect

**NOTE** *Unfortunately, Internet Explorer is currently out of the picture as far as CSS 3 transitions go, with even the IE9 beta not supporting them. So users of this browser will simply see instant changes rather than animated transitions. Let's hope that this powerful feature is added to IE soon.*

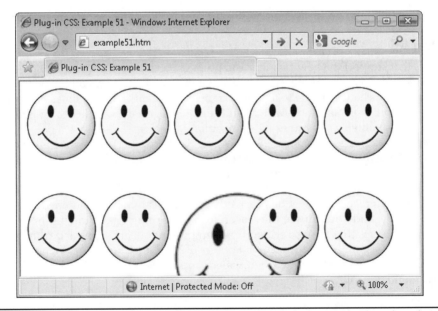

**FIGURE 7-7**   If you do not separate objects that are scalable, they can obscure each other when viewed in Internet Explorer.

## Classes and Properties

| | |
|---|---|
| `transitionall`<br>`transitionall_1` | Classes for apply transitions of 0.7 seconds duration to all changed properties of an object (`transitionall`), or to do so but with linear rather than easing movement (`transitionall_1`) |
| `transitionallslowest`<br>`transitionallslow`<br>`transitionallfast`<br>`transitionallfastest` | Classes – as `transitionall` and `transitionall_1`, but for durations of 2.0, 1.5, 0.3, and 0.1 seconds duration, including _1 versions for linear movement |
| `-moz-transition` | Property for transitioning properties of an object over a set duration in Firefox and other Mozilla browsers |
| `-webkit-transition` | Property for transitioning properties of an object over a set duration in Safari and Chrome |
| `-o-transition` | Property for transitioning properties of an object over a set duration in Opera |
| `transition` | Property for transitioning properties of an object over a set duration in all other browsers (except IE) |

## About the Classes

These classes apply transitions to all of an object's properties that change. This change is usually a result of the `:hover` pseudo class, as used by the _h versions of the classes in this book, or it can be a change instigated through the use of JavaScript, as implemented in the remaining chapters.

The transition is applied to an object using a CSS rule such as the following (or browser-specific variants of the property name like those that begin `-moz-`, `-webkit-`, or `-o-`):

```
transition:all .7s;
```

Browsers that do not support transitions will ignore this and just change properties immediately, without transitioning.

## How to Use Them

To use these classes, add them to the `class` argument of an object and forget about them. Then, when any properties of the object are changed that can transition, they will be animated over the period of time specified, rather than changing immediately.

For example, here's the example HTML from Plug-in 49, but modified to change all the hover effects to transitions of differing durations:

```
<img src='smiley.gif' class='scaleup1_h transitionallslowest' />
<img src='smiley.gif' class='scaleup2_h transitionallslow' />
<img src='smiley.gif' class='scaleup3_h transitionall' />
<img src='smiley.gif' class='scaleup4_h transitionallfast' />
<img src='smiley.gif' class='scaleup5_h transitionallfastest' />
<br /><br /><br />
```

```
<img src='smiley.gif' class='scaleup6_h transitionallslowest_l' />
<img src='smiley.gif' class='scaleup7_h transitionallslow_l' />
<img src='smiley.gif' class='scaleup8_h transitionall_l' />
<img src='smiley.gif' class='scaleup9_h transitionallfast_l' />
<img src='smiley.gif' class='scaleup10_h transitionallfastest_l' />
```

The first set of five images use the default easing transition, in which the animation starts slow, increases in speed and then slows again at the end. The second set uses the _l versions of the plug-ins to specify linear motion for the animation, where there is no speeding up and slowing down.

---

*TIP* *You will find you can add transitions to a wide range of the classes in this book that provide _h hover versions. This includes changing colors, position, dimensions, shadows, opacity, borders, and many more properties. All right, users of Internet Explorer won't get to see these nice transitions (yet), but for the sake of adding a simple extra class to your HTML, all other browser users (which as of late 2010 looks set to become the majority) will enjoy a much more sophisticated environment on their web pages.*

## The Classes

```
.transitionall {
    -moz-transition    :all .7s;
    -webkit-transition:all .7s;
    -o-transition      :all .7s;
    transition         :all .7s;
}
.transitionallslowest {
    -moz-transition    :all 2s;
    -webkit-transition:all 2s;
    -o-transition      :all 2s;
    transition         :all 2s;
}
.transitionallslow {
    -moz-transition    :all 1.5s;
    -webkit-transition:all 1.5s;
    -o-transition      :all 1.5s;
    transition         :all 1.5s;
}
.transitionallfast {
    -moz-transition    :all .3s;
    -webkit-transition:all .3s;
    -o-transition      :all .3s;
    transition         :all .3s;
}
.transitionallfastest {
    -moz-transition    :all .1s;
    -webkit-transition:all .1s;
    -o-transition      :all .1s;
    transition         :all .1s;
}
```

```
.transitionall_1 {
   -moz-transition    :all .7s linear;
   -webkit-transition:all .7s linear;
   -o-transition      :all .7s linear;
   transition         :all .7s linear;
}
.transitionallslowest_1 {
   -moz-transition    :all 2s linear;
   -webkit-transition:all 2s linear;
   -o-transition      :all 2s linear;
   transition         :all 2s linear;
}
.transitionallslow_1 {
   -moz-transition    :all 1.5s linear;
   -webkit-transition:all 1.5s linear;
   -o-transition      :all 1.5s linear;
   transition         :all 1.5s linear;
}
.transitionallfast_1 {
   -moz-transition    :all .3s linear;
   -webkit-transition:all .3s linear;
   -o-transition      :all .3s linear;
   transition         :all .3s linear;
}
.transitionallfastest_1 {
   -moz-transition    :all .1s linear;
   -webkit-transition:all .1s linear;
   -o-transition      :all .1s linear;
   transition         :all .1s linear;
}
```

## 52 Thumb View

This class provides a simple and effective way for users to browse large versions of photo thumbnails. In Figure 7-8, six thumbnails are displayed and the mouse is currently hovering over the second, which has caused the large version of the image to be displayed.

### Classes and Properties

| | |
|---|---|
| thumbview | Class to display a larger image of a thumbnail |
| position | Property containing the position of an object, such as relative or absolute |
| top | Property containing the vertical offset of an object from the top of its container |
| left | Property containing the horizontal offset of an object from the left of its container |
| display | Property specifying how an object is displayed, such as inline or block |

**FIGURE 7-8**   Use these classes to create a simple viewer for thumbnail images.

### About the Class

This class displays the contents of a `<span>` that accompanies a thumbnail image by hiding it using the `opacity` property and by scaling it to zero dimensions—until the mouse passes over the image, when the `<span>` is scaled back up again, and the opacity is restored to reveal it. The `<span>` is set to appear inset from the left of the container and down from the top by 30 pixels.

For some reason, the Opera browser doesn't vertically offset the same way that the other browsers do, so a browser-specific hack is used to change the `top` property of the `<span>` to a different value.

### How to Use It

Although this plug-in is intended mainly for displaying a large version of a thumbnail image, because it simply hides and displays a `<span>` on demand, you can place anything you like in it, meaning you can use it to display information on an image or other details.

Here is the HTML used for Figure 7-8:

```
<span class='thumbview'>
   <img class='bwidth1 bblack bsolid' src='t1.jpg' />
   <span><img class='bwidth2 bblack bsolid' src='i1.jpg' /></span>
</span>
<span class='thumbview'>
   <img class='bwidth1 bblack bsolid' src='t2.jpg' />
   <span><img class='bwidth2 bblack bsolid' src='i2.jpg' /></span>
</span>
```

```
<span class='thumbview'>
   <img class='bwidth1 bblack bsolid' src='t3.jpg' />
   <span><img class='bwidth2 bblack bsolid' src='i3.jpg' /></span>
</span><br />

<span class='thumbview'>
   <img class='bwidth1 bblack bsolid' src='t4.jpg' />
   <span><img class='bwidth2 bblack bsolid' src='i4.jpg' /></span>
</span>
<span class='thumbview'>
   <img class='bwidth1 bblack bsolid' src='t5.jpg' />
   <span><img class='bwidth2 bblack bsolid' src='i5.jpg' /></span>
</span>
<span class='thumbview'>
   <img class='bwidth1 bblack bsolid' src='t6.jpg' />
   <span><img class='bwidth2 bblack bsolid' src='i6.jpg' /></span>
</span>
```

The outer container of each thumbnail and image is a <span>, but it could equally be a <div> or other container. Within each container is an image followed by a <span>, in which a large version of each thumbnail image is placed. When the mouse passes over the outer container, the inner one is set to display, and when the mouse passes out, the inner one is hidden again.

---

**NOTE** *In Internet Explorer, what has been described here is pretty much what you will see. But on Opera 10, Firefox 4, Apple Safari 5, and Google Chrome 5, the images (or whatever is contained in the inner <span>) will fade and zoom in at the same time (and out again when the mouse passes away) due to the combined use of transitions, scaling, and opacity. If you can, try to view it in one of these browsers to see the impressive effect that results.*

## The Class

```
.thumbview {
     position:relative;
}
.thumbview span {
   position:absolute;
   top:-30px;
   left:30px;
   -moz-transition    :all .3s linear;
   -webkit-transition :all .3s linear;
   -o-transition      :all .3s linear;
   transition         :all .3s linear;
   -moz-transform     :scale(0);
   -webkit-transform  :scale(0);
   -o-transform       :scale(0);
   transform          :scale(0);
   opacity            :0;
   z-index            :0;
   filter             :progid:DXImageTransform.Microsoft.Matrix(
                        SizingMethod='auto expand', M11='0', M22='0');
}
```

```
.thumbview:hover span {
    -moz-transform    :scale(1);
    -webkit-transform :scale(1);
    -o-transform      :scale(1);
    transform         :scale(1);
    opacity           :1;
    z-index           :100;
    filter            :progid:DXImageTransform.Microsoft.Matrix(
                       SizingMethod='auto expand', M11='1', M22='1');
}

@media all and (-webkit-min-device-pixel-ratio:10000), /* Only  Opera */
    not all and (-webkit-min-device-pixel-ratio:0) { /* sees this hack */
    .thumbview span { top:30px; }
}
```

## PLUG-IN 53    Caption Image

Using this plug-in you can present your images with neat white borders and a shadowed caption on a thicker border at the picture's bottom. In Figure 7-9, the HTML from the previous example has been reused, with this class added to provide captions, and without the previous borders, since this class provides its own.

FIGURE 7-9    Use Plug-in 53 to add captions and interesting effects to images

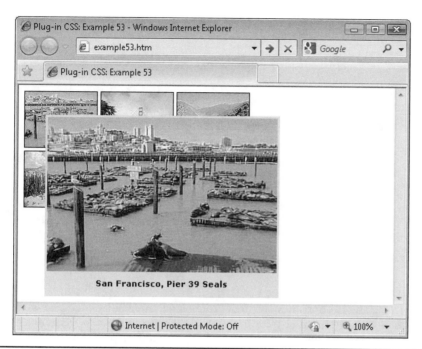

**FIGURE 7-10**    Displaying an image using a caption class in Internet Explorer

The screen grab was taken using Google Chrome, which is representative of the results you'll get with most browsers in that there is a smooth transition, the border of the photo is white and shadowed, and the caption is shadowed text on a translucent background.

However, in Internet Explorer it's not possible to achieve quite the same effect, mainly because IE dislikes using many of its features within a content property that is part of a pseudo class such as :before, or :after. Nevertheless, as you can see in Figure 7-10, it degrades reasonably well thanks to a few (unfortunately necessary) CSS hacks.

## Classes and Properties

| caption<br>caption_h | Classes to add a caption and other embellishments to an image (caption), or to do so only when the object is hovered over (caption_h) |
|---|---|
| position | Property containing the position of an object, such as absolute or relative |
| background | Property containing an object's background settings |
| padding | Property containing an object's padding settings |
| border | Property containing an object's border settings |
| color | Property containing the text color of an object |
| top | Property containing the vertical offset of an object from the top of its container |

| bottom | Property containing the vertical offset of an object from the bottom of its container |
|---|---|
| left | Property containing the horizontal offset of an object from the left of its container |
| height | Property containing the height of an object |
| line-height | Property containing the line height of an object |
| text-align | Property containing the alignment of the text in an object, such as left or right |
| font-size | Property containing the font size of an object |
| font-weight | Property containing the font weight of an object |
| font-family | Property containing the font family of an object |
| content | Property for adding content to an abject from CSS |
| opacity | Property containing the opacity (or invisibility) of an object |

## About the Classes

These classes frame and caption an image in a professional manner by changing various properties such as its borders, and by adding content taken from the alt argument.

The caption_h class applies the caption only when the mouse passes over the associated image, while the caption class applies it as soon as the larger image is displayed.

A few hacks must be used in the CSS to get Internet Explorer to display anything at all! These consist of affixing the \0 suffix to any rules that only IE should see. Also, to create the light ribbon behind the captions, the Unicode character 2588 (a solid block) is repeated 50 times in a :before set of rules. This block character string should be enough for reasonably wide pictures, but you can easily increase it if it isn't. Non-IE browsers do not see these :before rules.

## How to Use Them

To use these classes, you need to provide a caption for the image in the alt argument of its container (such as a <div> or <span>), and then use either the caption or caption_h class in the class argument, like this:

```
<span class='caption_h' alt='A caption'>
   <img src='myimage.jpg' />
</span>
```

For example, following is the HTML used for Figures 7-9 and 7-10, which combines the thumbview class with both the caption and caption_h classes:

```
<span class='thumbview'>
   <img class='bwidth1 bblack bsolid' src='t1.jpg' />
   <span class='caption' alt='San Francisco, Pier 39 Seals'>
      <img src='i1.jpg' />
   </span>
</span>
```

```
<span class='thumbview'>
   <img class='bwidth1 bblack bsolid' src='t2.jpg' />
   <span class='caption' alt='San Francisco Bay Bridge'>
      <img src='i2.jpg' />
   </span>
</span>
<span class='thumbview'>
   <img class='bwidth1 bblack bsolid' src='t3.jpg' />
   <span class='caption' alt='The San Francisco Peaks'>
      <img src='i3.jpg' />
   </span>
</span><br />

<span class='thumbview'>
   <img class='bwidth1 bblack bsolid' src='t4.jpg' />
   <span class='caption_h' alt='San Francisco Peaks Forest'>
      <img src='i4.jpg' />
   </span>
</span>
<span class='thumbview'>
   <img class='bwidth1 bblack bsolid' src='t5.jpg' />
   <span class='caption_h' alt='San Francisco Park Lake'>
      <img src='i5.jpg' />
   </span>
</span>
<span class='thumbview'>
   <img class='bwidth1 bblack bsolid' src='t6.jpg' />
   <span class='caption_h' alt='Las Vegas At Night'>
      <img src='i6.jpg' />
   </span>
</span>
```

The captions are immediately displayed when the larger version is shown of any of the top row of thumbnails, but the bottom row of icons only open up the large image. You need to move the mouse into this image to be shown the caption, too.

## The Classes

```
.caption, .caption_h {
   position:relative;
}
.caption img, .caption_h img {
   background:#000000;
   padding:3px;
}
.caption img, .caption_h:hover img {
   padding:0px;
   border:3px solid #ffffff;
   border:3px solid #eeeeee\0;                    /* IE hack */
   -moz-box-shadow    :3px 5px 9px #444;
   -webkit-box-shadow:3px 5px 9px #444;
   box-shadow         :3px 5px 9px #444;
}
```

```
.caption:before\0, .caption_h:hover:before\0 { /* IE hack section */
   position:absolute\0;
   color:#eeeeee\0;
   top:auto\0;
   bottom:3px\0;
   left:0px\0;
   font-size:20pt\0;
   font-weight:bold\0;
   font-family:Impact\0;
   content: '\2588\2588\2588\2588\2588\2588\2588\2588\2588\2588\2588\2588
   \2588\2588\2588\2588\2588\2588\2588\2588\2588\2588\2588\2588\2588\2588
   \2588\2588\2588\2588\2588\2588\2588\2588\2588\2588\2588\2588\2588\2588
   \2588\2588\2588\2588\2588\2588\2588\2588\2588\2588'; /* 1 long line */
}
.caption:after, .caption_h:hover:after {
   position:absolute;
   background:#ffffff;
   color:#000000;
   top:auto;
   bottom:3px;
   left:0px;
   width:100%;
   text-align:center;
   height:30px;
   line-height:30px;
   font-size:8pt;
   text-shadow:#888888 2px 2px 2px;
   font-weight:bold;
   font-family:Verdana, Helvetica, sans-serif;
   content:attr(alt);
   opacity:.9;
}
```

## PLUG-IN 54  Pointer

This pointer class is useful for making the mouse cursor change from an arrow to a pointing finger when it passes over an object, and is especially useful for attaching to buttons (which generally don't have this cursor behavior).

In Figure 7-11, two screen grabs have been taken with the mouse pointer enabled, and then merged to show the effect of passing the cursor over one object not using this class, and another that is. In the figure, the mouse cursor has changed to a pointing finger as it passes over the second button.

### Classes and Properties

| pointer | Class to change the mouse cursor to a pointing finger when it passes over an object |
|---------|-----------------------------------------------------------------------------------|
| cursor  | Property for changing the mouse cursor |

PART II

**FIGURE 7-11**
This class lets you
alert users that an
object is clickable.

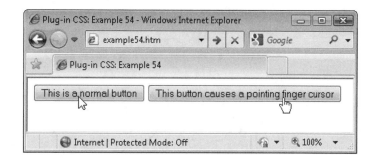

## About the Class

This short and sweet class simply sets the cursor property of an object to the value
pointer, so that the mouse cursor will change to a pointing finger when it passes over
the object.

## How to Use It

Following is the HTML used for Figure 7-11, in which the class has been assigned to one of
two buttons:

```
<button>This is a normal button</button>
<button class='pointer'>This button causes a pointing finger cursor
</button>
```

## The Class

```
.pointer { cursor:pointer; }
```

# 55 Rotation

With these classes, you can rotate an image by 90, 180, or 270 degrees, as shown in Figure 7-12
in which a smiley face appears 12 times. The first four instances are the four possible
clockwise rotations (the first being unrotated), the second group is the same, except that
the rotation occurs only when the mouse passes over an image, and the third is the same as
the second group, except that the rotations are counterclockwise. In the figure, the second
smiley on the third row is currently being hovered over and has rotated counterclockwise
by 90 degrees.

---

***TIP***   *If you need to rotate by different amounts than intervals of 90 degrees, see Chapter 8 for a
JavaScript-aided solution.*

**Figure 7-12**
These classes let
you display images
in any of four
different rotations.

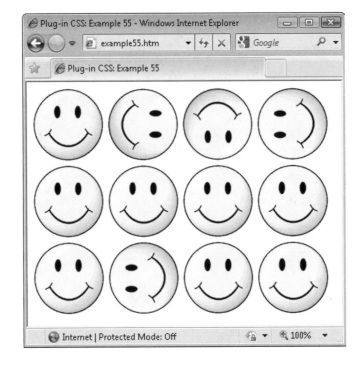

## Classes and Properties

| | |
|---|---|
| `rotatec90`<br>`rotatec90_h` | Classes to rotate an image clockwise by 90 degrees (`rotatec90`), or to do so only when the object is hovered over (`rotatec90_h`) |
| `rotatec180`<br>`rotatec270` (etc...) | Classes – as `rotatec90` but for rotating an object by 180 or 270 degrees, including `_h` classes for doing so only when hovered over |
| `rotatea90`<br>`rotatea270` (etc...) | Classes – as `rotatec90` but for rotating an object counterclockwise by 180 or 270 degrees, including `_h` classes for doing so only when hovered over |
| `-moz-transform` | Property used by Firefox and other Mozilla browsers to transform an object |
| `-webkit-transform` | Property used by Safari and Chrome to transform an object |
| `-o-transform` | Property used by Opera to transform an object |
| `transform` | Property used by all other browsers to transform an object (but not IE) |
| `filter` | Property used by IE to rotate an image, among many other features |

## About the Classes

These classes take an object and apply a rotation of 90, 180, or 270 degrees to it. The transforms used rotate in either a clockwise or counterclockwise direction so, for example, the `rotatec90` class uses this CSS rule:

```
transform:rotate(90deg);
```

...and the `rotatea90` class uses this rule (the a standing for the initial letter of the European term anticlockwise, since c is already taken for clockwise):

```
transform:rotate(-90deg);
```

The reason for providing both clockwise and counterclockwise methods is to allow the use of the `transitionall` classes (Plug-in 51) with these classes. When combined, on browsers that support transitions, the image will rotate smoothly in the direction supplied, rather than immediately change.

The Internet Explorer browser doesn't support transitions but does change the object to the required rotation.

## How to Use Them

To use these classes, enter them into the `class` argument of an object, like this:

```
<img class='rotatec90' src='myphoto.jpg' />
```

Browsers other than Internet Explorer support the rotating of any object such as a `<span>` or `<div>`, which means complete sections of text and HTML can be rotated. But IE is limited to only images.

Here is the HTML used to create Figure 7-12:

```
<img src='smiley.gif' />
<img class='rotatec90' src='smiley.gif' />
<img class='rotatec180' src='smiley.gif' />
<img class='rotatec270' src='smiley.gif' /><br />

<img src='smiley.gif' />
<img class='transitionall rotatec90_h' src='smiley.gif' />
<img class='transitionall rotatec180_h' src='smiley.gif' />
<img class='transitionall rotatec270_h' src='smiley.gif' /><br />

<img src='smiley.gif' />
<img class='transitionall_l rotatea90_h' src='smiley.gif' />
<img class='transitionall_l rotatea180_h' src='smiley.gif' />
<img class='transitionall_l rotatea270_h' src='smiley.gif' />
```

The first group instantly rotates the images and the second one rotates them only when the mouse hovers over an image. This group also implements the `transitionall` class, so that browsers that support it will animate the rotation.

The final group is the same as the second except that the images rotate counterclockwise, and the `transitionall_l` class is used for a linear, rather than easing, movement to the animation.

## The Classes

```
.rotatec90,.rotatec90_h:hover {
   -webkit-transform:rotate(90deg);
   -moz-transform  :rotate(90deg);
   -o-transform    :rotate(90deg);
   transform       :rotate(90deg);
   filter:progid:DXImageTransform.Microsoft.BasicImage(rotation=1);
}
.rotatec180, .rotatec180_h:hover {
   -webkit-transform:rotate(180deg);
   -moz-transform  :rotate(180deg);
   -o-transform    :rotate(180deg);
   transform       :rotate(180deg);
   filter:progid:DXImageTransform.Microsoft.BasicImage(rotation=2);
}
.rotatec270, .rotatec270_h:hover {
   -webkit-transform:rotate(270deg);
   -moz-transform  :rotate(270deg);
   -o-transform    :rotate(270deg);
   transform       :rotate(270deg);
   filter:progid:DXImageTransform.Microsoft.BasicImage(rotation=3);
}
.rotatea90,.rotatea90_h:hover {
   -webkit-transform:rotate(-90deg);
   -moz-transform  :rotate(-90deg);
   -o-transform    :rotate(-90deg);
   transform       :rotate(-90deg);
   filter:progid:DXImageTransform.Microsoft.BasicImage(rotation=3);
}
.rotatea180, .rotatea180_h:hover {
   -webkit-transform:rotate(-180deg);
   -moz-transform  :rotate(-180deg);
   -o-transform    :rotate(-180deg);
   transform       :rotate(-180deg);
   filter:progid:DXImageTransform.Microsoft.BasicImage(rotation=2);
}
.rotatea270, .rotatea270_h:hover {
   -webkit-transform:rotate(-270deg);
   -moz-transform  :rotate(-270deg);
   -o-transform    :rotate(-270deg);
   transform       :rotate(-270deg);
   filter:progid:DXImageTransform.Microsoft.BasicImage(rotation=1);
}
```

## PLUG-IN 56 Odd and Even Text Colors

When you wish to present a table in a more easy-to-read format, you can use the classes in this plug-in to alternate the color of each row by adding a class to the `<table>` tag, as

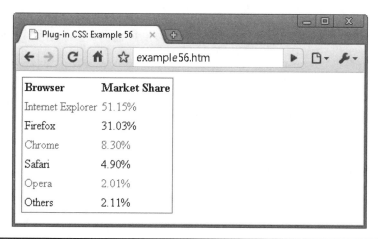

**FIGURE 7-13**  Using the Plug-in 56 classes to create alternately colored rows of text in tables

shown in Figure 7-13 (a screen grab from Google Chrome), where the text color in the odd rows has been changed to green.

These classes work in all the latest browsers except for Internet Explorer (even the IE9 beta), although it is rumored that the final release of IE9 may support the properties these classes rely on. IE8 and lower will simply display tables the normal way.

## Classes and Properties

| | |
|---|---|
| `aqua_o`<br>`aqua_e` | Classes to change the text color of either all odd rows in a table to aqua (`aqua_o`), or all even rows (`aqua_e`) |
| `black blue brown`<br>`fuchsia gold gray`<br>`green khaki lime`<br>`maroon navy olive`<br>`orange pink purple`<br>`red silver teal`<br>`white yellow (etc...)` | Classes – as `aqua_o` and `aqua_e`, but for the colors shown |
| `nth-child()` | Pseudo class used with the values odd or even for accessing odd or even numbered rows |
| `color` | Property containing the text color of an object |

## About the Classes

These classes change the text color of either the odd- or even-numbered rows in a table by using the `nth-child` pseudo class, like this:

```
.aqua_o tr:nth-child(odd) { color:#0ff; }
```

For example, this rule sets the class `aqua_o` to change the text color of all odd table rows to aqua, using the `tr:` part of the rule, in conjunction with the `:nth-child(odd)` pseudo class. For even rows, the `odd` parameter is changed to `even`.

## How to Use Them

To use these classes, simply mention them in the class argument of a table, as in the following, which will change the text color of all even rows to green:

```
<table class='green_e'>
```

Here's the HTML used to create Figure 7-13:

```
<table class='bsolid bwidth1 green_e' cellspacing='0' cellpadding='3'>
    <tr class='green_e'>
        <td><b>Browser</b></td>
        <td><b>Market Share</b></td>
    </tr>
    <tr>
        <td>Internet Explorer</td>
        <td>51.15%</td>
    </tr>
    <tr>
        <td>Firefox</td>
        <td>31.03%</td>
    </tr>
    <tr>
        <td>Chrome</td>
        <td>8.30%</td>
    </tr>
    <tr>
        <td>Safari</td>
        <td>4.90%</td>
    </tr>
    <tr>
        <td>Opera</td>
        <td>2.01%</td>
    </tr>
    <tr>
        <td>Others</td>
        <td>2.11%</td>
    </tr>
</table>
```

This example displays the market share of the main web browsers in July 2010 according to Wikipedia. It starts by creating a solid black border around the table with a width of one pixel, and then uses the `green_e` class to set the color of all even rows in the table to green. The table's `cellspacing` and `cellpadding` arguments are also set to 0 and 3, respectively, for improved styling.

A color class with the suffix `_o` could also be used if the odd row color needed changing from the default of black.

## The Classes

```
.aqua_o    tr:nth-child(odd),   .aqua_e    tr:nth-child(even)
  { color:#0ff }
.black_o   tr:nth-child(odd),   .black_e   tr:nth-child(even)
  { color:#000 }
.blue_o    tr:nth-child(odd),   .blue_e    tr:nth-child(even)
  { color:#00f }
.brown_o   tr:nth-child(odd),   .brown_e   tr:nth-child(even)
  { color:#c44 }
.fuchsia_o tr:nth-child(odd),   .fuchsia_e tr:nth-child(even)
  { color:#f0f }
.gold_o    tr:nth-child(odd),   .gold_e    tr:nth-child(even)
  { color:#fc0 }
.gray_o    tr:nth-child(odd),   .gray_e    tr:nth-child(even)
  { color:#888 }
.green_o   tr:nth-child(odd),   .green_e   tr:nth-child(even)
  { color:#080 }
.khaki_o   tr:nth-child(odd),   .khaki_e   tr:nth-child(even)
  { color:#cc8 }
.lime_o    tr:nth-child(odd),   .lime_e    tr:nth-child(even)
  { color:#0f0 }
.maroon_o  tr:nth-child(odd),   .maroon_e  tr:nth-child(even)
  { color:#800 }
.navy_o    tr:nth-child(odd),   .navy_e    tr:nth-child(even)
  { color:#008 }
.olive_o   tr:nth-child(odd),   .olive_e   tr:nth-child(even)
  { color:#880 }
.orange_o  tr:nth-child(odd),   .orange_e  tr:nth-child(even)
  { color:#f80 }
.pink_o    tr:nth-child(odd),   .pink_e    tr:nth-child(even)
  { color:#f88 }
.purple_o  tr:nth-child(odd),   .purple_e  tr:nth-child(even)
  { color:#808 }
.red_o     tr:nth-child(odd),   .red_e     tr:nth-child(even)
  { color:#f00 }
.silver_o  tr:nth-child(odd),   .silver_e  tr:nth-child(even)
  { color:#ccc }
.teal_o    tr:nth-child(odd),   .teal_e    tr:nth-child(even)
  { color:#088 }
.white_o   tr:nth-child(odd),   .white_e   tr:nth-child(even)
  { color:#fff }
.yellow_o  tr:nth-child(odd),   .yellow_e  tr:nth-child(even)
  { color:#ff0 }
```

# Odd and Even Background Colors

These classes complement those in Plug-in 56 by enabling the changing of a table row's odd or even background colors as shown in Figure 7-14, in which the background colors have been styled to alternate between lime green and aqua.

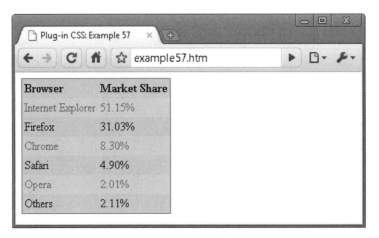

FIGURE 7-14   The table from the previous plug-in, now styled with alternating background colors

As with the odd and even text color classes, these classes will not work with Internet Explorer, although they may do so in the full release of IE9. In IE8 and earlier, the table will simply display as normal; therefore, you may wish to apply a standard background color to your tables as a fallback.

## Classes and Properties

| | |
|---|---|
| `aqua_bo`<br>`aqua_be` | Classes to change the background color of either all odd rows in a table to aqua (`aqua_bo`), or all even rows (`aqua_be`) |
| `black blue brown`<br>`fuchsia gold gray`<br>`green khaki lime`<br>`maroon navy olive`<br>`orange pink purple`<br>`red silver teal`<br>`white yellow (etc...)` | Classes – as `aqua_bo` and `aqua_be`, but for the colors shown |
| `nth-child()` | Pseudo class used with the values `odd` or `even` for accessing odd or even numbered rows |
| `background` | Property containing the background color of an object |

## About the Classes

These classes work in the same way as those in the previous plug-in group, except that they change the `background` instead of the `color` property.

## How to Use Them

To use these classes, simply mention them in the class argument of a table as in the following, which will change the background color of all even rows to aqua:

```
<table class='aqua_be'>
```

Here's the HTML used to create Figure 7-14:

```
<table class='bsolid bwidth1 green_e aqua_be lime_bo'
   cellspacing='0' cellpadding='3'>
   <tr class='green_e'>
      <td><b>Browser</b></td>
      <td><b>Market Share</b></td>
   </tr>
   <tr>
      <td>Internet Explorer</td>
      <td>51.15%</td>
   </tr>
   <tr>
      <td>Firefox</td>
      <td>31.03%</td>
   </tr>
   <tr>
      <td>Chrome</td>
      <td>8.30%</td>
   </tr>
   <tr>
      <td>Safari</td>
      <td>4.90%</td>
   </tr>
   <tr>
      <td>Opera</td>
      <td>2.01%</td>
   </tr>
   <tr>
      <td>Others</td>
      <td>2.11%</td>
   </tr>
</table>
```

This example adds the classes aqua_be and lime_bo to the previous example to change the background colors of the table rows. Although the colors in this example may look garish when you run them on your computer, I chose them because they convert well to the gray scale printing used in this book—and it's easy enough for you to change them anyway.

---

**NOTE**  *This concludes the standard CSS plug-ins. In the next chapter, I'll introduce Dynamic classes and show what you can do when you add a little JavaScript to your CSS.*

## The Classes

```
.aqua_bo    tr:nth-child(odd), .aqua_be    tr:nth-child(even)
   { background:#0ff }
.black_bo   tr:nth-child(odd), .black_be   tr:nth-child(even)
   { background:#000 }
.blue_bo    tr:nth-child(odd), .blue_be    tr:nth-child(even)
   { background:#00f }
.brown_bo   tr:nth-child(odd), .brown_be   tr:nth-child(even)
   { background:#c44 }
```

```
.fuchsia_bo tr:nth-child(odd), .fuchsia_be tr:nth-child(even)
   { background:#f0f }
.gold_bo    tr:nth-child(odd), .gold_be   tr:nth-child(even)
   { background:#fc0 }
.gray_bo    tr:nth-child(odd), .gray_be   tr:nth-child(even)
   { background:#888 }
.green_bo   tr:nth-child(odd), .green_be  tr:nth-child(even)
   { background:#080 }
.khaki_bo   tr:nth-child(odd), .khaki_be  tr:nth-child(even)
   { background:#cc8 }
.lime_bo    tr:nth-child(odd), .lime_be   tr:nth-child(even)
   { background:#0f0 }
.maroon_bo  tr:nth-child(odd), .maroon_be tr:nth-child(even)
   { background:#800 }
.navy_bo    tr:nth-child(odd), .navy_be   tr:nth-child(even)
   { background:#008 }
.olive_bo   tr:nth-child(odd), .olive_be  tr:nth-child(even)
   { background:#880 }
.orange_bo  tr:nth-child(odd), .orange_be tr:nth-child(even)
   { background:#f80 }
.pink_bo    tr:nth-child(odd), .pink_be   tr:nth-child(even)
   { background:#f88 }
.purple_bo  tr:nth-child(odd), .purple_be tr:nth-child(even)
   { background:#808 }
.red_bo     tr:nth-child(odd), .red_be    tr:nth-child(even)
   { background:#f00 }
.silver_bo  tr:nth-child(odd), .silver_be tr:nth-child(even)
   { background:#ccc }
.teal_bo    tr:nth-child(odd), .teal_be   tr:nth-child(even)
   { background:#088 }
.white_bo   tr:nth-child(odd), .white_be  tr:nth-child(even)
   { background:#fff }
.yellow_bo  tr:nth-child(odd), .yellow_be tr:nth-child(even)
   { background:#ff0 }
```

# PART III
# The Dynamic Classes

# CHAPTER 8

## Dynamic Objects

Powerful as CSS is, it isn't really a language, as shown by the plug-ins in this book having to repeat large chunks of code where only a minor change is required between each, such as a color or width. A language, on the other hand, is very good at repeating things based on only a few lines of code. And that's where JavaScript fits in, because with it you can bring the dynamic interaction of a web page up an order of magnitude.

What's more, many of the classes in this chapter allow you to enter values as parameters to create exactly the result you want, including moving objects about in the browser, loading images in only when (or if) they are scrolled into view, fading images in and out over user-definable periods, resizing and rotating objects by any amount, and changing an object's text and background colors to all possible values.

## PLUG-IN 58 NoJS (nojs) and OnlyJS (onlyjs)

There is a downside to employing JavaScript-aided classes because some people have JavaScript turned off, generally due to a habit they got into when pop-up windows became so prevalent. But with the advent of pop-up blocking in all modern browsers, the percent of users with JavaScript disabled has dropped from a height of around 12–15 percent a decade ago, to an estimated 2 percent or so nowadays. It may not be a large number of users, but it's still enough that, where possible, care should be taken to offer fallback features for these users. And that's what this first dynamic plug-in helps with, providing you with an easy way to offer fallback HTML for browsers on which the dynamic classes fail.

You can use the `<noscript>` tag for this, but it requires you to place all the fallback sections of code within pairs of these tags, and there's no simple solution for hiding standard HTML from non-JavaScript browsers. However, by using the `nojs` class for any block of code that should be viewable only to non-JavaScript browsers, no extra tags are required. You simply use the name in the `class` argument of an object, and the `onlyjs` class is used to make any section of HTML visible only to JavaScript-enabled browsers.

For example, the screen grab in Figure 8-1 shows a sentence enclosed within a `<div>` using the `nojs` class, making the sentence visible only to users without JavaScript, or who have JavaScript disabled.

---

**TIP** *JavaScript can be disabled and reenabled in Internet Explorer by pressing* ALT-T, *selecting Internet Options, choosing the Security tab, clicking the Custom level button, and then scrolling down and checking Active Scripting: Disable or Enable. Different commands are required to do this on other browsers.*

---

**FIGURE 8-1**
The sentence in this window will be seen only on browsers without JavaScript.

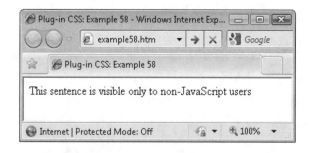

FIGURE 8-2
With JavaScript
enabled, a
different sentence
becomes visible.

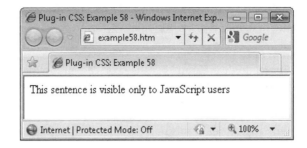

**FIGURE 8-2**
With JavaScript
enabled, a
different sentence
becomes visible.

Alternatively, in Figure 8-2, JavaScript is running in the browser and so a section of text for JavaScript-enabled browsers only is displayed.

## Variables, Functions, and Properties

| | |
|---|---|
| `classname` | String variable containing the name of the class—used by all these plug-ins so not mentioned again |
| `thistag` | Object referring to the current object—used by all these plug-ins so not mentioned again |
| `search()` | JavaScript function to search one string for another—used by all these plug-ins so not mentioned again |
| `Hide()` | Function to hide an object |
| `Show()` | Function to show an object |

## About the Classes

These classes provide complementary functionality to each other. The `nojs` class is ignored on non-JavaScript browsers; therefore, any object using the class is viewable. But on JavaScript-enabled browsers, the `nojs` class is acted upon by JavaScript and any object using it is hidden, so users who have JavaScript will not see any objects using the `nojs` class.

On the other hand, the `onlyjs` class should be used in conjunction with a `style` argument to hide an object from non-JavaScript browsers, but browsers with JavaScript enabled detect the class and unhide such objects so they become visible.

## How to Use Them

You will generally use these classes in pairs, so you can offer one set of HTML to users with JavaScript and another to those without, like this:

```
<div style='display:none;' class='onlyjs'>
   This sentence is visible only to JavaScript users
</div>
<div class='nojs'>
   This sentence is visible only to non-JavaScript users
</div>
```

In the first `<div>`, both the arguments `style='display:none'` and `class='onlyjs'` must be applied in order to make its contents visible only to browsers with JavaScript enabled.

For non-JavaScript browsers, you simply attach the argument class='nojs' to an object to ensure that only users without JavaScript enabled can see it.

### About the JavaScript

Don't worry if you don't program, because you can ignore these JavaScript code segments and skip to the next plug-in—they are included simply for programmers who may be interested in how they work.

The following partial JavaScript listing shows the main setup JavaScript code for all of the classes in the remainder of this book. It starts with initializing the *PJ.js* JavaScript library from my book *Plug-in JavaScript*. This is a library of JavaScript files that make using the language much simpler, especially for code that must run in a variety of modern browsers. As with all the other files used in this book, *PJ.js*, is available as part of the download at the companion web site at *plugincss.com*.

```
Initialize()

OnDOMReady(function()
{
    var gfurl     = 'http://fonts.googleapis.com/css?family='
    var wheight   = GetWindowHeight()
    var tags      = document.getElementsByTagName("*")
    var numtags   = tags.length
    var font      = ''
    var elems     = []
    var gfonts    = []
    var cites     = []
    var refers    = []
    var sclasses  = []
    var gfindex   = 0
    var cindex    = 0
    var demand    = false
    var index, index2, thistag, regex, oldclassname

    loadsclasses(sclasses)

    for (index = 0 ; index < numtags ; ++ index)
    {
        thistag         = tags[index]
        var tagname     = thistag.tagName.toLowerCase()
        var tagtype     = (thistag.type) ? thistag.type.toLowerCase() : ''
        var classname   = thistag.className.toLowerCase()
        var cnamecopy   = classname
        var origcname   = thistag.className
        var repeat      = true
```

After initializing the *PJ.js* library (which provides much of the functionality of these dynamic classes), the OnDOMReady() function is called, which sets up the code after it in such a way that the classes become active only once the entire web page is loaded (but before any images or other embedded objects), so that all objects in it can then be referenced at the earliest possible opportunity.

After that, a number of variables used by JavaScript are declared. If you load the code into an editor, you can issue a quick search to see which variables are used by which routines.

Next, the superclasses referred to in Chapter 12 are loaded using the `loadsclasses()` function, and then the main loop controlling the dynamic classes begins, in which every single `class=` argument in the web page is examined one at a time and, if it matches one of the new dynamic classes, the code to handle it is activated.

In the case of the two classes in this plug-in group, the code used follows. It simply employs a regular expression to find the class names (highlighted in bold) and, if found, acts on them by calling either the `Hide()` function to hide the object using the class, or the `Show()` function to reveal it. The variable `thistag` refers to the current object whose `class` argument is being examined.

---

*TIP*  *Remember that to function correctly, all the files used by the plug-ins must be loaded in at the start of each web page within `<head>` tags, like the following example which pulls in the PC.css style sheet and the PJ.js and PC.js JavaScript libraries:*

```
<head>
    <link rel='stylesheet' type='text/css' href='PC.css' />
    <script src='PJ.js'></script><script src='PC.js'></script>
</head>
```

### The JavaScript

```
if (classname.search(/\bnojs\b/, 0)    != -1) Hide(thistag)

if (classname.search(/\bonlyjs\b/, 0) != -1) Show(thistag)
```

---

## PLUG-IN 59   Middle (middle)

This class is particularly suitable in cases when standard CSS doesn't have the effect you want because instead of using values of `auto`, it calculates the correct margins by querying the dimension of the parent object and uses those values to force the desired behavior (as do the `middle`, `center`, `top`, `bottom`, `left`, and `right` plug-in classes).

What this class does is vertically align an object by finding out the height of the object immediately enclosing it (its parent) and then placing it directly between the upper and lower boundaries. In Figure 8-3, a 300 × 100–pixel `<div>` contains another object that has been vertically centered using this class.

**FIGURE 8-3**
Vertically centering one object inside another

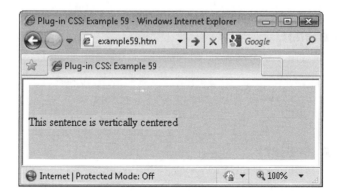

## Variables, Functions, and Properties

| parentnode | Object containing the parent of the current object |
|---|---|
| H() | Function to return the height of an object |
| O() | Function to return an object – used by most of these dynamic classes and therefore will not be mentioned again |
| Px() | Function to add the suffix px to a value – used by many of these dynamic classes and therefore will not be mentioned again |
| marginTop | Property containing the object's top margin |
| marginBottom | Property containing the object's bottom margin |

## About the Class

After looking up the height of the parent object, this class then sets the marginTop and marginBottom JavaScript equivalents of the CSS margin-top and margin-bottom properties to equal values sufficient to display the object exactly in the middle.

---

**NOTE**　*Wherever you see a JavaScript property that starts with a lowercase letter and has an uppercase one in the middle, you can convert it to a CSS property by changing the uppercase letter to lowercase and placing a hyphen before it. Therefore, marginBottom becomes margin-bottom, and so on.*

## How to Use It

In order to use this class, the parent object needs to already have a position other than static, such as relative or absolute, and the object to be moved should be given an absolute position, like this:

```
<div style='width:400px; height:100px;' class='relative lime_b'>
   <div class='absolute aqua_b middle'>
      This sentence is vertically centered
   </div>
</div>
```

This example sets the outer <div> to a width of 400 and a height of 100 pixels, gives it relative positioning and sets the background to lime. The inner <div> is given absolute positioning, a background color of aqua, and is assigned the middle class.

## The JavaScript

```
if (classname.search(/\bmiddle\b/, 0) != -1)
{
   S(thistag).marginTop = S(thistag).marginBottom =
      Px((H(thistag.parentNode) - H(thistag)) / 2)
}
```

 **Center (center)**

Plug-in 60 is similar to the middle class, but it centers an object horizontally. In Figure 8-4, the previous example has been extended to also center the inner object using this class.

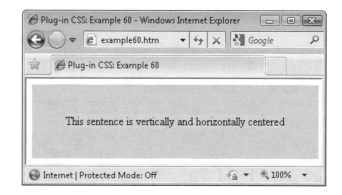

FIGURE 8-4
The example from the previous plug-in is now also centered horizontally.

## Variables, Functions, and Properties

| parentnode | Object containing the parent of the current object |
|---|---|
| W() | Function to return the width of an object |
| marginLeft | Property containing the object's left margin |
| marginRight | Property containing the object's right margin |

## About the Class

By looking up the width of the parent object, this class then sets the marginLeft and marginRight properties of the object to equal values sufficient to display the object exactly in the center.

## How to Use It

In order to use this class, the parent object needs to already have a position other than static, such as relative or absolute, and the object to be moved should be given an absolute position, like this:

```
<div style='width:400px; height:100px;' class='relative lime_b'>
   <div class='absolute middle center aqua_b'>
      This sentence is vertically and horizontally centered
   </div>
</div>
```

This example sets the outer <div> to a width of 400 and a height of 100 pixels, gives it relative positioning, and sets the background to lime. The inner object is given absolute positioning, a background color of aqua, and is assigned both the center and middle classes.

## The JavaScript

```
if (classname.search(/\bcenter\b/, 0) != -1)
{
   S(thistag).marginLeft = S(thistag).marginRight =
      Px((W(thistag.parentNode) - W(thistag)) / 2)
}
```

## Top (top)

This class attaches an object to the top of its parent, as shown in Figure 8-5, in which the previous example is top- instead of middle-aligned.

### Variables, Functions, and Properties

| parentnode | Object containing the parent of the current object |
|---|---|
| H() | Function to return the height of an object |
| marginTop | Property containing the object's top margin |
| marginBottom | Property containing the object's bottom margin |

### About the Class

By looking up the height of the parent object, this class then sets the marginTop property to 0 pixels and the marginBottom property of the object to the value required to ensure it stays at the top of its containing object.

### How to Use It

In order to use this class, the parent object needs to already have a position other than static, such as relative or absolute, and the object to be moved should be given an absolute position, like this:

```
<div style='width:400px; height:100px;' class='relative lime_b'>
   <div class='absolute top center aqua_b'>
      This sentence is top aligned and horizontally centered
   </div>
</div>
```

Here, the inner object is given absolute positioning, a background color of aqua, and is assigned both the top and center classes.

### The JavaScript

```
if (classname.search(/\btop\b/, 0) != -1)
{
   S(thistag).marginTop    = '0px';
   S(thistag).marginBottom = Px(H(thistag.parentNode) -H(thistag))
}
```

**FIGURE 8-5**
The inner object is top-aligned using this class.

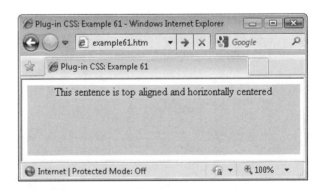

# Bottom (bottom)

This class attaches an object to the bottom of its parent, as shown in Figure 8-6, in which the previous example is bottom- instead of top-aligned.

## Variables, Functions, and Properties

| parentnode | Object containing the parent of the current object |
|---|---|
| H() | Function to return the height of an object |
| marginTop | Property containing the object's top margin |
| marginBottom | Property containing the object's bottom margin |

## About the Class

By looking up the height of the parent object, this class then sets the marginBottom property to 0 pixels and the marginTop property of the object to the value required to ensure it stays at the bottom of its containing object.

## How to Use It

The following example is the same as the previous one, with just one class change:

```
<div style='width:400px; height:100px;' class='relative lime_b'>
   <div class='absolute bottom center aqua_b'>
      This sentence is bottom aligned and horizontally centered
   </div>
</div>
```

Here the inner object is assigned both the bottom and center classes.

## The JavaScript

```
if (classname.search(/\bbottom\b/, 0) != -1)
{
   S(thistag).marginTop    = Px(H(thistag.parentNode) -H(thistag))
   S(thistag).marginBottom = '0px';
}
```

**FIGURE 8-6**
The inner object is bottom-aligned using this class.

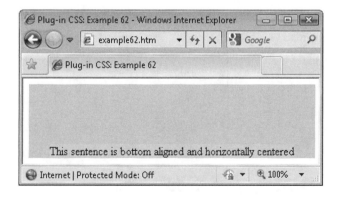

## Left (left)

Plug-in 63 is similar to the `center` class, but it aligns an object to the left. In Figure 8-7, the previous example has been modified to left-align the inner object using this class, rather than centering it. The object is also middle-aligned vertically.

### Variables, Functions, and Properties

| | |
|---|---|
| `Parentnode` | Object containing the parent of the current object |
| `W()` | Function to return the width of an object |
| `marginLeft` | Property containing the object's left margin |
| `marginRight` | Property containing the object's right margin |

### About the Class

By looking up the width of the parent object, this class then sets the `marginLeft` property to 0 pixels and the `marginRight` property of the object to the value required to ensure it stays at the left of its containing object.

### How to Use It

The following example is the same as the previous one, with just one class change:

```
<div style='width:400px; height:100px;' class='relative lime_b'>
   <div class='absolute left middle aqua_b'>
        This sentence is left aligned and vertically centered
   </div>
</div>
```

Here the inner `object` is assigned both the `left` and `middle` classes.

### The JavaScript

```
if (classname.search(/\bleft\b/, 0) != -1)
{
   S(thistag).marginLeft  = '0px';
   S(thistag).marginRight = Px(W(thistag.parentNode) - W(thistag))
}
```

**FIGURE 8-7**
The example from the previous plug-in is now left-aligned and centered vertically.

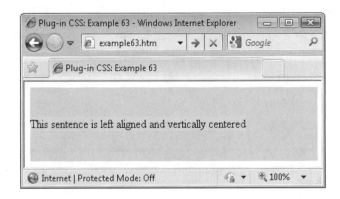

# Right (right)

Plug-in 64 is similar to the `left` class, but it aligns an object to the right. In Figure 8-8, the previous example has been modified to right-align the inner object using this class, rather than left-aligning it.

## Variables, Functions, and Properties

| | |
|---|---|
| `parentnode` | Object containing the parent of the current object |
| `W()` | Function to return the width of an object |
| `marginLeft` | Property containing the object's left margin |
| `marginRight` | Property containing the object's right margin |

## About the Class

By looking up the width of the parent object, this class then sets the `marginRight` property to 0 pixels and the `marginLeft` property of the object to the value required to ensure it stays at the right of its containing object.

## How to Use It

The following example is the same as the previous one, with just one class change:

```
<div style='width:400px; height:100px;' class='relative lime_b'>
    <div class='absolute right middle aqua_b'>
        This sentence is right aligned and vertically centered
    </div>
</div>
```

Here the inner `object` is assigned both the `right` and `middle` classes.

## The JavaScript

```
if (classname.search(/\bright\b/, 0) != -1)
{
    S(thistag).marginLeft  = Px(W(thistag.parentNode) - W(thistag))
    S(thistag).marginRight = '0px';
}
```

**FIGURE 8-8**
The example from the previous plug-in is now right-aligned.

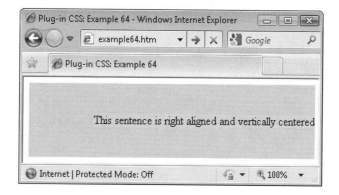

## On Demand (ondemand)

Have you noticed how Flash programs and movies generally don't load until you scroll them into view? The idea behind this is to save on downloading data unnecessarily, thus decreasing the provider's bandwidth fees and speeding up your browsing.

Well, with this class you can provide the same feature for your images. When you use it, only those images already in view when a page loads are downloaded. Then, as you scroll, when each new image comes into view it is quickly downloaded and displayed. And, because only one image is fetched at a time, rather than as part of the initial flurry of downloads accompanying a page load, it's actually very fast and looks good too since they fade into view.

With it, you'll save on your bandwidth bills and speed up your web pages at the same time, as shown in Figure 8-9, in which the photo is being faded in after being scrolled into view.

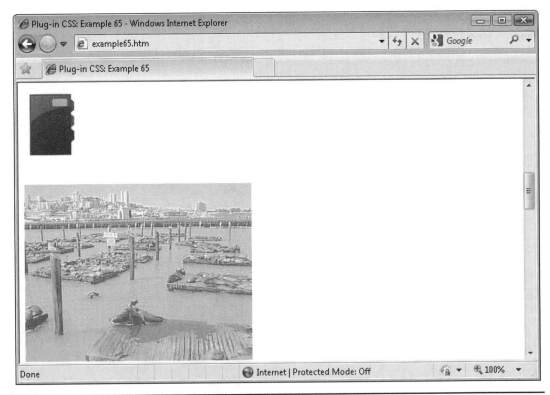

**FIGURE 8-9**   Using this plug-in, pictures are downloaded only when required.

## Variables, Functions, and Properties

| tagname | String variable containing the name of the tag, such as img |
|---|---|
| SCROLL_Y | Global integer variable containing the amount by which the browser has scrolled (global variables are always all uppercase in this program) |
| wheight | Integer variable containing the height of the browser viewport |
| index | Integer variable used for iterating through all the classes found in a web page |
| elems[] | String Array containing the sources of all images yet to be loaded |
| thistag.alt | String variable (and a property of thistag) containing the alternate text for the current image |
| thistag.src | String variable (and a property of thistag) containing the source of the current image |
| demand | Integer variable used as a flag and set to true if the ondemand class is being used on a web page |
| setTimeout() | JavaScript function to call a function after a set period |
| DoOnDemand() | Function to keep an eye on images and decide whether to load them |
| Opacity() | Function to set the opacity of an object |
| Y() | Function to return the height of an object |
| FadeIn() | Function to fade an object in over a set time |

### About the Class

This class checks all images in a web page to see whether they are using the ondemand class. Any that do have their position in the web page examined to see if they are within view. If they are, then the image locations are loaded in from the alt arguments and placed in the src arguments to download them. But any that are not yet in view have their opacity set to zero so that the broken image icon will not display.

Later in the program, a function will be set up to keep an eye on these images, and download and fade them in gently as they come into view.

### How to Use It

To use this class, all you need to do is attach the ondemand class to any images you have decided should use this feature, and use the alt argument for the image URL *not* the *src* argument (this is important), like this:

```
<img class='ondemand' alt='myphoto.jpg' />
```

The image will then only be downloaded and faded in when it is scrolled into view.

For programmers interested in the JavaScript code that later monitors the images (towards the end of the *PC.js* file), here it is (non-programmers can skip ahead to the next plug-in):

```
if (demand) setTimeout(DoOnDemand, 10)
```

This line checks whether the variable demand has a value of true. If so, then the ondemand class has been used at least once in the web page and so the function DoOnDemand() is set to be called in 10 milliseconds. That function looks like this:

```
function DoOnDemand()
{
    demand = false

    for (index = 0 ; index < numtags ; ++index)
    {
        thistag = tags[index]

        if (elems[index])
        {
            demand = true

            if (Y(thistag) < (SCROLL_Y + wheight))
            {
                thistag.onload = function() { FadeIn(this, 500) }
                thistag.src    = elems[index]
                elems[index]   = ''
            }
        }
    }

    if (demand) setTimeout(DoOnDemand, 10)
}
```

What it does is iterate through the array elems[], which has previously been assigned the locations of all ondemand images, and checks whether the image is in view. If so, then the FadeIn() function is set to be called as soon as the image is loaded, and then the image's src= argument is given the location of the image, so it can be fetched. Once an image is loaded, its entry in the elems[] array is removed so it won't be looked up again.

After this, if the variable demand is true, then the interrupt is set up to call the function in a further 10 milliseconds (and so on until all images are downloaded). If it is not true, then no more images require loading in, and so no more calls are made to the interrupt function.

Following is the initial code that locates instances of the ondemand class and acts on them.

---

**CAUTION** *Remember that you must use the alt argument of an image not its src argument when using the ondemand class. This is to prevent fast browsers that may have already parsed the full HTML from trying to load images in until the program lets it. With no URLs in the src arguments, the browser will skip them.*

## The JavaScript

```
if (classname.search(/\bondemand\b/, 0) != -1 && tagname == 'img')
{
    if (Y(thistag) > (SCROLL_Y + wheight))
```

```
    {
        elems[index] = thistag.alt
        demand       = true
        Opacity(thistag, 0)
    }
    else thistag.src = thistag.alt
}
```

# 66 Fadein (fadein[*n*])

Using this plug-in, you can fade in an object over a length of time of your choosing. This is the first dynamic plug-in in which you'll see how to pass values to those classes that use them. For example, the image in Figure 8-10 has been set to fade in over 2,000 milliseconds (or 2 seconds) and is now in the process of fading.

## Variables, Functions, and Properties

| arguments[1] | JavaScript array element containing the duration value |
| --- | --- |
| cnamecopy | String variable containing a copy of the class name |
| replace() | JavaScript function to replace values found in a string with other values |
| Opacity() | Function to set the opacity of an object |
| FadeIn() | Function to fade an object in over a set time |

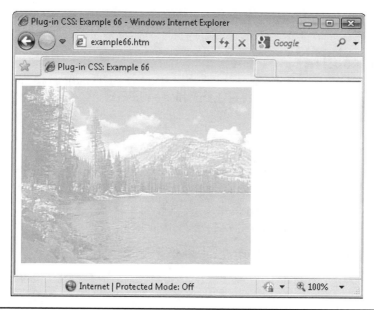

**FIGURE 8-10** Using this class to fade in images over a period of time

### About the Class

This class uses the JavaScript replace() function on a copy of the class name, and specifies an anonymous, inline function for handling the replacement. But, rather than replacing, the function only wants access to the matched string, which it receives in the array element arguments[1]. It then sets the opacity of the object to 0 and calls the FadeIn() function (from *PJ.js*), passing it the object to fade and the value in arguments[1], which is the number of milliseconds the fade should take.

### How to Use It

To make an object fade in, use this dynamic class in its class argument, as in the following (ensuring that duration of the fade in milliseconds is placed within a pair of square brackets):

```
<img class='fadein[2000]' src='i5.jpg' />
```

Any value from 0 upwards is acceptable for the duration length, and the argument and square brackets may not be omitted.

### The JavaScript

```
if (classname.search(/\bfadein\b/, 0) != -1)
{
    cnamecopy.replace(/fadein\[(([^\]]*)\]/, function()
    {
        Opacity(thistag, 0);
        FadeIn(thistag, arguments[1])
    } )
}
```

---

## 67  Fadeout (fadeout[*n*])

**PLUG-IN**

Plug-in 67 offers the inverse functionality to the fadein[] class by fading out an object over a set period of time, as shown in Figure 8-11, in which a photo is in the process of fading out using this class.

### Variables, Functions, and Properties

| | |
|---|---|
| arguments[1] | JavaScript array element containing the fade duration length |
| cnamecopy | String variable containing a copy of the class name |
| replace() | JavaScript function to replace values found in a string with other values |
| Opacity() | Function to set the opacity of an object |
| FadeOut() | Function to fade out object over a set time |

### About the Class

This class uses the JavaScript replace() function in the same way as the fadein[] plug-in to pass a duration interval to the FadeOut() function.

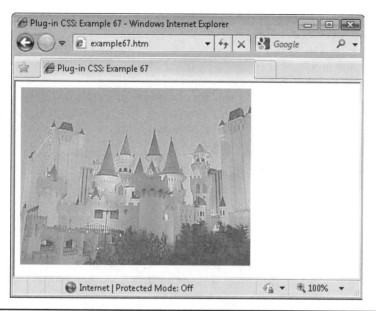

**FIGURE 8-11**   You can also fade out objects with the fadeout class.

## How to Use It

To make an object fade out, use this dynamic class in its `class` argument, like this (ensuring that duration of the fade in milliseconds is placed within a pair of square brackets):

```
<img class='fadeout[2000]' src='i6.jpg' />
```

Any value from 0 upwards is acceptable for the duration length, and the argument and square brackets may not be omitted.

---

**TIP**   *You can fade out any object, not just images. Beware, however, because Internet Explorer removes the ClearType setting on any text that has its opacity changed, making it appear more jagged. One solution is to fade a white object in and out that you place over another. The one underneath will then appear to fade out and in, and no fonts will be affected.*

## The JavaScript

```
if (classname.search(/\bfadeout\b/, 0) != -1)
{
    cnamecopy.replace(/fadeout\[([^\]]*)\]/, function()
    {
        FadeOut(thistag, arguments[1])
    } )
}
```

# PLUG-IN 68 Resize Textarea (resizeta[*n*|*n*])

Choosing the right dimensions for a `<textarea>` input tag can be difficult. Make it too small and there is not much room for the user. But if it's too large, it may appear daunting to the user, who will feel they need to fill the space.

Thankfully, the `resizeta[]` class provides an answer, allowing you to set up a `<textarea>` with an initial number of rows. This class will then monitor it for the minimum and maximum values you give it, contracting and expanding the area according to how many lines of text have been input, as shown in Figure 8-12.

## Variables, Functions, and Properties

| | |
|---|---|
| `tagname` | String variable containing the name of the tag, such as `img` |
| `cnamecopy` | String variable containing a copy of the class name |
| `arguments[1]` | JavaScript array element containing the minimum number of rows |
| `arguments[2]` | JavaScript array element containing the maximum number of rows |
| `replace()` | JavaScript Function to replace values found in a string with other values |
| `ResizeTextarea()` | Function to automatically resize a textarea as necessary |

## About the Class

This class uses the JavaScript `replace()` function on a copy of the class name, and specifies an anonymous inline function for handling the replacement. But, rather than replacing, the function only wants access to the matched string, which it receives in the array elements `arguments[1]` and `arguments[2]`. It then passes these values to the `ResizeTextarea()` function, which continuously monitors the textarea, contracting and expanding it as necessary.

## How to Use It

To use this class, set up a `<textarea>` tag with the required number of rows and columns, then place the `resizeta[]` class in the class argument and provide the minimum and

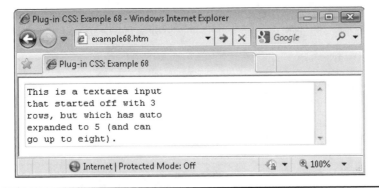

**FIGURE 8-12** A textarea that was originally three rows high has expanded to five.

maximum number of rows within the square brackets. These two values must be separated with a | symbol, which is the standard way to separate values passed in these dynamic classes. The result looks like this:

```
<textarea class='resizeta[3|8]' rows='3' cols='50'></textarea>
```

This example creates a 3-row by 50-column `<textarea>`, which can expand up to 8 and retract back to 3 rows.

### The JavaScript

```
if (classname.search(/\bresizeta\b/, 0) != -1 &&
    tagname == 'textarea')
{
    cnamecopy.replace(/resizeta\[([^\|]*)\|([^\]]*)\]/, function()
    {
        ResizeTextarea(thistag, arguments[1], arguments[2])
    } )
}
```

## PLUG-IN 69  Rotate (rotate[*n*])

This class starts to use a little meatier code. It's a more powerful version of the rotatec... and rotatea... classes from Plug-in 55 in Chapter 7, because it supports rotating an object between 1 and 359 degrees or –1 and –359 degrees.

For example, the image of the hand in Figure 8-13 has been rotated by –45, –22.5, 0, 22.5, and 45 degrees, respectively.

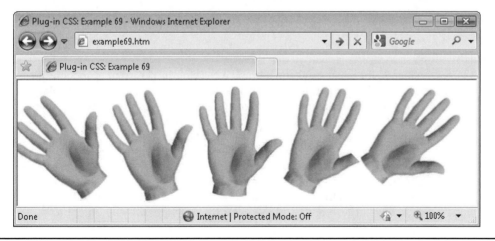

**FIGURE 8-13**  Using this class, you can rotate any object clockwise or counterclockwise, by any amount.

## Variables, Functions, and Properties

| cnamecopy | String variable copy of the class name |
|---|---|
| arguments[1] | JavaScript array element containing the amount of rotation |
| r | Array copy of the JavaScript arguments[] array, the amount by which to rotate the object |
| rad cosrad sinrad | Floating point variables used for calculating rotation values for Internet Explorer |
| w h | Integer variables containing the width and height of the object |
| REL | Global string variable containing the value "relative" |
| replace() | JavaScript function to replace values found in a string with other values |
| W() | Function to get the width of an object |
| H() | Function to get the height of an object |
| S() | Function to set the style properties of an object |
| Locate() | Function to move an object to a new location |
| MozTransform | Property for setting up a transformation on Firefox and other Mozilla-based browsers |
| WebkitTransform | Property for setting up a transformation on the Safari and Chrome browsers |
| OTransform | Property for setting up a transformation on the Opera browser |
| transform | Property for setting up a transformation on all other browsers (except IE) |
| filter | Property used by Internet Explorer for image transformations, among other features |

## About the Class

This class uses the JavaScript replace() function on a copy of the class name, and specifies an anonymous inline function for handling the replacement. However, rather than replacing, the function only wants access to the matched string, which it receives in the array element arguments[1]. If the browser is not Internet Explorer, it then passes this value to the S() function to modify the correct transform property for the browser.

If the browser is IE (determined by checking for the existence of the filter property), a series of calculations are made to determine the correct values for the matrix function IE uses to rotate an object. The matrix is then applied by assigning it to the filter property using the S() function, and then the object is moved to a relative location that will make the rotation appear to have occurred around its center (to match the way all other browsers rotate).

## How to Use It

To use this class, enter its name in the `class` argument of the object to be rotated, ensuring you pass the amount of rotation required within a pair of square brackets, like the following, which rotates the image clockwise by 17 degrees:

```
<img class='rotate[17]' src='image.jpg' />
```

Here, for example, is the HTML used to create Figure 8-13:

```
<img class='rotate[-45]'   src='hand.jpg' />
<img class='rotate[-22.5]' src='hand.jpg' />
<img                       src='hand.jpg' />
<img class='rotate[22.5]'  src='hand.jpg' />
<img class='rotate[45]'    src='hand.jpg' />
```

---

***CAUTION*** *On all recent browsers other than Internet Explorer, you can rotate any object. But because IE has to use the* `filter` *property for this effect, it will only work on images.*

## The JavaScript

```
if (classname.search(/\brotate\b/, 0) != -1)
{
    cnamecopy.replace(/rotate\[([^\]]*)\]/, function()
    {
        var r = arguments[1]

        S(thistag).MozTransform    = 'rotate(' + r + 'deg)'
        S(thistag).WebkitTransform = 'rotate(' + r + 'deg)'
        S(thistag).OTransform      = 'rotate(' + r + 'deg)'
        S(thistag).transform       = 'rotate(' + r + 'deg)'

        if (typeof S(thistag).filter != UNDEF)
        {
            var rad    = r * (Math.PI * 2 / 360)
            var cosrad = Math.cos(rad)
            var sinrad = Math.sin(rad)
            var w      = W(thistag)
            var h      = H(thistag)
            var filter = 'progid:DXImageTransform.Microsoft.' +
                'Matrix(M11=' + cosrad + ', M12=' + -sinrad    +
                ',      M21=' + sinrad + ', M22=' +  cosrad    +
                ", SizingMethod='auto expand')"

            S(thistag).filter = filter
            Locate(thistag, REL, -((W(thistag) - w) / 2),
                                 -((H(thistag) - h) / 2))
        }
    } )
}
```

**70**  ## Width (w[*n*])

Throughout this book, there have been examples where the width of an object has required changing, and this has been achieved using a `style` argument. However, with this class you can specify the width of an object as a dynamic class parameter, as shown in Figure 8-14, in which the width of the `<div>` has been set to 450 pixels.

### Variables, Functions, and Properties

| | |
|---|---|
| Cnamecopy | String variable copy of the class name |
| arguments[1] | JavaScript array element containing the new width |
| replace() | JavaScript function to replace one section of a string with another |
| S() | Function to modify a style property of an object |
| width | Property containing the width of an object |

### About the Class

This class uses the `replace()` function to pass the width from the class argument to the `S()` function in order to modify the object's width by changing the `width` property.

### How to Use It

To use this class, enter the width amount in pixels within square brackets after the class name like this, which sets the width of the `<div>` to 450 pixels:

```
<div class='w[450] yellow red_b'>Hello</div>
```

No measurements other than pixels are supported, and you must enter a number greater than 0 in the square brackets.

### The JavaScript

```
if (classname.search(/\bw\b/, 0) != -1)
{
    cnamecopy.replace(/w\[([^\]]*)\]/, function()
```

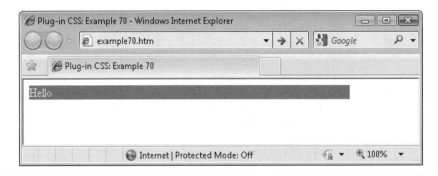

**FIGURE 8-14**    Using this class to change the width of an object

```
        {
            S(thistag).width = Px(arguments[1])
        } )
    }
```

# 71 Height (h[*n*])

With this class, you can specify the height of an object as a dynamic class parameter, as in the case of Figure 8-15, in which the example in the previous plug-in has also had its height set to 70 pixels.

## Variables, Functions, and Properties

| cnamecopy | String variable copy of the class name |
|---|---|
| arguments[1] | JavaScript array element containing the new height |
| replace() | JavaScript function to replace one section of a string with another |
| S() | Function to modify a style property of an object |
| height | Property containing the height of an object |

## About the Class

This class uses the replace() function to pass the width from the class argument to the S() function in order to modify the object's height by changing the height property.

## How to Use It

To use this class, enter the height amount in pixels within square brackets after the class name like this, which sets the height of the <div> to 70 pixels:

```
<div class='h[70] yellow red_b'>Hello</div>
```

No measurements other than pixels are supported, and you must enter a number greater than 0 in the square brackets.

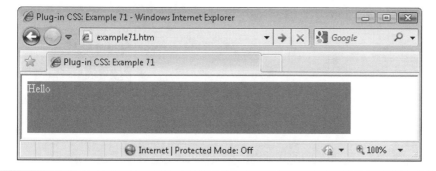

FIGURE 8-15    Using this class to change the height of an object

### The JavaScript

```
if (classname.search(/\bh\b/, 0) != -1)
{
    cnamecopy.replace(/h\[([^\]]*)\]/, function()
    {
        S(thistag).height = Px(arguments[1])
    } )
}
```

## PLUG-IN 72 X (x[*n*])

Once you free an object from the flow of a web page by giving it a position other than static (such as relative or absolute), you can move it where you like on a page (or within its containing object). Using this class, you can change an object's horizontal position on the page as shown in Figure 8-16, in which a 115 × 115–pixel object has been inset from the left of the browser by 475 pixels.

### Variables, Functions, and Properties

| cnamecopy | String variable copy of the class name |
|---|---|
| arguments[1] | JavaScript array element containing the new offset |
| replace() | JavaScript function to replace one section of a string with another |
| S() | Function to modify a style property of an object |
| left | Property containing the left offset of the object |

### About the Class

This class uses the replace() function to pass the horizontal location from the class argument to the S() function in order to modify the object's left offset by changing its left property.

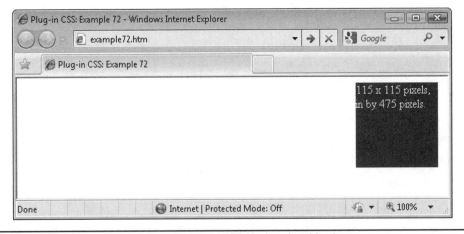

**FIGURE 8-16** The box has been inset from the left by 475 pixels using this class.

## How to Use It

To use this class, enter the left offset amount in pixels within square brackets after the class name like this, which sets the left offset of the <div> to 475 pixels (and also sets the width and height to 115 pixels each):

```
<div class='absolute w[115] h[115] x[475] yellow blue_b'>
   115 x 115 pixels, in by 475 pixels.
</div>
```

No measurements other than pixels are supported, and you must enter a number greater than 0 in the square brackets.

## The JavaScript

```
if (classname.search(/\bx\b/, 0) != -1)
{
   cnamecopy.replace(/x\[([^\]]*)\]/, function()
   {
      S(thistag).left = Px(arguments[1])
   } )
}
```

## PLUG-IN 73   Y (y[*n*])

This is the partner class for x[]; it moves an object down by the amount specified in the parameter in square brackets. Figure 8-17 shows the example from the previous plug-in, but with its vertical offset set to 53 pixels.

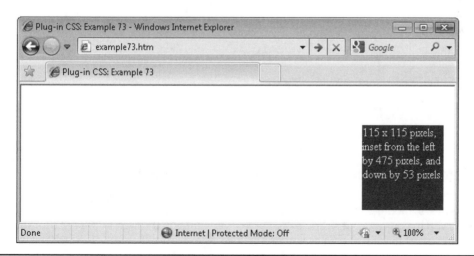

**FIGURE 8-17**   The object has now been moved down by 53 pixels.

## Variables, Functions, and Properties

| | |
|---|---|
| cnamecopy | String variable copy of the class name |
| arguments[1] | JavaScript array element containing the new offset |
| replace() | JavaScript function to replace one section of a string with another |
| S() | Function to modify a style property of an object |
| top | Property containing the top offset of the object |

## About the Class

This class uses the replace() function to pass the vertical location from the class argument to the S() function in order to modify the object's top offset by changing its top property.

## How to Use It

To use this class, enter the top offset amount in pixels within square brackets after the class name like this, which sets the top offset of the <div> to 53 pixels (and also sets the width and height to 115 pixels each and the left offset to 475 pixels):

```
<div class='absolute w[115] h[115] x[475] y[53] yellow blue_b'>
    115 x 115 pixels, inset from the left by 475 pixels, and
    down by 53 pixels.
</div>
```

No measurements other than pixels are supported, and you must enter a number greater than 0 in the square brackets.

---

***TIP***  *You can also use negative values on objects with relative position to move them both to the left and up in the browser.*

## The JavaScript

```
if (classname.search(/\by\b/, 0) != -1)
{
    cnamecopy.replace(/y\[([^\]]*)\]/, function()
    {
        S(thistag).top = Px(arguments[1])
    } )
}
```

## **74** Text Color (color[*colorname*/*#nnnnnn*/*#nnn*])

Although previous chapters have introduced a basic set of 21 color names that you can use within classes, sometimes you need much finer color control, which is what this class provides. With it, you can choose any color value from #000000 through to #ffffff (or the #000 to #fff short forms), as well as any pre-defined color names that browsers understand, such as blue, green, or violet. In Figure 8-18, six different color values have been selected using this class.

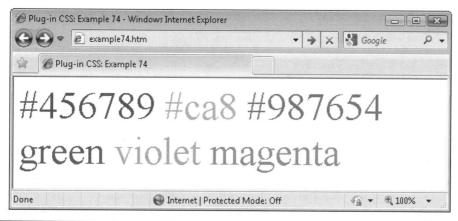

**FIGURE 8-18**   The result of using this class on six different values

## Variables, Functions, and Properties

| | |
|---|---|
| cnamecopy | String variable copy of the class name |
| arguments[1] | JavaScript array element containing the new color |
| replace() | JavaScript function to replace one section of a string with another |
| S() | Function to modify a style property of an object |
| color | Property containing the text color of an object |

## About the Class

This class uses the replace() function to pass the color value from the class argument to the S() function in order to modify the object's color by changing its color property.

## How to Use It

To use this class to change the color of some text, place it in the class argument of the containing object and enter the color value you want within a pair of square brackets following the class name, as in the following HTML, which was used for the screen grab in Figure 8-18:

```
<span class='pt40'>
   <span class='color[#456789]'>#456789</span>
   <span class='color[#ca8]    '>#ca8    </span>
   <span class='color[#987654]'>#987654</span><br />
   <span class='color[green]'  >green   </span>
   <span class='color[violet]' >violet </span>
   <span class='color[magenta] '>magenta</span>
</span>
```

### The JavaScript

```
if (classname.search(/\bcolor\b/, 0) != -1)
{
    cnamecopy.replace(/color\[([^\]]*)\]/, function()
    {
        S(thistag).color = arguments[1]
    } )
}
```

## PLUG-IN 75 Background Color (bcolor[#nnnnnn])

This class provides the same functionality as the `color[]` class, except for changing the background color of an object, as shown in Figure 8-19, in which the same six color values from the previous example have now been applied to the background properties of the objects.

### Variables, Functions, and Properties

| cnamecopy | String variable copy of the class name |
|---|---|
| arguments[1] | JavaScript array element containing the new color |
| replace() | JavaScript function to replace one section of a string with another |
| S() | Function to modify a style property of an object |
| backgroundColor | Property containing the background color of an object |

### About the Class

This class uses the `replace()` function to pass the color value from the class argument to the `S()` function in order to modify the object's background color by changing its `backgroundColor` property.

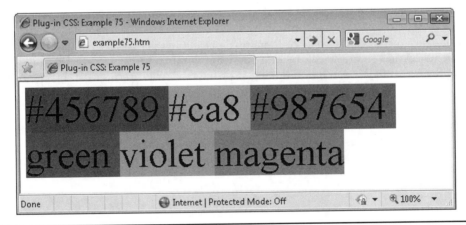

FIGURE 8-19   This class lets you change the background of any object to any color.

## How to Use It

To use this class to change the background color of some text, place it in the `class` argument
of the containing object and enter the color value you want within a pair of square brackets
following the class name, as in the following HTML, which was used for the screen grab in
Figure 8-19:

```
<span class='pt40'>
   <span class='bcolor[#456789]'>#456789 </span>
   <span class='bcolor[#ca8]'    >#ca8     </span>
   <span class='bcolor[#987654]'>#987654 </span><br />
   <span class='bcolor[green]'  >green   </span>
   <span class='bcolor[violet]' >violet  </span>
   <span class='bcolor[magenta]'>magenta </span>
</span>
```

## The JavaScript

```
if (classname.search(/\bbcolor\b/, 0) != -1)
{
   cnamecopy.replace(/bcolor\[([^\]]*)\]/, function()
   {
      S(thistag).backgroundColor = arguments[1]
   } )
}
```

# CHAPTER 9

## Dynamic Text and Typography

This chapter explores a range of dynamic classes for enhancing the way you use text in a web page, including a typewriter or teletype effect, a way of cleaning up strings by removing unwanted characters and whitespace, automatically loading Google fonts in from the Google servers when you reference them, vertically aligning text within an object, and creating glow effects by cycling the foreground and background colors of objects.

## PLUG-IN 76 Typetext (typetext[*n*])

Plug-in 76 displays the contents of an object as if it is being typed out on a typewriter or teletype machine. The class also takes a parameter specifying the duration of the animation so you can specify the exact time you require.

For example, in Figure 9-1 the poem "The Tyger" by William Blake is being typed to the screen over the course of 60 seconds.

### Variables, Functions, and Properties

| Cnamecopy | String variable copy of the class name |
|-----------|----------------------------------------|
| arguments[1] | JavaScript array element containing the animation duration |
| replace() | JavaScript function to replace one section of a string with another |
| TextType() | Function to modify a style property of an object |

### About the Class

This class removes the contents of the object it applies to and then replaces it over a time duration passed to it.

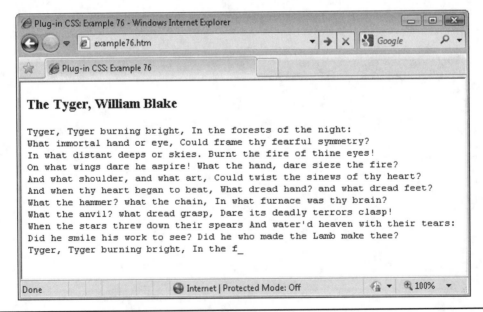

**FIGURE 9-1** Displaying a poem like a typewriter using this plug-in

## How to Use It

To use this class, enter its name into the `class` argument of the containing object, along with the animation duration within square brackets, as with the following example, which was used for the screen grab in Figure 9-1:

```
<pre><div class='typetext[60000]'>
Tyger, Tyger burning bright, In the forests of the night:
What immortal hand or eye, Could frame thy fearful symmetry?
In what distant deeps or skies. Burnt the fire of thine eyes!
On what wings dare he aspire! What the hand, dare sieze the fire?

And what shoulder, and what art, Could twist the sinews of thy heart?
And when thy heart began to beat, What dread hand? and what dread feet?
What the hammer? what the chain, In what furnace was thy brain?
What the anvil? what dread grasp, Dare its deadly terrors clasp!

When the stars threw down their spears And water'd heaven with their ears:
Did he smile his work to see? Did he who made the Lamb make thee?
Tyger, Tyger burning bright, In the forests of the night:
What immortal hand or eye, Dare frame thy fearful symmetry?</div></pre>
```

## The JavaScript

```
if (classname.search(/\btypetext\b/, 0) != -1)
{
    cnamecopy.replace(/typetext\[([^\]]*)\]/, function()
    {
        TextType(thistag, 1, arguments[1])
    } )
}
```

## PLUG-IN 77    Digits Only (digitsonly)

Plug-in 77 removes any characters from an input field that are not digits or whitespace. For example, in Figure 9-2 the user has been asked for their credit card number and has also entered some irrelevant text.

**FIGURE 9-2**    The user has input more than just a card number.

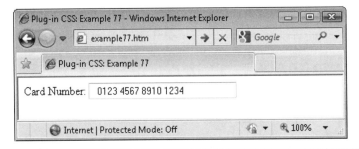

FIGURE 9-3   The unwanted characters have now been removed.

But in Figure 9-3, as soon as the user moves the mouse away, all the erroneous characters are automatically removed, leaving behind only the numbers and whitespace.

## Variables, Functions, and Properties

| onchange | JavaScript event that triggers when the contents of a field changes |
|---|---|
| onmouseout | JavaScript event that triggers when the mouse moves away from an object |
| onsubmit | JavaScript event that triggers when a form is submitted |
| CleanupString() | Function to clean up a string in a variety of different ways |
| this.value | Property containing the contents of the input field |

## About the Class

This class is triggered whenever the mouse moves out of the object employing it, at which point it calls the CleanupString() function (from the *PJ.js* library) to strip out all characters that are not digits or whitespace.

## How to Use It

When you want to ensure that an input field contains only digits or whitespace, place this class name in the class argument of the element, like this:

```
<input name='creditcard' class='digitsonly' size='30' />
```

The field will be automatically cleaned up for you with no further effort on your part.

## The JavaScript

```
if (classname.search(/\bdigitsonly\b/, 0) != -1)
{
    thistag.onchange = thistag.onmouseout =
        thistag.onsubmit = function()
    {
        this.value = CleanupString(this.value, 0, 0, 1, 1)
    }
}
```

## Text Only (textonly)

Plug-in 78 is similar to the previous one in that it removes all characters that are not text or whitespace from an input field. For example, in Figure 9-4 the user has entered some numbers into the field, which are not allowed.

However, in Figure 9-5 only the text and whitespace remain once the mouse is moved out of the field.

### Variables, Functions, and Properties

| | |
|---|---|
| onchange | JavaScript event that triggers when the contents of a field change |
| onmouseout | JavaScript event that triggers when the mouse moves away from an object |
| onsubmit | JavaScript event that triggers when a form is submitted |
| CleanupString() | Function to clean up a string in a variety of different ways |
| this.value | Property containing the contents of the input field |

### About the Class

This class is triggered whenever the mouse moves out of the object employing it, at which point it calls the CleanupString() function to strip out all characters that are not text or whitespace.

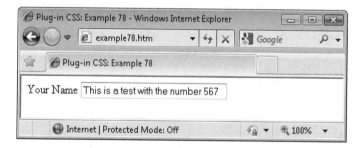

FIGURE 9-4    The user has entered numbers, which are not allowed.

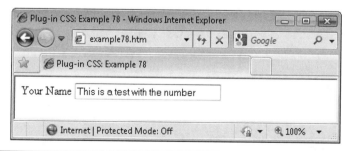

FIGURE 9-5    The field has been cleaned up by removing the numbers.

## How to Use It

When you want to ensure that an input field contains only text or whitespace, place this class name in the `class` argument of the element, like this:

```
<input name='name' class='textonly' size='30' />
```

The field will be automatically cleaned up for you with no further effort on your part.

## The JavaScript

```
if (classname.search(/\btextonly\b/, 0) != -1)
{
    thistag.onchange = thistag.onmouseout =
        thistag.onsubmit = function()
    {
        this.value = CleanupString(this.value, 1, 1, 0, 1)
    }
}
```

# 79 No Spaces (nospaces)

**PLUG-IN**

With Plug-in 79, you can remove all the spaces from an input field. It is probably most useful for stripping spaces out of credit card numbers. For example, how often have you entered your credit card online only to have a form re-presented to you advising that the input was invalid because spaces are not allowed? It's certainly happened a few times to me, and it's so unnecessary because it's an easy problem to fix on behalf of the user. For example, in Figure 9-6 a credit card number has been entered with spaces.

However, once the user moves the mouse away, clicks into another field, or submits the form, the whitespace is removed (see Figure 9-7).

## Variables, Functions, and Properties

| onchange | JavaScript event that triggers when the contents of a field change |
| onmouseout | JavaScript event that triggers when the mouse moves away from an object |
| onsubmit | JavaScript event that triggers when a form is submitted |
| CleanupString() | Function to clean up a string in a variety of different ways |
| this.value | Property containing the contents of the input field |

**FIGURE 9-6**   A credit card number containing spaces has been entered.

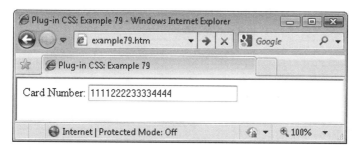

**FIGURE 9-7**   Now the spaces have been automatically removed.

## About the Class

This class is triggered whenever the mouse moves out of the object employing it, at which point it calls the `CleanupString()` function to strip out all whitespace from it.

## How to Use It

To remove the whitespace from a field, place this class name in the `class` argument of the element, as in the following example, in which both the `digitsonly` and `nospaces` classes have been used (they generally go well together when used for inputting credit card details):

```
<input name='creditcard' class='digitsonly nospaces' size='30'/>
```

The field will be automatically cleaned up for you by removing all non-digits and all whitespace.

## The JavaScript

```
if (classname.search(/\bnospaces\b/, 0) != -1)
{
    thistag.onchange = thistag.onmouseout =
        thistag.onsubmit = function()
    {
        this.value = CleanupString(this.value, 1)
    }
}
```

## No Punctuation (nopunct)

Sometimes you want just the bare text to be posted to a web form, and not any punctuation like exclamation points and question marks. You can do this easily with Plug-in 80, which strips them all out for you.

For example, in Figure 9-8 the user is being prompted for a reminder phrase that will be used to prompt them if they forget their password.

FIGURE 9-8   This input contains several punctuation characters.

But in Figure 9-9 the user has moved the mouse away and so the punctuation has been automatically filtered out.

## Variables, Functions, and Properties

| onchange | JavaScript event that triggers when the contents of a field change |
| onmouseout | JavaScript event that triggers when the mouse moves away from an object |
| onsubmit | JavaScript event that triggers when a form is submitted |
| CleanupString() | Function to clean up a string in a variety of different ways |
| this.value | Property containing the contents of the input field |

## About the Class

This class is triggered whenever the mouse moves out of the object employing it, at which point it calls the CleanupString() function to strip out all punctuation characters from it.

## How to Use It

To remove the punctuation characters from a field, place this class name in the class argument of the element, as in the following example:

```
<input name='reminder' class='nopunct' size='30'/>
```

The field will be automatically cleaned up for you by removing all the punctuation.

FIGURE 9-9   The punctuation has now been removed.

## The JavaScript

```
if (classname.search(/\bnopunct\b/, 0) != -1)
{
   thistag.onchange = thistag.onmouseout =
      thistag.onsubmit = function()
   {
      this.value = CleanupString(this.value, 0, 0, 0, 1)
   }
}
```

## Minimum Whitespace (minwhitespace)

Using Plug-in 81, you can remove all the additional whitespace characters users sometimes enter, replacing any groups of more than one whitespace character with a single space.

For example, in Figure 9-10 a `<textarea>` has been created in which a user is entering their bio, with a somewhat messy use of whitespace.

However, after passing the mouse away, the extra whitespace is removed, leaving a much better formatted text (see Figure 9-11).

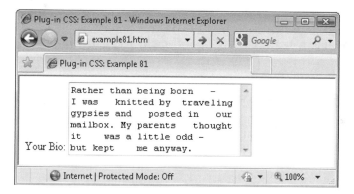

**Figure 9-10**   This <textarea> contains a lot of unnecessary whitespace.

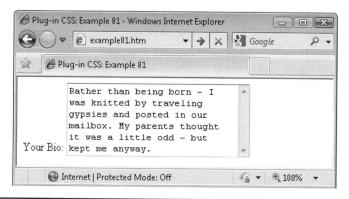

**Figure 9-11**   Now the text has been stripped of unnecessary extra whitespace.

## Variables, Functions, and Properties

| onchange | JavaScript event that triggers when the contents of a field change |
|---|---|
| onmouseout | JavaScript event that triggers when the mouse moves away from an object |
| onsubmit | JavaScript event that triggers when a form is submitted |
| CleanupString() | Function to clean up a string in a variety of different ways |
| this.value | Property containing the contents of the input field |

### About the Class

This class is triggered whenever the mouse moves out of the object employing it, at which point it calls the CleanupString() function to strip out all extra whitespace characters from it.

### How to Use It

To remove the extra whitespace from a field, place this class name in the class argument of the element, as in the following example:

```
<textarea class='minwhitespace' rows='6' cols='30'></textarea>
```

The field will be automatically cleaned up for you by removing all the extra whitespace.

### The JavaScript

```
if (classname.search(/\bminwhitespace\b/, 0) != -1)
{
    thistag.onchange = thistag.onmouseout =
        thistag.onsubmit = function()
    {
        this.value = CleanupString(this.value, 0, 0, 0, 0, 0, 0, 1)
    }
}
```

## PLUG-IN 82 Google Font (gfont[*n*])

In Plug-in 28 of Chapter 4, you saw how to incorporate Google fonts into your web pages. Unfortunately, you have to fiddle around with it a bit since you must add a <link rel...> tag for every font you include. But using this class, you simply mention a Google font by name, and if it hasn't been loaded in yet, it is fetched automatically for you.

Figure 9-12 is similar to Figure 4-9 but was achieved using this plug-in, and without having to manually load in all the fonts.

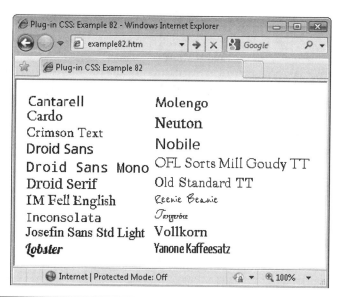

**FIGURE 9-12**   This class makes using Google fonts even easier.

## Variables, Functions, and Properties

| | |
|---|---|
| `arguments[1]` | JavaScript array element containing the font name to use |
| `font` | String variable containing the full font name |
| `window[font]` | Array attached to the window object instead of using a global array, containing the value true if a Google font is already due to be loaded |
| `gfonts` | Local array containing the Google fonts to be loaded |
| `gfindex` | Integer variable containing the number of Google fonts to load |
| `index` | Integer variable used for iterating through an array |
| `newcss` | Object containing a new style sheet to append to the DOM |
| `index` | Integer variable used for iterating through an array |
| `Index` | Integer variable used for iterating through an array |
| `replace()` | JavaScript function to replace a section of one string with another |
| `createElement()` | JavaScript function to create a new element object |
| `setAttribute()` | JavaScript function to set an attribute of an object |
| `appendChild( ()` | JavaScript function to add a new element to the DOM |
| `fontFamily` | Property containing the font family of an object |
| `window.opera` | Property only set in the Opera browser; used for determining whether the browser requires a redraw |
| `document.body. style` | Property that, if changed, forces a browser redraw in Opera |

## About the Class

This is a very easy class to use but a little complicated to explain. If you are interested only in how you can use it, then skip to the next section.

This class works by making a note of every `class` argument you use that mentions the `gfont[]` class name. Then, if the font required has not been marked to be fetched from Google's servers, the full font name is added to the `gfonts[]` array, and the `fontFamily` property is set to the font to use.

Later on, the fonts are all loaded in from Google's servers, but only after all the dynamic functions have been processed. This is because the act of loading in the new style sheets changes the document object model (DOM) by adding new elements to it which, if done before the HTML processing is complete, would corrupt the array of elements to be processed each time a new font is fetched.

## How to Use It

To use this class to access Google's fonts, just mention it in a `class` argument, supplying the shorthand name of the font from Table 9-1 in the following square brackets, like this:

```
<div class='gfont[crimson]'>Crimson Text</div>
```

| Shorthand | Font Name |
|---|---|
| cantarell | Cantarell |
| cardo | Cardo |
| crimson | Crimson Text |
| droidsans | Droid Sans |
| droidsansm | Droid Sans Mono |
| droidserif | Droid Serif |
| imfell | IM Fell English |
| inconsolata | Inconsolata |
| josefin | Josefin Sans Std Light |
| lobster | Lobster |
| molengo | Molengo |
| neuton | Neuton |
| nobile | Nobile |
| oflsorts | OFL Sorts Mill Goudy TT |
| oldstandard | Old Standard TT |
| reenie | Reenie Beanie |
| tangerine | Tangerine |
| vollkorn | Vollkorn |
| yanone | Yanone Kaffeesatz |

TABLE 9-1    The Google Font Families and Shorthand Class Argument Names

### About the JavaScript

Once all the dynamic classes used in a web page have been processed, the following JavaScript code is run to load in all the Google fonts from Google's servers that were accessed in the page:

```
for (index = 0 ; index < gfindex ; ++index)
{
   var newcss = document.createElement('link')
   newcss.setAttribute('href',  gfurl + escape(gfonts[index]))
   newcss.setAttribute('rel',  'stylesheet')
   newcss.setAttribute('type', 'text/css')
   document.getElementsByTagName('head')[0].appendChild(newcss)
}
```

With the fonts loaded, all browsers that support these fonts will be displaying them, with the exception of Opera, which requires a nudge to redraw the browser, like this:

```
if (gfindex && window.opera) setTimeout(function()
   { document.body.style += "" }, 1)
```

Following is the code used in the main section of JavaScript to process just the gfont[] class.

## The JavaScript

```
if (classname.search(/\bgfont\b/, 0) != -1)
{
   cnamecopy.replace(/gfont\[([^\]]*)\]/, function()
   {
      switch(arguments[1])
      {
         case 'cantarell'  : font = 'Cantarell'; break
         case 'cardo'      : font = 'Cardo'; break
         case 'crimson'    : font = 'Crimson Text'; break
         case 'droidsans'  : font = 'Droid Sans'; break
         case 'droidsansm' : font = 'Droid Sans Mono'; break
         case 'droidserif' : font = 'Droid Serif'; break
         case 'imfell'     : font = 'IM Fell English'; break
         case 'inconsolata': font = 'Inconsolata'; break
         case 'josefin'    : font = 'Josefin Sans Std Light'; break
         case 'lobster'    : font = 'Lobster'; break
         case 'molengo'    : font = 'Molengo'; break
         case 'neuton'     : font = 'Neuton'; break
         case 'nobile'     : font = 'Nobile'; break
         case 'oflsorts'   : font = 'OFL Sorts Mill Goudy TT'; break
         case 'oldstandard': font = 'Old Standard TT'; break
         case 'reenie'     : font = 'Reenie Beanie'; break
         case 'tangerine'  : font = 'Tangerine'; break
         case 'vollkorn'   : font = 'Vollkorn'; break
         case 'yanone'     : font = 'Yanone Kaffeesatz'; break
      }
```

```
    if (!window[font])
    {
       window[font]    = true
       gfonts[gfindex++] = font
    }

    S(thistag).fontFamily = font

    if (window.opera) setTimeout(function() // Required by Opera
       { document.body.style += "" }, 1)    // to redraw window
  } )
}
```

## PLUG-IN 83 Text Middle (textmiddle)

Plug-in 83 vertically centers text using the trick of setting the CSS line-height property to that of the containing object. This is easy enough to do in your CSS on a single-element basis, but because exact heights must be entered, this class is superior since it does the calculation for you.

For example, the <div> in Figure 9-13 has been set to 100 pixels in height, and the text within it has been vertically centered using this plug-in.

### Variables, Functions, and Properties

| Px()       | Function to add the suffix px to a string          |
|------------|----------------------------------------------------|
| lineHeight | Property containing the line height of the object  |

### About the Class

This class looks up the height of the object and then sets the line height of its contents to the same as the object height, which has the effect of vertically centering the text.

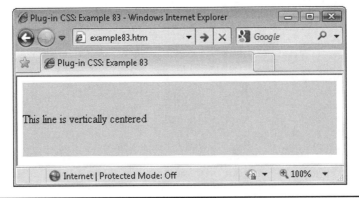

**FIGURE 9-13**    The text within the object has been vertically centered.

## How to Use It

To vertically center text within an object, mention this class in its `class` argument like in this example, which first sets the object height to 100 pixels, and the background to aqua, so you can clearly see the effect:

```
<div class='h[100] textmiddle aqua_b'>
   This line is vertically centered
</div>
```

## The JavaScript

```
if (classname.search(/\btextmiddle\b/, 0) != -1)
{
   S(thistag).lineHeight = Px(H(thistag))
}
```

# 84 Text Glow (textglow[#nnnnnn|#nnnnnn|n])

Plug-in 84 cycles between two colors over a time period you specify, providing a glowing effect. For example, in Figure 9-14 the text has been set to cycle through from yellow to red over the course of a second, and then back again, and so on.

## Variables, Functions, and Properties

| cnamecopy | String variable copy of the class name |
|---|---|
| arguments[1] | JavaScript array element containing the first color |
| arguments[2] | JavaScript array element containing the second color |
| arguments[3] | JavaScript array element containing the animation duration |
| replace() | JavaScript function to replace one section of a string with another |
| ColorFade() | Function to constantly fade between two colors |

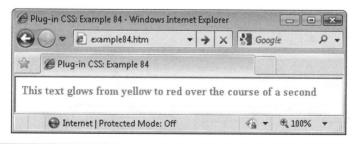

**FIGURE 9-14**   You can create a text glow effect with this class.

## About the Class

This class calls the `ColorFade()` function (from the *PJ.js* file) to constantly fade between two text colors. It uses the JavaScript `replace()` function to capture the values passed with the class, and then supplies them to `ColorFade()` via the `arguments[]` array.

## How to Use It

To use this class, you must specify two six-digit hex color numbers, prefaced by # symbols, as well as a duration for the animation in milliseconds. These parameters should be separated by | symbols and placed within square brackets following the class name that is passed in a `class` argument, like this:

```
<div class='textglow[#ffff00|#ff0000|1000] b'>
   This text cycles from yellow to red over the course of a second
</div>
```

This example cycles between the colors yellow and red over the course of a second (1000 milliseconds), and then back over the same duration, at which point the animation begins again.

## The JavaScript

```
if (classname.search(/\btextglow\b/, 0) != -1)
{
    cnamecopy.replace(/textglow\[([^\|]*)\|([^\|]*)\|([^\]]*)\]/,
        function()
    {
        ColorFade(thistag, arguments[1], arguments[2], 'text',
            arguments[3])
    } )
}
```

## Background Glow (backglow[*#nnnnnn*| *#nnnnnn*| *n*])

Plug-in 85 is similar to the previous one, but it provides a glow effect to the background color property of an object, as shown in Figure 9-15. This is the same as the previous example, except that a background glow from lime green to blue over 1.5 seconds has been added.

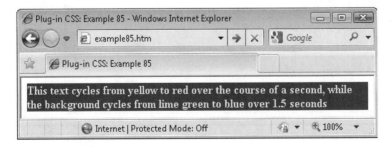

**FIGURE 9-15**   Combining background and foreground color glows

## Variables, Functions, and Properties

| | |
|---|---|
| `cnamecopy` | String variable copy of the class name |
| `arguments[1]` | JavaScript array element containing the first color |
| `arguments[2]` | JavaScript array element containing the second color |
| `arguments[3]` | JavaScript array element containing the animation duration |
| `replace()` | JavaScript function to replace one section of a string with another |
| `ColorFade()` | Function to constantly fade between two colors |

## About the Class

This class calls the `ColorFade()` function with slightly different arguments to constantly fade between two background colors. It uses the JavaScript `replace()` function to capture the values passed with the class, and then supplies them to `ColorFade()` via the `arguments[]` array.

## How to Use It

To use this class, you must specify two six-digit hex color numbers, prefaced by # symbols, as well as a duration for the animation in milliseconds. These parameters should be separated by | symbols and placed within square brackets following the class name passed in a class argument, like this:

```
<div class='textglow[#ffff00|#ff0000|1000] b
   backglow[#00ff00|#0000ff|1500] b'>
   This text cycles from yellow to red over the course of a
   second, while the background cycles from lime green to blue
   over 1.5 seconds
</div>
```

This example cycles between the text colors yellow and red over the course of a second (1000 milliseconds), and then back over the same duration, at which point the animation begins again. At the same time, the background color cycles from lime green to blue over 1.5 seconds, and back again, and so on.

---

**CAUTION**  *Due to the way the two color glow functions operate, they require six-digit hex color values, and will not accept three-digit or name color values.*

## The JavaScript

```
if (classname.search(/\bbackglow\b/, 0) != -1)
{
   cnamecopy.replace(/backglow\[([^\|]*)\|([^\|]*)\|([^\]]*)\]/,
      function()
   {
      ColorFade(thistag, arguments[1], arguments[2], '',
         arguments[3])
   } )
}
```

# CHAPTER 10

## Dynamic Interaction

The classes in this chapter are designed to offer features that could only otherwise be created using JavaScript. For example, both the HTML5 `placeholder` and `autofocus` attributes have been emulated as dynamic classes, so you can now offer these features on most JavaScript-enabled browsers.

Also, there is a powerful system for adding citations to a web page, and automatically creating a list of them all at the article end, giving you the ability to use names to refer to objects, which are then automatically converted into numbers you can use to create labels or captions such as Figure 1, Table 3, and so on. During this, the numbering is kept consistent even if you move the referenced objects about on the page.

Finally, there's a simple class for preventing casual users from trying to copy and paste the contents of your web page.

## Placeholder (placeholder[*prompt*])

Plug-in 86 provides similar functionality to the HTML5 placeholder attribute for input fields. With it, you can specify default text you would like to appear in a field that has no input— for use as a prompt for the user—as shown in Figure 10-1.

In Figure 10-2, once the user starts entering data into the field, the placeholder is forgotten and will not reappear unless the data entered is deleted by the user.

**Figure 10-1**    A placeholder prompt is displayed in an empty field.

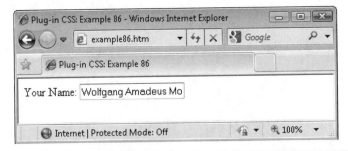

**Figure 10-2**    The placeholder prompt is removed when data is entered into the field.

## Variables, Functions, and Properties

| | |
|---|---|
| `tagname` | String variable containing the name of the current tag, such as `input` |
| `origcname` | String variable containing an exact copy of the class name before the class name is converted to lowercase |
| `arguments[1]` | JavaScript array element containing the placeholder text |
| `replace()` | JavaScript function to replace a section of text in a string with another |
| `FieldPrompt()` | Function (from *PJ.js*) to activate a placeholder in a field |
| `placeholder` | HTML 5 Property containing any placeholder text |

## About the Class

This class uses the `replace()` function to pass the argument containing the placeholder text to the `FieldPrompt()` function, via the `arguments[]` array. The `origcname` string variable is used for the `replace()` function, rather than the usual `cnamecopy` string, since it retains any uppercase characters that should be used in the placeholder. But before applying the placeholder text to a field, it checks whether the browser already has an HTML5 placeholder value set, and if so, it does nothing, allowing that to override this class.

## How to Use It

To insert a placeholder prompt in a field, place the prompt text within square brackets following the class name, in the `class` argument of an object, like this:

```
<input type='text' name='name' class='placeholder[Enter your name]' />
```

## The JavaScript

```
if (classname.search(/\bplaceholder\b/, 0) != -1 &&
   tagname == 'input')
{
   origcname.replace(/placeholder\[([^\]]*)\]/, function()
   {
      if (thistag.placeholder == '' ||
         typeof thistag.placeholder == UNDEF)
         FieldPrompt(thistag, arguments[1])
   } )
}
```

## 87 Autofocus (autofocus)

With Plug-in 87, you can specify which object should have focus when a page loads, in the same way that *google.com*, for example, automatically places the input cursor into the search field so it's ready for you to enter your search term.

In Figure 10-3, normally no field would have focus on page load, but by using this class the input field has been focused, and the text cursor is now displaying within it.

FIGURE 10-3    Use this class to give focus to any object you choose.

## Variables, Functions, and Properties

| `tagname` | Variable containing the tag name, such as `input` |
|---|---|
| `tagtype` | Variable containing the type of a tag, such as `hidden` |
| `focus()` | JavaScript function to provide focus to an object |

### About the Class

This class checks whether the tag name is one of `input`, `select`, `textarea`, or `button`, and proceeds only if it is. Next it checks whether the tag type has the value `hidden`, and if so, it then uses the `focus()` function to give the tag focus.

### How to Use It

To use this class, enter its name into the `class` argument of any `<input>`, `<select>`, `<textarea>`, or `<button>` object, like this:

```
<input type='text' name='name' class='autofocus' />
```

### The JavaScript

```
if (classname.search(/\bautofocus\b/, 0) != -1 &&
    tagname == 'input'    || tagname == 'select' ||
    tagname == 'textarea' || tagname == 'button')
{
    if (tagtype != 'hidden') thistag.focus()
}
```

## PLUG-IN 88 Cite (cite[*citation*])

Using Plug-in 88, you can easily add citations as you compile an article, which will then be automatically numbered, hyperlinked in superscript text, and referenced at the end of the article. For example, Figure 10-4 features a short biography of Sir Timothy Berners-Lee (inventor of the World Wide Web) that incorporates two references to articles on other sites, which have been marked as they occur in the text and detailed at the article end.

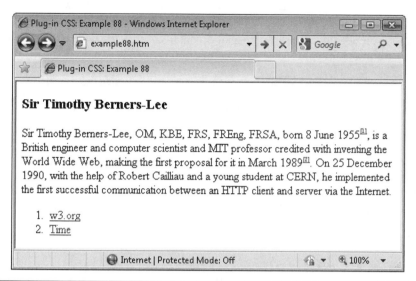

**FIGURE 10-4**    This class makes handling citations extremely easy.

## Variables, Functions, and Properties

| | |
|---|---|
| origcname | String variable containing an exact copy of the class name before the class name is converted to lowercase |
| arguments[1] | JavaScript array element containing the citation details |
| Cites[] | Array containing the list of citation details |
| cindex | Integer variable containing the number of citations |
| replace() | JavaScript Function to replace a section of text in a string with another |
| Html() | Function (from *PJ.js*) to read or write the HTML contents of an object |
| InsVars() | Function (from *PJ.js*) for inserting one or more values into a string |
| verticalAlign | Property containing the vertical alignment of an object |
| textDecoration | Property containing the text decoration of an object, such as underline |
| fontSize | Property containing the font size of an object |

## About the Class

This class makes a note of all cite[] class references as they occur and places the citation details from each into the array cites[]. A superscript link is then made to the list of citations, which will appear once all have been processed. Using these links, you can jump directly to the matching citation later in the web page.

## How to Use It

To use this class, you need to include some citation details within the square brackets of a `cite[]` class argument, like this:

```
Global warming may be increasing<span class='cite[Wikipedia]'></span>.
```

Or you can include a link within the citation details if you prefer, like this:

```
Global warming may be increasing<span class="cite[<a href='
http://en.wikipedia.org/wiki/Global_warming'>Wikipedia</a>]"></span>.
```

In this case, the `class` argument is enclosed in double quotation marks so that the URL within it can be placed in single quotation marks.

Once you have placed all your citations in the article text, you must then place an object with the ID name of `citations` somewhere on your web page, which will then be used for placing the citation details in once they have all been processed, like this:

```
<div id='citations'></div>
```

To see this work in practice, here is the HTML used for Figure 10-4:

```
<h3>Sir Timothy Berners-Lee</h3>

Sir Timothy Berners-Lee, OM, KBE, FRS, FREng, FRSA, born 8 June 1955<span
class="cite[<a href='http://www.w3.org/People/Berners-Lee/Longer.html'>
w3.org</a>]"></span>, is a British engineer and computer scientist and
MIT professor credited with inventing the World Wide Web, making the
first proposal for it in March 1989<span class="cite[<a href='http://205.
188.238.181/time/time100/scientist/profile/bernerslee.html'>Time</a>]">
</span>. On 25 December 1990, with the help of Robert Cailliau and a
young student at CERN, he implemented the first successful communication
between an HTTP client and server via the Internet.

<div id='citations'</div>
```

### The JavaScript that Creates the Citation List

If you are interested in how this works, the following code runs after all the dynamic classes in a web page have been processed, but only if `cindex` has a value greater than 0 (indicating there is at least one citation):

```
if (cindex > 0)
{
   var html = '<ol>'

   for (index = 0 ; index < cindex ; ++index)
      html += InsVars('<a name=cite#1></a><li>#2</li>',
         index + 1, cites[index])

   if (typeof O('citations') != UNDEF) Html('citations', html + '</ol>')
}
```

It then creates an unordered list and iterates through the cites[] array extracting all the citations into the object that has been given the ID of citations (if it exists).

The code that first processes the cite[] class is shown next.

## The JavaScript

```
if (classname.search(/\bcite\b/, 0) != -1)
{
    cnamecopy.replace(/cite\[(([^\]]*)\]/, function()
    {
        cites[cindex++]           = arguments[1]
        S(thistag).verticalAlign   = 'super'
        S(thistag).textDecoration  = 'none'
        S(thistag).fontSize        = '50%'

        Html(thistag, Html(thistag) +
            InsVars("<a href='#cite#1'>[#1]</a>", cindex))
    } )
}
```

---

**PLUG-IN 89**

# Reference (ref[*type* | *name*])

Using Plug-in 89, you can refer to sections of an article by special names, and when the article is viewed by a user, all the references are changed to numbers, in the same way that figures in this chapter have numbers that run in order to easily identify them. This means you can relocate the references and sections to which they refer within an article without worrying about having to renumber them all.

For example, in Figure 10-5 there are two figures and one section that are referenced by the main text. Even though these objects do not appear in the same order in which they are referred, they have been given identifying numbers in the correct sequence.

**FIGURE 10-5**
This class keeps track of referenced objects, renumbering them for you.

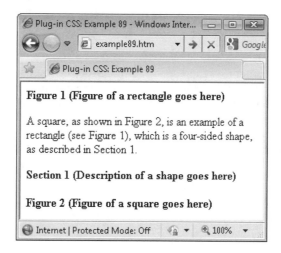

## Variables, Functions, and Properties

| | |
|---|---|
| cnamecopy | String variable containing a copy of the class name |
| arguments[1] | JavaScript array element containing the reference object type |
| arguments[2] | JavaScript array element containing the reference object name |
| a1<br>a2 | Variable copies of arguments[1] and arguments[2] used as shorthand to simplify the code |
| refers[] | Array containing all the references |
| replace() | JavaScript function to replace a section of text in a string with another |
| Html() | Function (from *PJ.js*) to read or write the HTML contents of an object |

## About the Class

This class takes an object type and an object name and then keeps track of where these are used throughout a web page. They are then given numerical values according to the order in which they are encountered, such that (for example) the first figure object is given the value 1, the second is given the value 2, and so on.

## How to Use It

To use this class, you must give every object you reference a unique name, so that whenever it is mentioned, the correct number can be placed with it. You also need to specify the type of each object so you can, for instance, have figures and tables, and as many other object types as you need.

So, for example, to announce that an object is a figure, you might use code such as this:

```
<b>Figure <span class='ref[fig|uniquename]'></span><br />
<img src='animage.jpg' />
```

In this case, the unique name is uniquename, and the object type is fig. To now reference this figure from anywhere in the web page, you would use code such as this:

```
(see Figure <span class='ref[fig|uniquename]'></span>)
```

Leave the contents of the <span> (or other object you use) empty because the class will place the number to display inside it, overwriting anything already there.

Once you have done this, you can move the figure and any references to it to any other places in the article and they will still correctly reference each other—and, if necessary, they will be renumbered should the figure be moved before or after another figure.

Here's another example that uses this class, and which creates the result seen in Figure 10-5:

```
<b>Figure <span class='ref[fig|rect]'></span>
(Figure of a rectangle goes here)</b>
```

```
<p>A square, as shown in Figure <span class='ref[fig|square]'></span>,
is an example of a rectangle (see Figure <span class='ref[fig|rect]'>
</span>), which is a four-sided shape, as described in Section <span
class='ref[sec|shape]'></span>.</p>

<b>Section <span class='ref[sec|shape]'></span>
(Description of a shape goes here)</b><br /><br />

<b>Figure <span class='ref[fig|square]'></span>
(Figure of a square goes here)</b>
```

I have highlighted the references in bold so you can quickly see them. Three objects in total are referenced:

- fig|rect
- fig|square
- sec|shape

Two of the objects are of type fig and the other is of type sec. What the class does is allocate the fig object numbers in the order in which they first appear in the document (and would do the same for the sec objects, except there is only one).

Therefore, if fig|square is encountered first, it will become Figure 1, but if fig|rect is the first one found, then *it* will be Figure 1. This means that all the objects will always be ordered correctly according to where they appear in an article (no matter where you move them to), making it easy for your readers to locate them.

## The JavaScript

```
if (classname.search(/\bref\b/, 0) != -1)
{
   cnamecopy.replace(/ref\[([^\|]*)\|([^\]]*)\]/, function()
   {
      var a1 = arguments[1]
      var a2 = arguments[2]

      if (typeof refers[a1] == UNDEF)
      {
         refers[a1]            = Array()
         refers[a1]['count'] = 1
         refers[a1][a2]       = 1
      }
      else if (typeof refers[a1][a2] == UNDEF)
         refers[a1][a2] = ++refers[a1]['count']

      Html(thistag, refers[a1][a2])
   } )
}
```

# 90 No Copy (nocopy)

Sometimes you want to prevent idle copying and pasting of your work, or simply wish to prevent the ugly effect that a highlighted section of text might have on your design. You can do so using Plug-in 90, as shown in Figure 10-6, in which the first section of text can be copied, but the second cannot.

## Variables, Functions, and Properties

| PreventAction() | Function (from *PJ.js*) to prevent drag and copy actions |
|---|---|

## About the Class

This class prevents the use of drag and drop on an object. It works well on most browsers but there is a bug in Internet Explorer in which you can commence a drag operation outside of an object that uses this class and the browser will allow you to continue the drag into it. But IE does correctly prevent starting a drag operation from within objects using this class.

## How to Use It

To prevent an object from allowing drag-and-copy operations, mention this class name in the object's class argument, like this:

```
<p class='nocopy'>This text is uncopyable</p>
```

However, due to the Internet Explorer bug, you will have the best results if you attach this class to the <body> section of a web page, like this (so that nothing on a web page can be copied):

```
<body class='nocopy'>
    ... Your web page contents
</body>
```

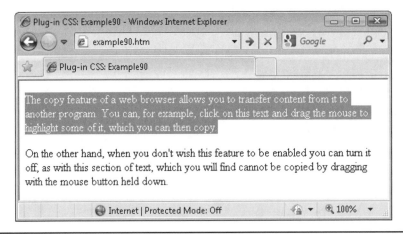

FIGURE 10-6    Prevent sections of text from being copied with this plug-in.

Here is the HTML used for Figure 10-6:

```
<p>The copy feature of a web browser allows you to transfer content from
it to another program. You can, for example, click on this text and drag
the mouse to highlight some of it, which you can then copy.</p>

<p class='nocopy'>On the other hand, when you don't wish this feature
to be enabled, you can turn it off, as with this section of text, which
you will find cannot be copied by dragging with the mouse button held
down.</p>
```

## The JavaScript

```
if (classname.search(/\bnocopy\b/, 0) != -1)
{
   PreventAction(thistag, 'both', true)
}
```

# CHAPTER 11

## Incorporating JavaScript

Even if you are not a programmer, or not familiar with JavaScript, you can still make use of this powerful language using the classes in this chapter. With them, you can embed simple calculations or complex expressions within an object, just by placing them within a pair of special tokens.

You can also use these plug-ins to leverage the power of JavaScript for creating sections of conditional HTML, whether based on expressions of your choice, or using a special global keyword to identify the browser in use (such as Firefox, or Internet Explorer, and so on).

Once you've used these classes, I think you may find them so handy you'll wonder how you ever managed without them.

## PLUG-IN 91 Embed JavaScript (embedjs)

Using Plug-in 91, you can embed snippets of JavaScript within an object, without having to use `<script>` tags. This makes it easy for you to display the result of a calculation, or anything else that can be displayed by JavaScript.

For example, in Figure 11-1 a number of code snippets have been embedded within a paragraph of text, which have been evaluated with the results then inserted in their place.

### Variables, Functions, and Properties

| `replace()` | JavaScript function to replace one section of text with another |
|---|---|
| `Html()` | Function to get or set the HTML contents of an object |
| `try() ... catch()` | JavaScript functions to try an expression and, if there is an error, catch it quietly without throwing an error |
| `Eval()` | JavaScript function to evaluate an expression |

### About the Class

When this class is encountered, the object using it is parsed to see whether it has any sections embedded within `[[` and `]]` tags. If so, these sections are evaluated as JavaScript code and the result returned by the evaluation is substituted for the entire section from the opening `[[` to the closing `]]`.

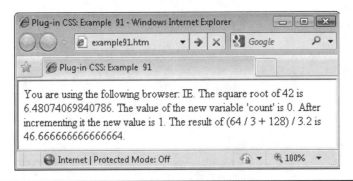

FIGURE 11-1   A paragraph with several JavaScript snippets embedded in it

## How to Use It

With this class, you have the ability to easily embed any JavaScript inline with text. For example, you might want to display the result of a simple calculation and can do so like this:

```
<div class='embedjs'>The result of 23.2 * 7 is [[23.2 * 7]].</div>
```

As you can see, you don't need to know anything about JavaScript to use this class to display the result of arithmetic calculations. You can also access the global variable BROWSER, which is used by the *PJ.js* file to keep track of the current browser type. It will have a value such as "IE", "Opera", "Firefox", and so on, and can be displayed like this:

```
<div class='embedjs'>Your browser is [[BROWSER]].</div>
```

You can also embed much larger sections of code by separating the expressions from each other with a semicolon, like this:

```
<div class='embedjs'> The multiplication table for the number 12 is
[[mystr = ''; for (myvar = 1 ; myvar &lt; 13 ; ++myvar) mystr += myvar
* 12 + ' '; mystr]]</div>
```

Or, if you prefer, you can format the contents like program code as follows (still ensuring that there are semicolons at the end of each statement except the final one, which is optional):

```
<div class='embedjs'>The multiplication table for the number 12 is
[[
    mystr = '';
    for (myvar = 1 ; myvar &lt; 13 ; ++myvar)
        mystr += myvar * 12 + ' ';
    mystr
]]
</div>
```

The output from this example is:

**The multiplication table for the number 12 is 12 24 36 48 60 72 84 96 108 120 132 144**

---

**CAUTION**  *In the* `for()` *loop of this example, the* `&lt;` *entity is used instead of the* `<` *symbol because placing the* `<` *within HTML confuses browsers, which expect an HTML tag to follow it. Likewise, you must use the* `&gt;` *entity where you need a* `>` *symbol. The only way you can use the* `<` *and* `>` *symbols is if the entire JavaScript snippet is encased in quotation marks, like this:* `"[[76 < 83.3]]"`*, which will return the value* `true`*.*

Here's the HTML used for Figure 11-1, in which I have highlighted the embedded JavaScript snippets in bold:

```
<div class='embedjs'>
    You are using the following browser: [[BROWSER]]. The square root of
    42 is [[Math.sqrt(42)]]. The value of the new variable 'count' is
    [[count = 0]]. After incrementing it the new value is [[++count]].
    The result of (64 / 3 + 128) / 3.2 is [[(64 / 3 + 128) / 3.2]].
</div>
```

As you can see, you can also create a new variable (such as count, in the preceding example), and then refer to it later in a web page (as long as you don't make it local by prefacing it with the var keyword, in which case it will work only in the current code snippet).

If you make a mistake, such as introducing a syntax error, an error message will be displayed in red, instead of the result you were expecting. For example, the following is invalid:

```
<div class='embedjs'>The result of 66 x 87 is [[66 x 87]].</div>
```

The problem is that the x symbol is not a valid operator in JavaScript, and it should be replaced with a * symbol. Therefore, because the parser was expecting a semicolon following the 66, the preceding snippet will generate an output similar to the following:

**The result of 66 x 87 is** [SyntaxError: missing ; before statement]

### The JavaScript

```
if (classname.search(/\bembedjs\b/, 0) != -1)
{
    Html(thistag, Html(thistag).replace(/\[\[([^\]]*)\]\]/g,
        function()
    {
        arguments[1] = arguments[1].replace(/&lt;/g, '<')
        arguments[1] = arguments[1].replace(/&gt;/g, '>')

        try
        {
            return eval(arguments[1])
        }
        catch(e)
        {
            return "<span class='red'>[" + e + "]</span>"
        }
    } ))
}
```

## PLUG-IN 92 If (if[*expr*])

If you've ever wished you could write conditional HTML, then you should find this class very handy, because with it you can display an object only if an expression evaluates to true. For example, in Figure 11-2, the screen grab was taken after midday; therefore, it displays the phrase "Good Afternoon".

### Variables, Functions, and Properties

| | |
|---|---|
| replace() | JavaScript function to replace one section of text with another |
| Html() | Function to get or set the HTML contents of an object |
| Eval() | JavaScript function to evaluate an expression |

**FIGURE 11-2**    Using this class, you can display objects only when conditions are satisfied.

## About the Class

This class evaluates the expression following the class name and then displays the object only if the expression evaluates to `true`. If it is `false`, to prevent the object's display it is simply encased within `<!--` and `-->` HTML comment tags.

## How to Use It

Use this class when you want to display objects only when certain conditions are met. For example, the following object is displayed only after midday:

```
<span class='if[now = new Date(); now.getHours() > 11]'>Afternoon</span>
```

What is going on here is that a new object called `now` is created from the current date and time using the `Date()` function. Then, the `getHours()` method of the `now` object is used to return the current hour between 0 and 23. This value is compared with the number 11 and, if it is greater, the contents of the `<span>` is displayed, which in this case is the word "Afternoon".

---

**NOTE**   *Unlike its use in objects implementing the* `embedjs` *class, the direct use of the* `>` *symbol is acceptable in this case, because the entire contents of the class argument are enclosed within quotation marks, and therefore the* `>` *cannot be mistaken for part of an HTML tag.*

---

### Using the BROWSER Global Variable with this Class

Because browsers all work differently, the *PJ.js* library of JavaScript functions needs to know which browser is running, and therefore tweaks can be made to ensure all the functions have the same (or nearly the same) effect. You can use the global variable BROWSER that it creates for your own purposes, too.

For example, if you have written an application for the iPad tablet that you want to advertise, you could use the following code to display details about it only to people browsing your web page using that device:

```
<div class="if[BROWSER == 'iPad']">
   Check out our special app for iPad users...
   etc...
</div>
```

| Value | Browser/Device Type |
|---|---|
| IE | Internet Explorer |
| Opera | Opera |
| Chrome | Google Chrome |
| iPod | Apple iPod Touch |
| iPhone | Apple iPhone |
| iPad | Apple iPad |
| Android | Google Android |
| Safari | Apple Safari |
| Firefox | Mozilla Firefox |
| UNKNOWN | No known browser type identified |

**TABLE 11-1**   The possible values of the BROWSER variable

Table 11-1 lists all the values that BROWSER may have, in order of determination. For example, if an iPod Touch device is detected, then the string "iPod" is assigned to BROWSER, even though the browser running is a version of Safari.

Here is the code used for Figure 11-2:

```
Good
<span class='if[now = new Date(); now.getHours() < 12]'>Morning</span>
<span class='if[now = new Date(); now.getHours() > 11]'>Afternoon</span>
```

### The JavaScript

```
if (classname.search(/\bif\b/, 0) != -1)
{
    origcname.replace(/(if|IF)\[([^\]]*)\]/, function()
    {
        if (!eval(arguments[2]))
            Html(thistag, '<!-- ' + Html(thistag) + ' -->')
    } )
}
```

## PLUG-IN 93  If Not (ifnot[*expr*])

Plug-in 93 provides the inverse of the if[] class and is useful for implementing the equivalent of an if... else... block of code. For example, in Figure 11-3 this class is used in conjunction with the if[] class, and you can see the different results displayed in the Apple Safari browser and in Internet Explorer (the inset).

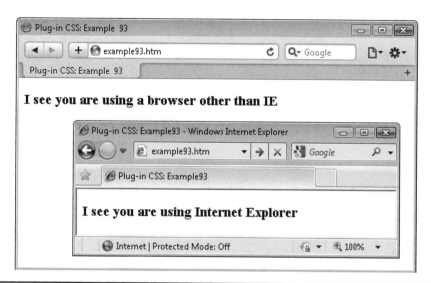

**FIGURE 11-3**    Using both the if[] and ifnot[] classes to target different browsers

## Variables, Functions, and Properties

| `replace()` | JavaScript function to replace one section of text with another |
|---|---|
| `Html()` | Function to get or set the HTML contents of an object |
| `Eval()` | JavaScript function to evaluate an expression |

## About the Class

This class evaluates the expression following the class name and then displays the object only if the expression evaluates to `false`. If it is `true`, to prevent the object's display it is simply encased within `<!--` and `-->` HTML comment tags.

## How to Use It

You use this class in the same manner as the `if[]` class, except that the object will be displayed only if the result of the expression in the square brackets evaluates to `false`. For example, here is the code used for the screen grabs in Figure 11-3:

```
I see you are using
<span class="   if[BROWSER == 'IE']">Internet Explorer</span>
<span class="ifnot[BROWSER == 'IE']">a browser other than IE</span>
```

Of course, you could replace the second line with the following, in which the `if[]` class is used in place of `ifnot[]`, but with a modified expression:

```
<span class="if[BROWSER != 'IE']">a browser other than IE</span>
```

But the point of the `ifnot[]` class is that you don't have to rewrite an expression that was used in an `if[]` class; you can simply copy the entire expression and place it within an `ifnot[]` class to achieve the inverse effect of the original, which is very handy if the expression is quite complex.

---

**NOTE** *This completes all the dynamic classes in this book. In the next and final chapter, I'll show you how you can combine any of these classes together to create superclasses, which have the combined functionality of many classes at once.*

## The JavaScript

```
if (classname.search(/\bifnot\b/, 0) != -1)
{
    origcname.replace(/(ifnot|IFNOT)\[([^\]]*)\]/, function()
    {
        if (eval(arguments[2]))
            Html(thistag, '<!-- ' + Html(thistag) + ' -->')
    } )
}
```

# CHAPTER 12

**Superclasses**

N ow that you have access to the almost 1800 classes from the previous chapters, this chapter focuses on combining them in combinations to make superclasses—single classes with the functionality of several classes at once. These superclasses include creating an RSS button, applying simple borders, handling rollovers, horizontal and vertical animated tabs, and more.

You'll also discover how easy it is to create your own superclasses using simple <meta . . . > statements to help make building dynamic web pages the easiest it has ever been.

## What Is a Superclass?

Superclasses are classes that contain groups of other classes. For example, the first superclass in this chapter, `clickable`, contains the `nooutline` and `pointer` classes (Plug-ins 19 and 54).

Seven superclasses have been predefined for you in the *PC.js* file, and you can easily create your own using the <meta . . . > tag, like this:

```
<meta http-equiv='sclass' name='clickable' content='nooutline pointer' />
```

In this example, the superclass `clickable` is created by placing the argument `http-equiv='sclass'` within a <meta . . . > tag, followed by the argument specifying the name of the superclass, `name='clickable'`, and finally the classes to put in the superclass, `content='nooutline pointer'`.

Here's another example:

```
<meta http-equiv='sclass' name='yellowonblue' content='yellow blue_b' />
```

This creates the new superclass `yellowonblue` which will set the foreground color of the object to which it applies to yellow, and the background to blue.

> **NOTE** *You can include as many classes in a superclass as you like, as well as any combination of normal and dynamic classes from this book, or even throw in your own classes created either within <style> tags or from a style sheet.*

## Clickable (clickable)

The purpose of Plug-in 94 is to clearly indicate that objects, and buttons in particular, are clickable. It does this by removing any outline that may be placed around the object when it has the focus, and by turning the mouse cursor into a pointer when it hovers over the object.

In Figure 12-1, two rows of buttons have been created. The first row doesn't use this superclass, but the second does.

In the screen grab, you can clearly see the dotted outline that has been applied to the first Cancel button, but which will not appear over the second one. Also, the mouse cursor will change to a pointer when over the second row, but not the first.

### Classes

| | |
|---|---|
| `nooutline` | Plug-in 19: Prevents a dotted outline being placed over an object in focus |
| `pointer` | Plug-in 54: Turns the mouse cursor into a pointer when it hovers over the object |

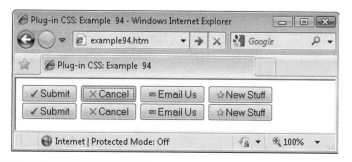

FIGURE 12-1  This superclass removes outlines and changes the mouse cursor to a pointer.

## About the Superclass

By combining the effects of two other classes, this superclass helps to clearly indicate when an object is clickable.

## How to Use It

To use this superclass, enter its name into the class argument of an object. For example, the following code was used to create the screen grab in Figure 12-1:

```
<button class='check_h'>Submit</button>
<button class='cross_h'>Cancel</button>
<button class='email_h'>Email Us</button>
<button class='star_h' >New Stuff</button><br />

<button class='check_h clickable'>Submit</button>
<button class='cross_h clickable'>Cancel</button>
<button class='email_h clickable'>Email Us</button>
<button class='star_h clickable' >New Stuff</button>
```

Try passing your mouse over the different rows and clicking various buttons to see the differences between them.

## 95 RSS Button (rssbutton)

Plug-in 95 creates a great looking RSS button without the need for including an image. For example, Figure 12-2 shows it being applied to both a <button> and a <span> object in both the Chrome and Internet Explorer browsers. Although there are minute differences between them, all the buttons look quite respectable.

## Classes

| carrot1 | Plug-in 4: Changes the background to the gradient carrot1 |
|---|---|
| carrot2_a | Plug-in 5: Changes the background to the gradient carrot2 when the object is clicked |
| smallestround | Plug-in 8: Applies a 2-pixel rounded border |

| b | Plug-in 21: Changes the font weight to bold |
|---|---|
| white | Plug-in 24: Changes the foreground color to white |
| yellow_h | Plug-in 24: Changes the hover color to yellow |
| smallbutton | Plug-in 33: Creates a button with a 75 percent font size, and 2 pixels of padding |
| clickable | Plug-in 94: Indicates that the object is clickable |

## About the Superclass

This superclass brings together a large number of CSS rules from several different classes, even including the previous superclass, `clickable`, to create a dynamic, 3D-effect RSS button.

## How to Use It

To use this superclass, you will need to surround it with an `<a href='...'>` tag pointing to your RSS feed, like this:

```
<a class='n' href='myfeed.xml'>
   <span class='rssbutton'>RSS FEED</span>
</a>
```

The first line references the RSS feed and uses the n class to suppress the underline that would otherwise appear under the button. The middle line applies the rssbutton superclass to a `<span>` tag, and supplies the string "RSS FEED" to it.

You can also use the `<button>` tag by placing it in a form like this:

```
<form method='get' action='myfeed.xml'>
   <button class='rssbutton'>RSS FEED</button>
</form>
```

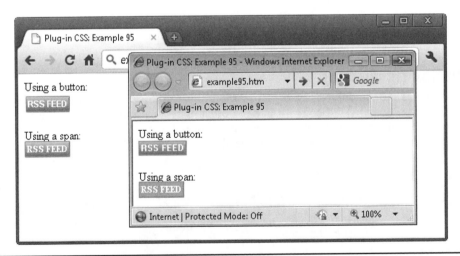

FIGURE 12-2    The RSS button superclass used on different objects in different browsers

*CAUTION When using the <button> tag, Internet Explorer will submit the text between the <button> and </button> tags, while other browsers will submit the contents of its* value *attribute (if any).*

# 96

# Border (border)

Often, you want to quickly add a border to an object and Plug-in 96 will do the job for you, instead of having to supply a set of CSS rules. For example, in Figure 12-3 a photograph is displayed twice, the second time using this superclass.

## Classes

| bsolid | Plug-in 16: Sets the object's border to solid |
|--------|-----------------------------------------------|
| bwidth1 | Plug-in 17: Sets the object's border width to 1 pixel |
| bblack | Plug-in 18: Sets the object's border color to black |

## About the Superclass

This superclass uses all three border classes to create a simple, 1-pixel black border around the object.

## How to Use It

When you want to quickly add a border to an object, just enter this superclass name in its class argument, like this:

```
<img class='border' src='myphoto.jpg' />
```

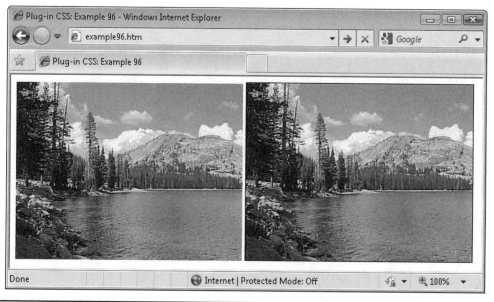

**FIGURE 12-3**    Displaying an image without and with the border superclass

# PLUG-IN 97
## Absolute Top Left (abstopleft)

Whenever you create a rollover or need to align objects on top of each other, the process is the same. All objects after the first one should be moved to the top left corner of the containing object, and Plug-in 97 makes doing so quick and easy.

You can see this superclass in use in Figure 12-4, where the boat image has been superimposed over the photograph.

### Classes

| absolute | Plug-in 1: Gives an object absolute positioning |
|----------|--------------------------------------------------|
| totop    | Plug-in 13: Moves an object to the top of its container |
| toleft   | Plug-in 13: Moves an object to the left of its container |

### About the Superclass

This superclass applies three classes to give an object absolute positioning, and to move it to its containing object's top left corner.

### How to Use It

To use this superclass, you will need a container object with a position other than static in which to place your objects. Then, the second object onward must apply the superclass, as in the following example, which was used for Figure 12-4:

```
<div class='relative'>
   <img class='trans07' src='i2.jpg' />
   <img class='abstopleft trans06' src='boat.png' />
</div>
```

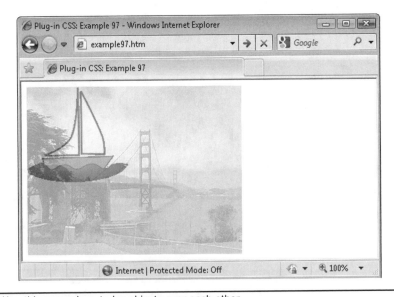

FIGURE 12-4   Use this superclass to lay objects over each other.

In this example, the larger image is given a transparency level of 7 and the boat a transparency of 6 and they have been superimposed over each other. Reasons you would want to do this include creating slideshows and rollovers, as in the following plug-in.

## PLUG-IN 98

## Rollover (rollover)

Plug-in 98 makes it very easy for you to create rollover effects, as shown in Figure 12-5, in which two face images are displayed that, when moused over, turn from happy to sad, and vice versa.

### Classes

| trans00 | Plug-in 9: Sets the transparency of an object to fully visible |
|---------|---------------------------------------------------------------|
| trans00_h | Plug-in 9: Sets the transparency of an object to fully visible when the mouse cursor passes over it |
| trans10 | Plug-in 9: Sets the transparency of an object to completely invisible |
| trans10_h | Plug-in 9: Sets the transparency of an object to completely invisible when the mouse cursor passes over it |
| abstopleft | Plug-in 97: Gives an object absolute positioning and moves it to the top left corner of its container |

### About the Superclasses

These two superclasses are intended to be used together. The `rollover` superclass should be applied to the first of a rollover pair of objects, and `rollover_h` to the second. Once implemented, whenever the mouse passes over the objects, the first one is set to transparent and the second to fully visible so the one you can see swaps. When the mouse is moved away, the first object becomes visible again and the second invisible.

In another illustration of superclasses being used as members of other superclasses, the `abstopleft` superclass is used as one of the members of this superclass pair.

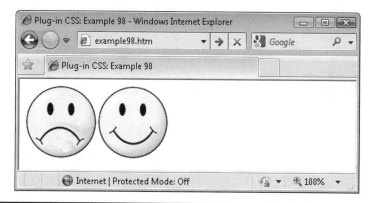

**FIGURE 12-5**   Creating rollover effects with this pair of superclasses

## How to Use Them

To use these superclasses, first create an object that has a positioning other than static, and then place two other objects within it, giving the first one the rollover superclass, and the second rollover_h, like this:

```
<div class='relative'>
    <img class='rollover'   src='frowney.gif' />
    <img class='rollover_h' src='smiley.gif'  />
</div>
```

The application of the relative class to the <div> ensures that it doesn't have a position of static, and therefore it will act as the containing object for the images within it. The rollover_h superclass makes use of the abstopleft superclass (among others), so there is no need to specify the positioning of the second image.

---

*TIP*  *You are not restricted to only images by these superclasses, and can use any types of objects for the rollover pairs.*

---

## PLUG-IN 99 Vertical Tab (vtab)

Plug-in 99 creates a tab that slides in from the left of the screen on browsers that support CSS transitions such as Opera 10, Firefox 4, Apple Safari 5 and Google Chrome 5. Sadly, the smooth transition doesn't work on Internet Explorer, but it does degrade to a simple in or out animation.

In Figure 12-6, a number of tabs have been created using this superclass, and the mouse is currently hovering over the "Politics" tab, which has popped out.

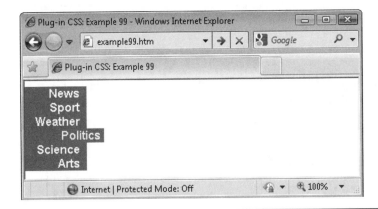

**FIGURE 12-6**   A number of pop-out tabs created using this superclass

## Classes

| | |
|---|---|
| `leftpadding10` | Plug-in 15: Applies 10 pixels of padding to the object's left side |
| `leftpadding40_h` | Plug-in 15: Applies 40 pixels of padding to the object's left side when it is hovered over by the mouse |
| `rightpadding5` | Plug-in 15: Applies 5 pixels of padding to the object's right side |
| `b` | Plug-in 21: Sets the object's font weight to bold |
| `transitionallfast_l` | Plug-in 51: Applies a linear transition of 0.3 seconds to any property changes that occur on the object (where supported by the browser) |

## About the Superclass

This is a great little superclass for creating a variety of animation and menuing effects. It works by changing the left padding of an object when the mouse passes over it. In conjunction with CSS3 transitions (on browsers that support them), the object will slide out and in smoothly over the course of 0.3 seconds. In Internet Explorer and other browsers that don't support transitions, the object will simply pop in and out.

## How to Use It

To use this superclass, first create a container object by giving it a position other than static. For example, here is the HTML used for Figure 12-6:

```
<div class='relative red_b leftby20 arial w[100]'>
   <div class='vtab white red_b yellow_h right w[80]'>News</div>
   <div class='vtab white red_b yellow_h right w[80]'>Sport</div>
   <div class='vtab white red_b yellow_h right w[80]'>Weather</div>
   <div class='vtab white red_b yellow_h right w[80]'>Politics</div>
   <div class='vtab white red_b yellow_h right w[80]'>Science</div>
   <div class='vtab white red_b yellow_h right w[80]'>Arts</div>
</div>
```

In the first line of this example, the `<div>` is given relative positioning, a red background color, is moved to the left by 20 pixels (to send it past the screen edge), its font family is set to Arial, and it is given a width of 100 pixels.

Inside it are six tabs, each of which uses the `vtab` superclass, and it is set to white text on a red background, which changes to yellow text when hovered over with the mouse. The text is also aligned to the right and the width of each tab is set to 80 pixels.

When you pass your mouse over the tabs on a browser that supports CSS3 transitions, you'll see them sliding in and out in a pleasing and professional manner. Even on IE and other browsers that do not support transitions, the effect still happens, although instantly rather than over time.

All the example now needs is for `<a href='...'>` tags to be placed around each tab (possibly including the use of the `n` class to suppress any underlines) and the menu will be complete. When you do this, ensure that the `<a href='...'>` and `</a>` are placed around the `<div>` (or other container), not within it.

PART III

# Horizontal Tab (htab)

Plug-in 100 is similar to the previous plug-in, except that it creates drop-down tabs, as shown in Figure 12-7 in which the "Science" tab is currently being hovered over, and has therefore slid down.

## Classes

| | |
|---|---|
| `absolute` | Plug-in 1: Gives an object absolute positioning |
| `toppadding20_h` | Plug-in 15: Applies 20 pixels of padding to the object's top when it is hovered over by the mouse |
| `b` | Plug-in 21: Sets the object's font weight to bold |
| `center` | Plug-in 22: Centers the object's contents |
| `transitionallfast_l` | Plug-in 51: Applies a linear transition of 0.3 seconds to any property changes that occur on the object (where supported by the browser) |

## About the Superclass

This superclass works by changing the top padding of an object when the mouse passes over it. In conjunction with CSS3 transitions (on browsers that support them), the object will slide down and up smoothly over the course of 0.3 seconds. In Internet Explorer and other browsers that don't support transitions, the object will simply pop down and back up again.

## How to Use It

To use this superclass, you need to first create a container object by giving it a position other than static. For example, here is the HTML used for Figure 12-7:

```
<div class='red_b arial'>
   <span class='htab white red_b yellow_h w[80] x[0]'  >News</span>
   <span class='htab white red_b yellow_h w[80] x[80]' >Sport</span>
   <span class='htab white red_b yellow_h w[80] x[160]'>Weather</span>
   <span class='htab white red_b yellow_h w[80] x[240]'>Politics</span>
   <span class='htab white red_b yellow_h w[80] x[320]'>Science</span>
   <span class='htab white red_b yellow_h w[80] x[400]'>Arts</span>
</div>
```

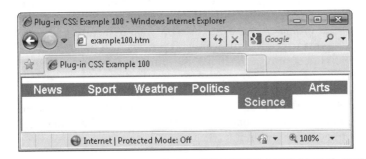

**FIGURE 12-7**   These pop-out tabs drop down vertically when hovered over.

In the first line of this example, the `<div>` is given a red background color, and its font family is set to Arial.

Inside it are six tabs, each of which uses the `htab` superclass, and is also set to white text on a red background, which changes to yellow text when hovered over with the mouse. The width of each tab is set to 80 pixels, and the horizontal location of each tab is moved in by 80 pixels from the previous one.

When you pass your mouse over the tabs on a browser that supports CSS3 transitions, you'll see them smoothly sliding down and up. In IE and other browsers, the tabs instantly pop down and up.

# Index